OUTWARD AND UPWARD MOBILITIES

International Students in Canada, Their Families, and
Structuring Institutions

EDITED BY ANN H. KIM AND
MIN-JUNG KWAK

Outward and Upward Mobilities

International Students in Canada, Their Families, and Structuring Institutions

UNIVERSITY OF TORONTO PRESS
Toronto Buffalo London

ISBN 978-1-4875-0462-5

Printed on acid-free, 100% post-consumer recycled paper with
vegetable-based inks.

Library and Archives Canada Cataloguing in Publication

Outward and upward mobilities : international students in Canada,
their families, and structuring institutions / edited by Ann H. Kim and
Min-Jung Kwak.

Includes bibliographical references and index.
ISBN 978-1-4875-0462-5 (hardcover)

1. Students, Foreign – Canada. 2. Students, Foreign – Education
(Higher) – Canada. 3. Students, Foreign – Family relationships – Canada.
4. Student mobility – Canada. 5. Social mobility – Canada. I. Kwak,
Min-Jung, 1971–, editor II. Kim, Ann H., 1972–, editor

LB2376.6.C3O98 2019   371.826'910971   C2018-905690-8

University of Toronto Press acknowledges the financial assistance to its
publishing program of the Canada Council for the Arts and the Ontario Arts
Council, an agency of the Government of Ontario.

**Canada Council   Conseil des Arts
for the Arts   du Canada**

**ONTARIO ARTS COUNCIL
CONSEIL DES ARTS DE L'ONTARIO**

an Ontario government agency
un organisme du gouvernement de l'Ontario

Funded by the   Financé par le
Government   gouvernement
of Canada   du Canada | Canada

Contents

List of Figures   vii

List of Tables   ix

Acknowledgments   xi

1. Introduction: Education Migration, Social Mobility, and Structuring Institutions   3
   ANN H. KIM AND MIN-JUNG KWAK

Part I: International Students in the Canadian Context

2. "International Students Are ... Golden": Canada's Changing Policy Contexts, Approaches, and National Peculiarities in Attracting International Students as Future Immigrants   25
   ROOPA DESAI TRILOKEKAR AND AMIRA EL MASRI

3. Explaining International Student Mobility to Canada: A Review   56
   ANN H. KIM AND GUNJAN SONDHI

4. Barriers to Knowledge on International Students and a Potential Opportunity   76
   ANN H. KIM, REEM ATTIEH, AND TIMOTHY OWEN

Part II: Integration and Adjustment in Educational Institutions

5. The International Undergraduate Experience through the Lens of Developmental Psychology   95
   MAXINE GALLANDER WINTRE, STELLA DENTAKOS, SAEID CHAVOSHI, ABIRAMI R. KANDASAMY, AND LORNA WRIGHT

6. Legal Status and School Experiences for Families with Young
Students 121
ANN H. KIM, MIN-JUNG KWAK, EUNJUNG LEE, WANSOO PARK, AND
SUNG HYUN YUN

Part III: Local Considerations: Ethnic Communities and Families

7. Adapting to China's Students at the Gateway: Student Stories
and the Trajectories of Chinese Community Associations in
Vancouver 139
JEAN MICHEL MONTSION

8. "Settlers" Meeting the "Settled": International Students
Encountering the South Asian "Diaspora" in Ontario,
Canada 159
GUNJAN SONDHI

9. Global Restructuring, Gender, and Education Migration: Chinese
Immigrant Women Professionals in Canada 177
GUIDA C. MAN AND ELENA CHOU

10. "A Typical *Girogi* Family Experience?" The Transnational Migration
and Heterogeneous Identity Formation of *Girogi* Families in
Toronto, Canada 197
MIN-JUNG KWAK, WANSOO PARK, EUNJUNG LEE, SANGYOO LEE, AND
JEONG-EUI LEE

Part IV: The Post-student Experience

11. Student Transitions: Earnings of Former International Students in
Canada's Labour Market 219
YUQIAN LU AND FENG HOU

12. Bumpy Roads: Tracing Pathways into Practice for International
Students in Nursing 246
MARGARET WALTON-ROBERTS AND JENNA HENNEBRY

Afterword: A Multi-level Perspective on Education Migration 266
MIN-JUNG KWAK AND ANN H. KIM

List of Contributors 279

Figures

1.1 International Student Arrivals as a Portion of All Temporary Residents and Permanent Residents, 2010–15   6

1.2 Temporary Resident Permit Stock (Not Unique Persons), 1995–2014   7

1.3 International Students and the Immigration-Economic-Education Policy Realms before and after the Development of Canada's National International Education Strategy   11

5.1 International Students' Rate of Communication with Their Parents by Gender   104

5.2 Differences in Preference and Use of Communication Mediums When Interacting with Parents   104

5.3 Developmental Sequence Model to University Adjustment   111

11.1 Cumulative Rates of Transition to Permanent Residence among International Students   225

11.2 Transition Rates and Source Country's Log GDP Per Capita   228

Tables

1.1 Top Ten Source Countries of International Students in Canada, 2006–15 8

2.1 CIC International Student Policy Changes, 2002–15 34

2.2 Summary of Federal IE and IS Approaches 40

4.1 Data Sources Containing Standard Immigration-Related Variables 80

4.2 Perceived Barriers of WES Clients 88

5.1 Socio-demographic Descriptors of Current Sample 100

5.2 Breakdown of Countries of Origin Included in Each Category 101

6.1 Legal Status and School-Related Experiences 133

6.2 Legal Status and School-Related Experiences, Newcomers 134

11.1 Demographic Characteristics of International Students at Their First Student Permits, Canada 222

11.2 Cumulative Transition Rates by the End of the Tenth Year since the First Student Permit 226

11.3 Demographic Characteristics at First Arrival among Immigrants Who Were Former International Students 230

11.4 Characteristics at Landing among Immigrants Who Were Former International Students 232

11.5 Regression Coefficients of Log Annual Earnings among Immigrants Who Were Former International Students 236

11.6 The Relative Importance of Predictors of Immigrant Earnings by Years after Immigration 242

12.1 Top Ten Countries of Last Residence for IENs Entering Canada, 2011 249

12.2   Country Where Applicants to the College of Nurses of Ontario
       were Originally Trained, 2014   249
12.3   Respondents' Intention to Remain Temporarily or Permanently
       in Canada   258
12.4   Percentage of Funds Borrowed   259

Acknowledgments

We would like to express our sincere appreciation to the Academy of Korean Studies and the Social Sciences and Humanities Research Council of Canada for funding this book as well as the September 2012 workshop – Outward and Upward Mobilities: Families from South Korea in a Transnational Era – that inspired us to pull this collection together. Other funders of the 2012 workshop include the Population Change and Lifecourse Strategic Knowledge Cluster at Western University in London, Ontario, the Faculty of Liberal Arts and Professional Studies at York University, and the York Centre for Asian Research. We would also like to thank Elena Chou for assistance in coordinating this book project, Alicia Filipowich for support and administrative assistance, and Esther Yu for assistance in editing. Bringing together a collection like this, with different working and writing styles, requires the efforts of numerous dedicated and detail-oriented people to whom we are very grateful.

OUTWARD AND UPWARD MOBILITIES

International Students in Canada, Their Families, and
Structuring Institutions

1 Introduction: Education Migration, Social Mobility, and Structuring Institutions

ANN H. KIM AND MIN-JUNG KWAK

People are moving out for education to move up in the world. As with the mobility of other migrant groups, student mobility is a form of social mobility. And like other migrant groups, international students are defined by their relationship to the state via immigration policy. Mediating this relationship are the institutions in which students are embedded, which can influence the processes of social mobility. As such, we cannot dissociate international students' identities and experiences from these structuring institutions. Thus, while "outward and upward" continues to be an apt description of international student mobility (ISM), meso- and macro-level factors complicate the attainability of geographic and social mobility for students and their families. This multi-level approach motivates our collection. In what follows we ask, What is the connection between students and these structuring institutions? Which institutions are significant in students' lives and how do they interact with student experiences?

Here we widen the net to consider international students, regardless of legal status, at all levels of education, along with their families, local communities, educational and professional institutions, and host-country governments. We explain educational migrants' individual and familial motivations and address how social and spatial mobilities shape and are shaped by policies and practices, social networks and local ethnic communities, local labour markets, educational institutions, and regulatory bodies. It is important to study student mobility from the perspective of the individuals and migrant groups that engage in the practice, and there is also good reason to go beyond the micro perspective to take a broader view and situate these experiences within an institutional framework. This is the primary aim of the current collection.

The chapters in this book respond to the need for an in-depth social study of the international student experience in Canada. Students, as much in the present as in the past, value and acquire class markers like education in a shifting social and spatial field. In the last several decades, we observed the increasingly international and transnational character of education (Kim 2013) and an intensifying global competition to meet the demand for international education. This competition is driven partly by a desire among advanced countries to entice the highly educated and highly skilled to their borders as one way of achieving economic goals, and partly by students in generally less advanced nations seeking an international education as a symbol of distinction and cosmopolitanism and/or a route to permanent residence abroad. The magnitude and uneven geographic patterns of student flows are the results of this ongoing competition.

Globally, the number of post-secondary-level international students – those who cross international borders for study purposes – more than doubled between 2000 and 2013 to reach 4.1 million (see the 2016 study by the UNESCO Institute for Statistics, "Global Flow of Tertiary-Level Students").[1] In 2013, the majority of international students originated from Asia, with seven countries receiving the largest share of all students: the United States, the United Kingdom, Australia, France, Germany, Japan, and Canada (OECD 2015). There is evidence that the competition to attract students is intensifying as the share of international students going to these places is declining (UNESCO Institute for Statistics 2016). International students are now migrating to an ever-widening network of countries, including places like China, Malaysia, South Korea, Singapore, New Zealand, and the Middle East (UNESCO Institute for Statistics 2016).

Canada continues to be an active participant in this skills race, particularly as a receiving country. The recruitment of international students fits within Canada's social development and nation-building goals, and it is in line with what Simmons (2010) notes as the shift in immigration policy in 2001 from a focus on skilled workers to highly skilled workers and on education. Although Simmons wrote about permanent residents as "designer immigrants," or those migrants "selected as if they were custom designed to meet the specific criteria of a neo-liberal nation intent

---

1 When we consider other types of education migrants, such as short-term program registrants and younger international students below the tertiary level, these numbers represent are a severe undercount of education migration.

on productivity, cost recovery, and immigrant self-settlement" (2010, 85), this is now an apt description of international students.

While international students have garnered an increasing level of attention from policymakers and scholars since the late 1980s, this interest has grown in recent years (Kim and Sondhi 2015). In 2008, the Canadian government, through a joint effort between the Department of Foreign Affairs and International Trade and the Council of Ministers of Education, Canada, launched its first international marketing campaign under the slogan "Imagine Education au/in Canada," and in 2013, the federal government committed $10 million over two years for other international marketing activities. (For an excellent discussion of Canada's policies related to ISM, see Trilokekar and El Masri in this volume as well as other work by Trilokekar and colleagues).

Although we do not have figures for the broader population of education migrants, we can observe trends in international student counts. According to Immigration, Refugees, and Citizenship Canada (IRCC; formerly Citizenship and Immigration Canada, or CIC), international students are defined as temporary residents on study permits (CIC 2015b).[2] And in accordance with policy objectives, the numbers of international students in Canada is steadily rising. Between 1995 and 2015, the number of student permits in a given year have more than trebled, from approximately 125,524 to nearly 460,000 (CIC 2015a; CIC 2015b). To place these figures in context, this represents between one-third and one-half of all temporary resident permits issued in a given year.[3] Figure 1.1 shows the number of student entries from 2010 to 2015 alongside the number of other temporary resident permits. What is notable is the parity of temporary permits for students and landed permanent residents as well as the large gap between total temporary and permanent residents.

In addition to the steady rise in the numbers of students arriving in Canada per year, the total stock of international students is also rising. Although one source puts the number of international students, across all levels, at over 350,000 in 2015 (Knight-Grofe and Rauh 2016), IRCC does not provide figures representing actual persons (some had multiple permits, and were thus counted more than once). Figure 1.2 displays the

---

2 Unlike the global figures, these numbers include secondary-level and younger students as well as tertiary-level students, but they are again limited to permit holders and not short-term students who may study in Canada without visas. We also include students who held work permits for study purposes.

3 Other temporary resident permits include those for work or humanitarian purposes.

Figure 1.1 International Student Arrivals as a Portion of All Temporary Residents and Permanent Residents, 2010–15

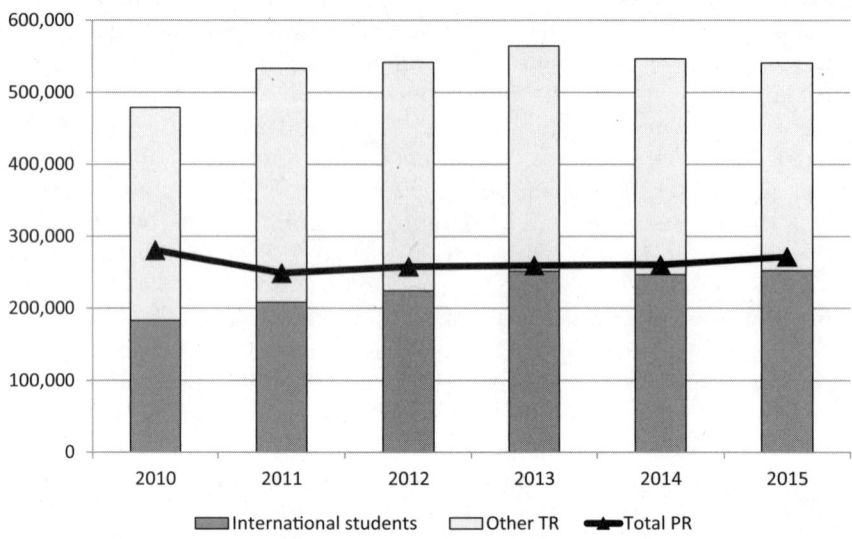

Source: Citizenship & Immigration Canada, RDM, February 2016 – Permanent residents; Citizenship & Immigration Canada, RDM, as of February, 2016 – Temporary residents

stock of temporary resident permits over time, which shows a threefold increase from 1995 to 2014, although the proportion of international student permits fluctuated during the same period between 35.5 to 43.4 per cent. According to one Statistics Canada estimate, the number of post-secondary international students enrolled in colleges and universities in Canada rose from roughly 150,000 in 1999 to close to 200,000 in 2013, or approximately 10 per cent of all post-secondary enrolments (CANSIM Table 477–0031). This suggests that the growth in the student population is consistent with the Canadian government's efforts to use the temporary resident stream to meet its stated economic goals, which are achieved when students and other highly skilled migrants transition or switch to permanent residence, a topic taken up by Lu and Hou in this volume.

Along with rising numbers, we have also seen a growth in the diversity of students' national origins. Canada receives students from 187 countries (Knight-Grofe and Rauh 2016), and the top 10 sources by citizenship are listed in Table 1.1. Based on counts of international students at

Figure 1.2 Temporary Resident Permit Stock (Not Unique Persons), 1995–2014

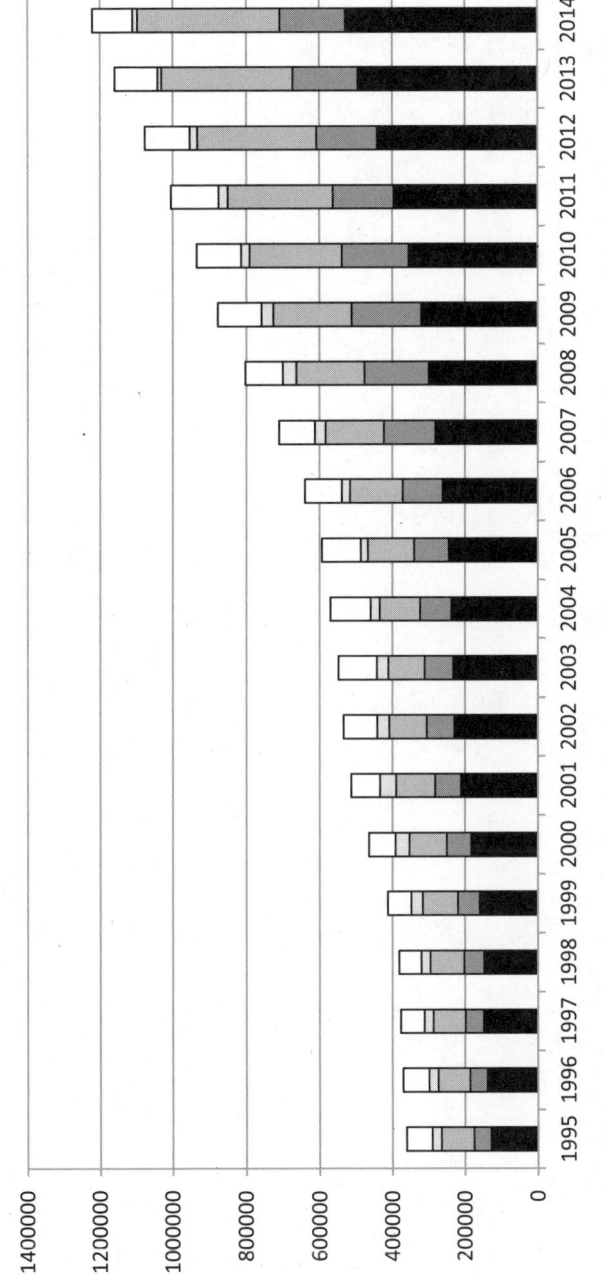

■ Total student permits ■ Temporary Foreign Worker Program ■ International Mobility Program □ Refugee claimants □ Others

Table 1.1 Top Ten Source Countries of International Students in Canada, 2006–15

Year	2005	2006	2007	2008	2009	2010	2011	2012	2013	2014	2015
China	48,074	49,544	50,905	55,017	61,043	68,360	79,857	93,777	110,285	126,053	139,872
India	9,232	10,161	10,604	11,376	14,592	24,028	33,262	41,503	46,315	51,646	62,367
South Korea	39,930	42,694	44,919	44,641	40,809	38,011	34,495	31,040	28,128	27,661	27,816
France	10,635	11,685	12,874	13,653	14,734	16,036	17,802	20,042	22,257	24,859	26,805
Saudi Arabia	1,526	1,741	2,484	5,155	9,394	14,737	17,969	18,408	17,858	17,435	16,434
United States	17,361	17,330	17,080	16,572	16,231	16,033	16,088	16,062	16,137	16,082	16,208
Brazil	2,129	2,622	3,204	4,120	4,558	4,844	5,691	8,254	12,241	14,316	13,720
Nigeria	1,990	2,077	2,382	2,674	3,406	4,341	5,288	6,455	8,120	9,983	11,966
Japan	14,394	13,839	12,783	11,416	10,309	9,642	9,769	10,269	10,782	10,994	11,427
Mexico	5,871	6,290	6,468	6,446	6,717	7,091	7,580	8,072	8,405	8,367	8,241
Total (all countries)	233,896	239,899	246,814	258,090	274,240	300,264	327,433	359,659	394,420	428,408	459,644

Source: Facts and Figures 2015: Immigration Overview - Temporary Residents - Annual IRCC Updates. International Students by Top 50 Countries of Citizenship. http://open.canada.ca/data/en/dataset/052642bb-3fd9-4828-b608-c81dff7e539c

Notes: Rank is based on 2015 figures. Figures reflect counts based on students' country of citizenship.

all levels with permits, rather than annual entries, the top source country, for over a decade, has been China. The number of international students from China increased each year over the 2005–15 period, and students from China also increased as a proportion of all students in the same period, from 21 to 30 per cent. While China's position as the top source country is relatively stable, there have been shifts in the rankings of the other main source countries over this period. At the beginning of the century, South Korea was an important source of international students overall, but their numbers have declined since 2008; the country is now ranked third, according to IRCC data, despite being the top source country of students in primary-level programs.

Another rapidly growing international student stream comes from India, now the second-ranked source country after growing from 10,000 students in 2006 to over 60,000 in 2015 (see Table 1.1). Less significant in terms of numbers but also growing over this period were students from France, Saudi Arabia, Brazil, Nigeria, and Mexico. Although the United States and Japan were also in the top ten, their numbers were relatively stable or faced slight declines.

Despite the diversity of national origins, the top three source countries accounted for more than 40 per cent of international students in a given year, and this figure surpassed 50 per cent in 2015. The presence of a large number of students from China, India, and South Korea explains the focus in the literature on students from these places, and this attention is evident in this volume. Although there are fewer than 10,000 students from each of the other countries in a given year, it is important to understand the experiences of groups with fewer numbers since their presence is nonetheless growing.

On a global scale, the growth in international students in Canada is also consistent with growth in other places such as the United States, which has roughly 800,000 international students, the United Kingdom, with over 400,000, and Australia, with roughly 250,000 (Choudaha 2017). The investments directed toward the recruitment of students from abroad and these students' growing presence in many countries justify increasing research attention on this important group as well as the institutions that structure and are also structured by the students, their families, and the education industry.

Shifting Institutional Arrangements and Policy Frameworks

The chapters in this volume make clear that the motivations for education migration among individuals and families are enduring: there are the shorter-term objectives of a high quality of education, of acquiring language skills and foreign credentials, and of lifestyle changes, as well as the longer-term goal of upward social mobility. To be sure, the belief persists across generations and cultures that the most effective and legitimate way to gain access to class resources – that is, to "move up in the world" – is to acquire cultural capital.

Less consistent are student experiences and less durable are student flows and volumes along with the institutional arrangements and policy frameworks that shape and respond to ideological shifts. This is no less true for Canada. In an increasingly interconnected world characterized by intensifying global competition, emerging economies and new competitors have begun to challenge existing hierarchies. This race is only expected to expand. Within the current global order of ISM, Canada's relatively stable place among the top six or seven host countries of international tertiary students is neither fixed nor guaranteed as new places like New Zealand, along with certain Asian and European countries, vie for their place among the top destinations.

Interestingly, this fierce global competition grew out of the neo-liberal period that began in the late 1970s, when differential tuition fees were established for international students in the United Kingdom and Canada. Currently, international students pay higher fees than domestic students in most countries of the OECD (OECD 2017), and in top destinations such as the United Kingdom, Australia, and Canada, the export education industry generates billions of dollars in economic value each year (Deloitte Access Economics 2015; Kunin and Associates 2016; Walker 2014). With the dampening effect of differential fees on enrolment rates, and budget cuts within institutions, aggressive recruitment of international students to boost revenues has marked the first two decades of the twenty-first century in many places (Choudaha 2017). These measures have been accompanied by calls for, and often the implementation of, a centralized recruitment effort by way of a state-funded national strategy with multi-sectoral coordination, three examples of which can be seen in the United Kingdom, Australia, and Canada.

The direct involvement of national governments in a formerly decentralized education sector has shifted policy frameworks such that an explicit overlap and integration of education with other policy realms has occurred. In Canada, the focus of this book, international students arrive at a juncture where education, immigration, and economic policies meet and overlap (see Figure 1.3) – an excellent case study of which is given in Walton-Roberts and Hennebry's chapter on international

Figure 1.3 International Students and the Immigration-Economic-Education
Policy Realms before and after the Development of Canada's National
International Education Strategy

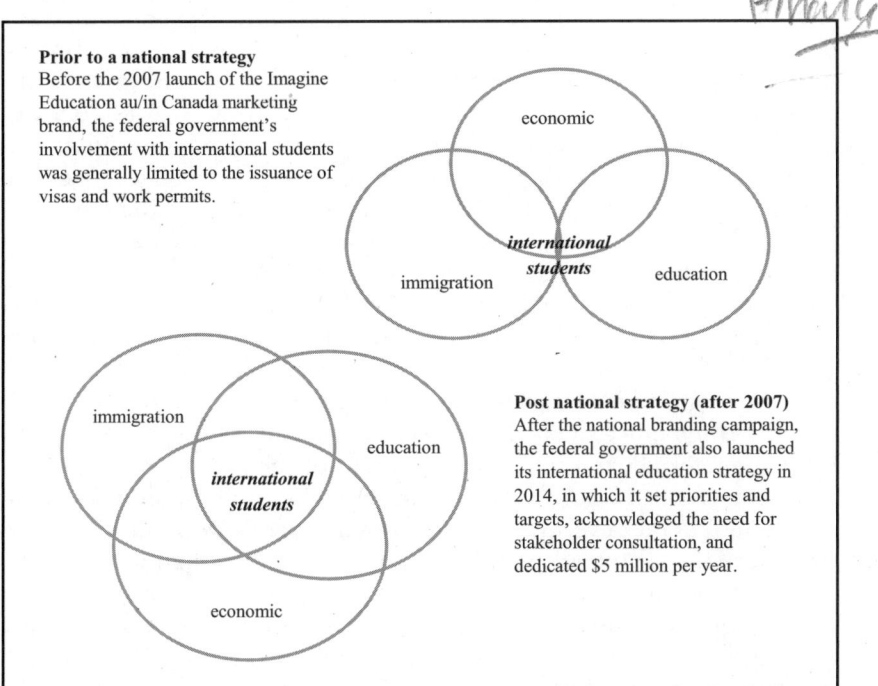

nurses in Canada. Although immigration policy in Canada has historically been a nation-building exercise, and has thus fit into a package of
policies on economic trade and development and ethnocultural relations (Simmons 2010), the explicit inclusion of education within this
immigration package is new. Prior to the implementation of Canada's
international education branding campaign in 2008, recognition of the
connection between immigration and education was generally limited to
the issuance of study and work permits for international students. In the
contemporary period, education migration, or "edugration," is increasingly linked to permanent residence and the vision of an economically
robust and multicultural society.

Traditionally, the Canadian government's involvement in post-
secondary education focused on indirect support through tax credits,

grants, and loans to individuals, contributions to federal research-funding bodies, and social transfers to provinces to support post-secondary institutions (Office of the Parliamentary Budget Officer 2016). And although the actual value of the federal government's contribution to post-secondary revenues changes from year to year, its relative contribution declined from 11.6 per cent in 2004–5 to 9.4 per cent in 2013–14. Non-federal government support also declined from 42.6 to 39.5 per cent. Post-secondary institutions are increasingly relying on tuition and other fees as well as investments, which rose as a percentage of college and university revenues from 23.8 to 31.4 per cent during the same ten-year period (Office of the Parliamentary Budget Officer 2016). Concomitant with the traditional forms of support for the post-secondary sector is the federal government's new push into international education at all levels. This began as a national branding campaign with Imagine Education au/in Canada in 2008 (now EduCanada) and culminated in the first international education strategy in 2014 (Foreign Affairs, Trade and Development Canada 2014). Trilokekar and El Masri's chapter in this volume briefly traces the development of the federal government's involvement in education and its links to labour and immigration policies. The federal government now explicitly recognizes and facilitates opportunities for international students to gain Canadian work experience and contribute to the economy and a highly skilled labour force. It also recognizes the need for a congruent immigration policy, particularly as it pertains to the processing of study (and work) permits and to the post-study transition from student to worker – and for many, the transition to permanent resident.

The intersectional space international students now occupy, which is both new and unstable, is undergoing constant transformation and policy tweaking. On the one hand, international students comprise one of the most desirable segments of migrants, and as such are the new "designer migrants," to borrow Simmons's term. They are highly motivated, highly skilled, and often arrive with significant financial resources. Their entry and temporary stay are vetted and regulated. A more compelling argument for the international student migration stream is that those students who are successful in the transition to the labour market can take up permanent residence, a relatively recent notion for a country historically built on the backs of working adults.

On the flipside, international students are viewed as foreigners less deserving of the same rights and entitlements as permanent residents and citizens, including access to social and health services, though like other migrants, they require support in adjustment (see Wintre et al.'s chapter in this volume, which looks at the factors associated with student adjustment, including university support and structure). Their enrolment in higher education institutions is also contentious as they are perceived by the public as occupying coveted and limited university spots. This is a long-standing issue, as evidenced in two examples from the mainstream media: a 1979 CTV *W5* episode called "Campus Give-away" and a 2010 Maclean's article formerly entitled "Too Asian? Some Frosh Don't Want to Study at an Asian University" and revised to "The Enrollment Controversy" after some public backlash.

International Education, Social Mobility, and Structuring Institutions

In taking an appropriate institutional perspective, this collection is not about institutions per se, which is to say that the institutions themselves are not under the microscope. Rather, this book is about how students interacted with institutions, how they were affected by them, and how they redefined them. Institutions, as described by the early sociologist Herbert Spencer, are "those more enduring structures that meet fundamental functional requisites of human organization and that regulate, control, and circumscribe the actions of individuals and groups in a society" (quoted in Turner 1985, 106). Spencer's conceptualization of institutions is broader than the formal institutions of higher education and the export education industry, and it allows for the inclusion of kinship ties, ethnic communities, and local labour markets. It is through such institutions – whether one perceives them as serving a functional or hegemonic purpose – that government policies are often communicated, interpreted, enacted, and enforced, and it is this student-institution nexus that helps us to understand the social realities in which international students operate.

If we can conceptualize interactions with institutions as falling on a spectrum from harmonious, which promotes social integration (Turner 1985, 112), to conflictual, which leads to the social isolation of individuals or the change of individuals or institutions, the contributions in this collection demonstrate that student interactions with institutions are rarely at either extreme, but fall all across the spectrum. This perspective goes beyond conceptualizing institutions as part of the supply-side of the ISM equation; they are more than drivers of ISM flows and international student recruitment.

With this institutional perspective in mind, we draw on a conceptual framework that bridges two perspectives: the link between social mobility and education migration, and a structuring institutional perspective of the international education industry.

Education provides a leveraging tool for students to perform better in the labour market and to overcome the disadvantages of social and economic status. On the other hand, education is also known to reinforce social inequalities by passing on benefits to a small segment of society. Critical scholarship emphasizes that such inequalities are shaped by differences in monetary affordability, the existence of social supports/networks, and proficiency of cultural knowledge. For example, Bourdieu (1984) observes that the consumption of high culture by the French bourgeoisie was closely related to the process of social reproduction. Echoing Bourdieu, Waters and Brooks (2011) reminds us that "capital," whether social, cultural, or economic, benefits students who have the means, and that education migration is used as a tool to accelerate this process.

Our understanding of the link between education and social mobility has developed in step with the development of an increasingly interconnected global order. While Bourdieu's earlier discussion was spatially limited to French upper-class society (1984, 1996), we have since witnessed a higher level of education migration for the purpose of foreign-language and credential acquisition. People are increasingly going across borders for educational purposes and to earn a foreign credential as a way to improve their social and economic conditions. Arguably, this has been the case for decades, and yet in the contemporary period a foreign education has become more accessible to more people.

Another development we are witnessing, and which is shown in this book, is that the trajectories of education migration as a path to social mobility have diversified as well. The following chapters represent the varied experiences of student groups coming to Canada under different levels of study (including younger students below the tertiary level), with different gender perspectives (including women and LGBTQ students), and with insights on parents/guardians and whole families. One of the key findings from these chapters is that education migration does not always provide a smooth ladder for upward social mobility. Kwak et al. and Kim et al. found that the educational journeys of different international student groups in Canada were accompanied by various types of barriers and resulted in mixed outcomes. Other groups (as shown in the chapter by Walton-Roberts and Hennebry) had to navigate constantly changing policies and negotiate between the competing interests of institutional stakeholders.

This leads to our second theme: the role of institutional actors, which concerns the rising importance of government and non-governmental institutions, labour market forces, religious organizations, ethnic communities, and professional regulatory bodies and the like, along with policies on international student recruitment and integration. The commercialization and marketization of education is known to be a driving force behind the national branding of the education industry in some Western countries (e.g., Johnstone and Lee 2014; Kwak 2013; Waters 2008; Waters and Brooks 2011). Relaxed visa entries for international students, aggressive marketing and recruitment, and implementation of retention strategies are all notable examples of such efforts. However, the ways in which institutional actors have responded to the growing demand for international education and the needs of local labour markets have by no means been uniformly and smoothly coordinated. In many cases, the ostensibly seamless growth of the international education industry masks many complex dynamics (Kwak 2013), and it shapes not only the composition of student flows to Canada but also students' lives. In Canada, our contributors found, different levels of governments have been working mostly independently but also in cooperation from time to time to deal with international education. However, the policies and practices of governments and professional regulatory organizations are not always harmonized with the wishes of international students and their families. This interaction between and tension among individuals, their self-construction, and the institutions that structure that construction are the focus of this collection.

The Collection in Four Parts

Part I contains three chapters that offer an introduction and overview of policies, explanations, and data on ISM to Canada. The chapter by Trilokekar and El Masri describes the changing policy context and approaches to international education in Canada. The authors first examine how the federal government came to recognize the need to adopt a fee system for international education in the 1980s as international students began to be perceived as an important source of revenue. In the early 2000s, the government made another important shift in its international education policy as it began to view international students as ideal future immigrants. As the global competition for foreign talent increased, the federal government joined the bandwagon by promoting Canadian education abroad and implementing favourable immigration policies for international students. Trilokekar and El Masri also document how these changes were implemented by different levels of government working both independently and cooperatively, paying particular attention to the changing global trends. The authors emphasize that Canada's particular historical, geopolitical, economic, and cultural context informed the government's adoption of a global policy discourse on international education and international student recruitment.

The other two chapters in Part I complement the policy discussion by focusing on what we know thus far about ISM to Canada and the data limitations that restrict an expansion of knowledge. Kim and Sondhi apply Findlay's (2011) framework of demand- and supply-side perspectives to review the literature that explains ISM to Canada. The review shows one body of work that sees student mobility as a choice and explains individual mobility by the push and pull forces experienced in each of the sending and host countries (the demand side). We learn that push forces tend to be connected to social, economic, and political conditions in sending societies and primarily to language barriers in host societies. Pull forces in sending countries are related to families and financial considerations, whereas in host countries they are related to academic offerings, the prestige of an overseas education, and the possibility of permanent residence. In addition, individual motivations differ by level of study, sending regions, and class background. On the supply side, the review emphasizes the importance of institutions and policies that direct international student flows and underscore the structured nature of student mobility. As Trilokekar and El Masri discuss in their chapter, the current structure of international student flows and education in Canada have been shaped by the policies and practices of different levels of government, non-governmental agencies, and educational institutions.

Providing a different type of review, the chapter by Kim, Attieh, and Owen examines the availability (or lack thereof) of national-level data on international students. Based on their review of nineteen surveys and other data sources offered by Statistics Canada and various other national bodies, the authors argue that the collection of data on migrants tends to reflect Canada's historical nation-building project, which views immigrants as permanent settlers. In other words, this view of migrants as permanent residents has been institutionalized in our data collection systems, and this established practice has consequences for informing our understanding of migrant populations as the temporary resident population expands. While the authors notice improvements and some opportunities for national-level analyses on international students (as demonstrated by Lu and Hou in their chapter), they make it clear that current measures have yet to capture the complex migration trajectories that characterize current population movements. Looking at these limitations, they consider whether records maintained by non-governmental organizations on individual users might provide a solution to these conceptual and data limitations. Using secondary data from World Education Services with caution, they show that international students face different types of barriers than other migrant groups. They conclude that such data have the potential to fill some gaps but that more work is needed.

Part II highlights the adaptation and integration of international students in educational institutions. The chapter by Wintre et al. looks at international undergraduate student adjustment at York University through the lens of developmental psychology. First, the authors argue that undergraduate students should be seen as emerging adults, as their study participants expressed motivations for international study that were consistent with themes characterizing the emerging adulthood stage: a desire for change, increased opportunities, independence, autonomy, concerns for the future, and new experiences. Participants also identified areas of concern relating to geographic separation, language, employment, and integration. Given this emerging-adulthood framework, the authors examined the factors associated with student adjustment using the Student Adaptation to College Questionnaire (SACQ). Their statistical analysis incorporated standard individual-level variables such as age and gender but also included others such as acculturation motivation and self-reported English abilities. Most relevant to the themes of this book, however, were those variables that accounted for the role of families, social networks, and universities. Interestingly, the results demonstrate that perceptions related to parental relationships, social support, and institutional support were important for international student adjustment.

Where most of the literature on ISM focus on tertiary-level students, Kim et al. ask how the legal status of younger students from South Korea shapes both the experiences of students and their parents. Despite the growth in the number of temporary residents in Canada, there is only very limited research comparing how permanent and temporary statuses are linked to particular kinds of psychosocial, social, and economic outcomes. Yet, many families are defined by their legal status, as this is how institutions often distinguish eligibility/membership criteria. As such, we would expect these institutional definitions and practices to affect integration patterns. Using data from a face-to-face survey conducted in the Korean community in Toronto, Kim et al. find that status was associated with academic and language difficulties, less parent-teacher interactions, and less participation in co- and extra-curricular activities, although the latter was evident only for first-born or single children. How to address these issues and whether these patterns apply to other communities are important questions.

Part III consists of four chapters and begins with local diasporic communities before moving on to a consideration of how families are implicated in international student experiences. Where Wintre et al.'s analysis shows that social support positively affects student adjustment, Montsion's chapter provides insight on this association by exploring how local Chinese community organizations and Christian churches in Vancouver are "filling the gaps" left by governments and educational institutions. He argues that the official branding of Vancouver as a gateway between Asia and Canada reflects a laissez-faire approach that has left non-governmental organizations to respond to students' needs. He describes how several students from Mainland China received support from local associations in broadening their social networks, offering opportunities to gain work-related experience (e.g., through volunteering and corporate connections), and reducing loneliness and isolation. Through his chapter, we learn that the institutional actors supporting international students range widely from well-established Chinese community associations, such as the United Chinese Community Enrichment Services Society (SUCCESS), to Chinese Christian churches, to newly created Mainlander organizations. Finally, Montsion shows that the influx of students from Mainland China contributes to a shifting landscape of local community politics that has been dominated historically by migrants from Hong Kong.

From the Chinese diasporic community in Vancouver, we move to the Indian diaspora in Toronto. The chapter by Sondhi explores two-way interactions between international students from India and the Indian community through the lens of gender. Drawing on the Butlerian vocabulary of the (un)intelligibility of gender performances, Sondhi recognizes the emerging heterogeneity of the Indian diaspora in Toronto. The sources of information utilized in this chapter include sixty-five in-depth, semi-structured interviews conducted in Toronto and New Delhi and an online survey that collected data on the socio-economic background and migration trajectories of the participants. The author pays particular attention to the stories of six students highlighting their experience with gender performance. While some students feel more at ease within the Indian community than in Western culture, other female students, especially those who were more social and career driven in India, have a hard time fitting in with the local Indian community. These students find that the Indian community in Toronto adheres to an older version of gender ideology and they choose to be "intelligible" (accepted) by performing conservative gender norms. In a number of other cases, participants who identified as queer made themselves "unintelligible" (not accepted) within the community and chose to withdraw from it. The analysis confirms a growing diversity among the students from India and the Indian diaspora in Toronto.

Man and Chou examine the immigration pathways of Chinese women who came to Canada for their own or their children's education. The authors explore the migration trajectories of sixteen Mainland Chinese women in the context of global economic restructuring. The women were especially good examples of transnational subjects for they actively weighed in on the benefits and challenges of education migration from China to Canada. The authors pay particular attention to the women's transnational strategies for social reproduction. Responding to rapid economic restructuring in China, newly emerging middle-class families have increasingly sought a better place for their children's education and social development. Despite struggling with de-skilling and precarious employment in Canada, and even separation from spouses through transnational family arrangements, most study participants still considered education migration a viable strategy to facilitate the social reproduction of their family's middle-class identity. Man and Chou's analysis is linked with the chapter by Kwak et al., which examines the diverse experiences of transnational family arrangements among Korean education migrants in Toronto.

Despite growing scholarship on dynamic and flexible views on identity formation, studies on minority and (im)migrant groups often reify a static and universal view of identity formation. This can be seen in the studies of *jogi yuhaksaeng* and *girogi gajok* (young Korean international students and their families, respectively). In their chapter, Kwak et al. examine the heterogeneous nature of transnational migrants and their identity formation, focusing on young (grades K–12) Korean students and their families in Toronto. Drawing upon twenty semi-structured interviews with *girogi* mothers and their children, the authors explore ways in which the students and their mothers flexibly negotiate and reconstruct their identities beyond the pervasive and typical preconceptions of separated families. Except for the commonality of being a family split between Korea and

Canada, the analysis of the interview data reveals that *girogi* families are varied in terms of their migration objectives, their perspectives on identity, and the trajectories of their changing family relations.

For many policymakers, a salient question concerns transitions from temporary to permanent residence and from school to work. Part IV addresses these topics. Lu and Hou, both researchers at Statistics Canada, examine transition rates as well as the factors associated with labour market performance among former international students who have been landed immigrants for at least ten years. They find that while there are some variations by gender, level of education, and source country, roughly 20 to 30 per cent of the 1990–2004 cohorts of international students had transitioned to permanent residence by the ten-year mark. To investigate the question of labour market insertion, they analyse a special data file called the Canadian Employer-Employee Dynamics Database (CEEDD) with linked administrative data that is not available through the Data Liberation Initiative at a Research Data Centre (see Kim, Reem, and Owen in this volume). They look specifically at the annual earnings of former international students and find that levels of education attained in Canada and subsequent work experience in the country were positively associated with earnings for both women and men.

Walton-Roberts and Hennebry examine the transition process of internationally educated nurses (IENs) who navigate through a complex system of regulations and requirements in order to practice in Canada. Despite the increase in the expected nursing shortfall in Canada, they found that many IENs face significant challenges when it comes to dealing with changing immigration policies and regulatory changes in the nursing profession. The delayed assessment of foreign credentials and the shortened absence period permitted by the College of Nurses of Ontario (CNO) are known to be major barriers for IENs seeking to complete licensing and registration. The conflicting requirements of the CNO and Citizenship and Immigration Canada (CIC) present a classic catch-22 problem as well. The authors draw on a study of ninety-two IENs from India to reinforce their point. They also provide recommendations for professional regulatory agencies and governments to harmonize the transition process from training to entry into the nursing profession for IENs.

We are fortunate in Canada to have a wide network of exemplary scholars who take up the question of ISM from different disciplinary perspectives while sharing research interests in how institutions influence the relationship between students and the state. Through this body of work representing communities across Canada, from Vancouver to Halifax, we learn that international students and their families participate in their local ethnic communities and their educational institutions in myriad ways, that their psychosocial development must be taken into consideration when asking questions about adaptation, that our systems and institutions (including our data systems) must also adapt to students and their families, and that transitions to the labour market, and permanent residence, are not without setbacks and difficulties. Most of all, this volume demonstrates the need to ask more critical questions about the short- and long-term effects of temporary legal status, how student and family experiences differ by educational level and region of settlement, the barriers to and facilitators of adaptation and integration, and, ultimately, to what extent and in what ways individual, familial, institutional, and state goals are in harmony and in discord.

References

Bourdieu, Pierre. 1984. *Distinction: A Social Critique of the Judgement of Taste.* Cambridge, MA: Harvard University Press.

Choudaha, Rahul. 2017. "Three Waves of International Student Mobility (1999–2020)." *Studies in Higher Education* 42 (5): 825–32. https://doi.org/10.1080/03075079.2017.1293872.

Citizenship and Immigration Canada (CIC). 2015a. *Facts and Figures 2014: Immigration Overview – Temporary Residents.* Citizenship and Immigration Canada: Research and Evaluation Branch.

– 2015b. *Facts and Figures 2015: Immigration Overview – Temporary Residents.* http://open.canada.ca/data/en/dataset/052642bb-3fd9-4828-b608-c81dff7e539c.

Deloitte Access Economics. 2015. *The Value of International Education to Australia. Report.* Australian Government.

Findlay, Allan M. 2011. "An Assessment of Supply and Demand-Side Theorizations of International Student Mobility." *International Migration (Geneva, Switzerland)* 49 (2): 162–90. https://doi.org/10.1111/j.1468-2435.2010.00643.x.

Foreign Affairs, Trade and Development Canada. 2014. *Canada's International Education Strategy: Harnessing Our Knowledge Advantage to Drive Innovation and Prosperity. Report.* Government of Canada.

Johnstone, Marjorie, and Eunjung Lee. 2014. "Branded: International Education and 21st-Century Canadian Immigration, Education Policy, and the Welfare State." *International Social Work* 57 (3): 209–21. https://doi.org/10.1177/0020872813508572.

Kim, Ann H. 2013. "Outward and Upward Mobilities: The Global Dispersion of Students from South Korea." *Asian and Pacific Migration Journal* 22 (4): 465–73. https://doi.org/10.1177/011719681302200401.

Kim, Ann H., and Gunjan Sondhi. 2015. "Bridging the Literature on Education Migration." *Population Change and Lifecourse Strategic Knowledge Cluster Discussion Paper Series/Un Réseau Stratégique de Connaissances Changements de Population et Parcours de vie Document de travail* (3): 1. http://ir.lib.uwo.ca/pclc/vol3/iss1/7.

Knight-Grofe, Janine, and Karen Rauh. 2016. *A World of Learning 2016: Canada's Performance and Potential in International Education.* Canadian Bureau for International Education Report.

Kunin, Roslyn, and Associates. 2016. *Economic Impact of International Education in Canada: An Update. Final Report, July.* Global Affairs Canada.

Kwak, Min-Jung. 2013. "Rethinking the Neo-Liberal Nexus of Education, Migration, and Institutions." *Environment & Planning A* 45 (8): 1858–72. https://doi.org/10.1068/a43493.

Office of the Parliamentary Budget Officer. 2016. *Federal Spending on Postsecondary Education.* Report. Ottawa, Canada.

Organisation for Economic Co-operation and Development (OECD). 2015. *Education at a Glance 2015: OECD Indicators.* Paris: OECD Publishing.

– 2017. "Tuition Fee Reforms and International Mobility." In *Education Indicators in Focus 51.* Paris: OECD Publishing.

Simmons, Alan. 2010. *Immigration and Canada: Global and Transnational Perspectives.* Toronto: Canadian Scholars' Press.

Statistics Canada. 2015. "Table 477–0031 – Postsecondary enrolments, by student status, country of citizenship and sex, annual (number)." *CANSIM Database.* http://www5.statcan.gc.ca/cansim/a26?lang=eng&retrLang=eng&id=4770031&pattern=students&tabMode=dataTable&srchLan=-1&p1=1&p2=49.

Turner, Johnathan H. 1985. *Herbert Spencer: A Renewed Appreciation.* Thousand Oaks, CA: Sage Publications.

UNESCO Institute for Statistics. 2016. "Global Flow of Tertiary-Level Students." http://uis.unesco.org/en/uis-student-flow.

Walker, Patricia. 2014. "International Student Policies in UK Higher Education from Colonialism to the Coalition." *Journal of Studies in International Education* 18 (4): 325–44. https://doi.org/10.1177/1028315312467355.

Waters, Johanna. 2008. *Education, Migration and Cultural Capital in the Chinese Diaspora: Transnational Students between Hong Kong and Canada.* New York: Cambria Press.

Waters, Johanna, and Rachel Brooks. 2011. "International/Transnational Spaces of Education." *Globalisation, Societies and Education* 9 (2): 155–60. https://doi.org/10.1080/14767724.2011.576933.

PART I

International Students in the
Canadian Context

2 "International Students Are … Golden": Canada's Changing Policy Contexts, Approaches, and National Peculiarities in Attracting International Students as Future Immigrants

ROOPA DESAI TRILOKEKAR AND AMIRA EL MASRI

Introduction

As an international student adviser in the mid- to late 1990s, first at Ryerson University and then at York University, I recollect "dual intent" being among *the* major issues facing international students (IS) applying for student visas.[1] That is, IS had to prove that they did not intend to both enter the country on a temporary basis and then immigrate permanently. The "burden of proof" was placed on IS to show that they intended to come to Canada *only* for study purposes and that they would return home after completing their studies. In radical opposition is Canada's first-ever international education strategy, Harnessing Our Knowledge Advantage to Drive Innovation and Prosperity, released in January 2014, which states:

> International students are a future source of skilled labour, as they may be eligible after graduation for permanent residence through immigration programs such as the Canadian Experience Class (introduced in 2008). International students are well positioned to immigrate to Canada as they have typically obtained Canadian credentials, are proficient in at least

The quotation in the title of this chapter is an excerpt from a confidential interview. All interviews referenced in this chapter were conducted by Paul Axelrod (principal investigator), Theresa Shanahan, Roopa Desai Trilokekar, and Richard Wellen (co-investigators) for *Making Policy in Canadian Post-secondary Education since 1990*, a project funded by the Social Sciences and Humanities Research Council of Canada (SSHRC) General Research Grant, 2008–11. The names of the interviewees have been withheld by agreement of both parties. The interview with Bob Rae was not confidential and is quoted with permission.

1 Reference made to first author Roopa Desai Trilokekar.

one official language and often have relevant Canadian work experience.
(DFATD 2014, 12)

What triggered such a profound change in the Canadian government's approach to IS over since the 1990s? How does Canada's policy
compare to those of other OECD countries, which, like Canada, actively
recruit IS? This chapter examines the changing international education (IE) policy context and approaches to IS in Canada via a historical
policy analysis to ascertain if and how Canadian policy either converges
or diverges from global trends, or if it is the result of the formation of a
hybrid policy.

Viewed against the backdrop of demographic challenges and economic restraints, there has been growing policy attention from advanced
economies to the recruitment and retention of IS as part of a broad
strategy to manage highly skilled migration (Becker and Kolster 2012;
OECD 2015; Riaño and Piguet 2016; She and Wotherspoon 2013). Several OECD countries are "engaged in marketing their higher education
institutions, easing entry and status extension regulations, allowing IS to
work during studies, and offering channels for them to change status and
stay as knowledge workers" (She and Wotherspoon 2013, 2). With more
intense and complex competition among these countries for IS, there
has been a resulting trend of both policy convergence and divergence,
with key national factors determining the shape of each government's
IS policy (Chaloff and Lemaître 2009; Choudaha, Li, and Kono 2013;
Santiago et al. 2008; Suter and Jandl 2006; Tremblay 2005). Researchers
note the importance of examining the various factors that shape government policies (see Ortiz, Chang, and Fang 2015; Riaño and Piguet 2016;
She and Wotherspoon 2013). This chapter aims to compliment those
studies that focus on national government policies on IS recruitment
and retention.

International Students, Globalization, and the
Internationalization of Higher Education

In the present context, internationalization is the "process of integrating an international, intercultural or global dimension into the purpose, functions or delivery of higher education at the institutional and
national levels" (Knight 2008, 21). IS "are defined as non-Canadian
students who do not have 'permanent resident' status and have had to
obtain the authorization of the Canadian government [typically a student visa] to enter Canada with the intention of pursuing an education"

(Statistics Canada 2010). The hosting of IS is associated with institutional strategies for internationalization. Universities Canada's[2] internationalization survey reports that 45 per cent of responding Canadian institutions identified the recruitment of IS as among their highest priorities, and 70 per cent included IS recruitment among their top five goals (AUCC 2014). Whereas Canadian universities acknowledge the value of IS in internationalizing their campuses, they also cite the revenue these students generate (AUCC 2014). Due a decline in public funding, cash-deprived universities "are looking for revenues from all sources ... and international students do help us do that" (Chignal 2015).

Internationalization is thus considered "one of the major forces impacting and shaping higher education in the 21st century," (Knight 2008, ix). Altbach, Reisberg, and Rumbley state that

> Globalization, a key reality in the 21st century, has already profoundly influenced higher education ... We define globalization as the reality shaped by an increasingly integrated world economy, new information and communications technology, the emergence of an international knowledge network, the role of the English language, and other forces beyond the control of academic institutions (2009, 7).

Clearly, both internationalization and globalization are seen as critical forces shaping higher education in the twenty-first century. Sometimes considered distinct yet interrelated, globalization and internationalization are more often than not used interchangeably to signify neo-liberal policy changes aimed at restructuring national higher education systems to secure a greater share of the global educational market (Currie and Newson 1998; Dolby 2011; Enders and Fulton 2002; Stromquist 2013; Wells 2005). Recruitment of IS is one such policy and practice adopted by nation states to meet these objectives (Altbach and Knight 2007; Dennison and Schuetze 2004; Dolby 2011; Marginson 2011; Rizvi 2011; Trilokekar and Kizilbash 2013).

In fact, it is suggested that national governments have developed a wide range of "more advanced or even highly sophisticated strategies" to both recruit and retain IS (Becker and Kolster 2012, 52). OECD countries are reported to attract over 70 per cent of all IS, with Australia, Canada, France, Germany, Japan, the United Kingdom, and the United States

---

2 Universities Canada was previously known as the Association of Universities and Colleges of Canada (AUCC).

together receiving more than 50 per cent of all IS worldwide (OECD 2015). Depending on the actual number of IS they host and their overall recruitment and retention policies, countries have been categorized as "major players" (the United States, the United Kingdom, and Australia); "middle powers" (Germany and France); "evolving destinations" (Japan, Canada, and New Zealand); and "emerging contenders" (Malaysia, Singapore, and China) (Verbik and Lasanowski 2007). Canada ranks as the world's seventh most popular destination for IS (CBIE 2016; ICEF 2013) and it holds a 5 per cent share of the global market for internationally mobile students (ICEF 2013). Becker and Kolster (2012) report on how these national IS policies are increasingly aligned with national economic strategies and foreign economic and cultural policies "focusing on increasing a country's international economic competitiveness by investing in knowledge, innovation and a highly-skilled workforce" (52). However, there are differentials in policy focus. The United Kingdom and Australia, for example, aim to recruit IS who can pay higher tuition fees because income from these fees accounts for a large proportion of many institutions' revenues. Hence, the United Kingdom and Australia are noted for their aggressive recruitment practices, which have resulted in the strongest growth in international undergraduate students (Choudaha et. al. 2013). On the other hand, countries such as Germany and Canada, given their declining or low birth rates and aging populations, are noted for attracting IS in an effort to address future labour market shortages and to boost the future national economy (Becker and Kolster 2012). Australia has witnessed a shift in its immigration policies to the extent that IS are now also viewed as a potential pool of qualified immigrants. Hence, IS are increasingly viewed as "ideal," "home-grown" alternatives to other immigrants (Gribble and Blackmore 2012; Hawthorne 2008a, 2008b; Johnstone and Lee 2014; Lowe 2010; Sá and Sabzalieva 2016). With better language skills and significantly more acculturation in host countries, they are considered an "attractive and efficient resource," as they are of "prime work-force age and have self-funded to meet domestic employer requirements" (Hawthorne 2012, 422). A similar rationale supports government policy across several countries, including the Netherlands, Sweden, and Ireland, to name just a few (de Wit 2011; Hawthorne 2008a, 2008b; Morris-Lange and Brands 2015; Sá and Sabzalieva 2016).

As countries acknowledge the risks associated with "uncontrollable and destabilizing migration flows," they develop "migration management" strategies to "both strictly control human mobility and organize it in a way that makes it compatible with a number of objectives pursued by both state and non-state actors" (Pécoud 2013, 1). Beine et al. (2015) note an emerging policy trend that separates high-skilled labour immigration (e.g., IS) from unwanted labour migration. As mentioned above, with several OECD countries facing similar demographic challenges, the new immigration pathway for IS as a way of addressing a country's immediate and projected labour market shortages has gained popularity (Becker and Kolster 2012; de Wit 2011; Hawthorne 2008a, 2008b; Riaño and Piguet 2016; She and Wotherspoon 2013; She 2011; Tremblay 2005). Riaño and Piguet (2016) report that IS are the fastest-growing immigrant group among all groups of migrants, including labour migrants, family migrants, and refugees. However, scholars indicate that countries differ in their overall approach to IS policies. Some are characterized by their "closed policy" approach – which is "legitimized, for example, by security issues as well as the fear that foreign students might crowd out natives from graduate programs and ultimately become competitors in the labour market" – while others exhibit more "open policy" approaches, which seek to "increase the number of highly skilled workers but also follow the idea that student migration is correlated with entrepreneurship, international trade, and investment" (Riaño and Piguet 2016, 17). For example, She and Wotherspoon (2013) suggest that the United States is inclined to have low openness to IS entry and high control on their settlement whereas Canada tends to act in the opposite way – that is, high openness to entry and low control on stay. Hence, scholars suggest that despite the overall convergence in IS policies across host countries, the detailed regulations, procedures, and mechanisms through which these policies are carried out differ from one country to another (Cornelius and Tsuda 2004).

Approach: Framework and Outline

We define policy as "any course of action (or inaction) relating to the selection of goals, the definition of values, or the allocation of resources" (Codd 1988, 235). To investigate how Canada's federal policy on IS and IE has been constructed and framed we adopt Gale's (2001) historiography methodological approach to policy analysis. Policy historiography is interested in tracing policy changes and the way those changes are addressed within a particular policy domain; exploring policies in their current form; and examining the nature of the change from earlier policies to the current one. When studying the construction of policy and its changes over time, it is important to remember that "policy documents ... are ideological texts that have been constructed within a particular context. The task of deconstruction begins with the recognition of that context" (Codd 1988, 243–4). This approach aids us in "highlight[ing] how policies come to be framed in certain ways – reflecting how economic, social, political and cultural contexts shape both the content and language of policy documents" (Taylor 1997, 28).

This chapter is divided into three sections. First, in keeping with Gale's (2001) approach to policy historiography, we start by examining the conditions and specific contexts (historical, economic, and political) that have led to the emergence of particular IE policy agendas and approaches. Focusing on the federal government, this chapter first analyzes how and to what end the state shapes such policies. We then examine whether global forces cause the state to reproduce global policy rhetoric as a "product of conscious adaptation, blind imitation or pressure to conform" (Stromquist quoted in Wells 2005, 110). Finally, in concerning itself with the effects or implications of federal policy at the national, provincial, and institutional levels, this chapter adopts a layered approach to understanding policy (Taylor 1997), engaging with what Marginson and Rhoades (2002) refer to as the "gloconal," or, as Marginson and Sawir (2005) explain, how IS and IE policy get taken up and constituted "by an amalgam of global, national and local factors in complex ways" (289) to produce specific practices and policies within a given context. This chapter thus attempts to address policy discourse through its core aspects: contexts, texts, and consequences (Taylor 1997).

Historical Development of Federal Policy on IS

Bond and Lemasson (1999) suggest that the two major formative strands of internationalization in Canadian universities are development cooperation and IS. The enrolment of IS at Canadian universities first began as part of Canada's Overseas Development Assistance (ODA) program. During the 1960s, IS came mainly from the developing world and they arrived with funding, including scholarships such as the Canadian Commonwealth Scholarship and Fellowship Program (CSFP). Beginning in the 1980s, however, there was a radical shift in government policy towards IS. This shift was evident in the third volume of the 1984 Commission on Canadian Studies report, *Some Questions of Balance: Human Resources, Higher Education and Canadian Studies*, which expressed concern over the fact that Canadians were spending approximately $300 million of their tax dollars on the education of IS in Canada (excluding fees). There was a growing sentiment during this period that IS should not be educated at the expense of Canadian taxpayers (DFAIT 1988,

217). In 1982–3, an estimated 65,000 IS were studying in Canada, 35,000 of them at universities. An outcome of this report was a complete shift to a fee-paying model for IS, with most provinces charging differential fees, though some had already initiated this prior to the report as early as the late 1970s (Canadian Federation of Students 2015).

This shift towards attracting more fee-paying IS, which was likely a result of an increase in "nationalistic" or "parochial" thinking on the part of the government, was also directly tied to the increased emphasis on an economic agenda in Canada's foreign policy. Beginning in the 1980s, the Department of Foreign Affairs and International Trade (DFAIT) highlighted the priority given to international trade in Canada's foreign policy. Within the context of an "international market place," Canadian higher education began to be viewed as a commodity (Joyal 1994, 6), and IS and IE were perceived as important mechanisms to secure Canada's national prosperity. In the late 1980s, a staff position was added to DFAIT for the exclusive purpose of "marketing … educational services" (DFAIT 1988, 3), with Minister of International Trade Sergio Marchi proclaiming, "Education is now an industry. Canada needs to approach the international market place for education services with the same discipline and commitment that we bring to other sectors" (Trilokekar 2007, 225). There was a direct policy link between IS recruitment, IE, and international trade. IS and IE became increasingly valuable in terms of their dollar contributions to the economy. For example, Jim Fox, president of the Canadian Bureau for International Education (CBIE) stated that, "for Canada, educational trade amounts to $1.5 billion. This relates to international students alone … Education, in fact, ranks as an export that is next to wheat in its importance to this country" (quoted in Joyal 1994, 19). By 1992, with Canadian universities now hosting 37,000 foreign students, the focus turned to substantially increasing IS numbers. Team Canada Missions abroad came to include university presidents, and in 1995, the first eight Canada Education Centres were established to market Canadian higher education. In 1998, a new Educational Marketing Unit was established within DFAIT and assigned the task of brand development for Canadian education abroad (Trilokekar 2007).

Another shift in IS policy was introduced with the release of Canada's Innovation Strategy in 2002. Having previously focused exclusively on recruiting IS, the government was now committed to attracting them as future immigrants. The new Immigration and Refugee Protection Act (IRPA) of 2001 put in place a series of measures that essentially enabled the retention of IS beyond their formal period of study – namely by establishing a new category of temporary residents, thereby allowing IS to more easily pursue study and/or work opportunities in Canada. In 2004, a pilot off-campus work project for IS was established, and Citizenship and Immigration Canada (CIC) began partnering directly with the post-secondary sector in programs such as the Student Partners Project in 2005 to further streamline and facilitate IS entry to Canada and their application for permanent residency.

This new push to attract IS as permanent residents resulted in further government investments in IS recruitment strategies. Advantage Canada, released in 2006 as Canada's economic action plan, explicitly stated that Canada's knowledge advantage was to be achieved by marketing higher education abroad and attracting the "best" foreign students to Canada. Also in 2006, DFAIT announced Edu-Canada, a new initiative aimed at promoting Canada as an educational destination. An investment of $1 million per year over five years was allocated to launch the Imagine Education in/au Canada brand and an associated marketing campaign. In 2008, the Global Commerce Strategy provided a further investment of $2 million for educational marketing. That same year, the off-campus work permit program was formally launched and a novel immigration category introduced, the Canadian Experience Class (CEC), which enabled temporary foreign workers, including IS with Canadian work experience, to apply for permanent residency (CIC 2010). The introduction of the CEC marked the start of an even more targeted approach to the wooing of IS as future permanent residents. By 2009, IS were able to extend their post-graduation work permits for to up to three years.

The government's attempt to invest in recruiting more IS was further legitimized by the resulting economic returns. Two government-commissioned reports, *Economic Impact of International Education in Canada* and *Best Practices on Managing the Delivery of Canadian Education Marketing*, both published in 2009, emphasized the economic advantage of hosting IS. The two reports also positioned Canada competitively in their assessment of global IS recruitment and retention best practices. In 2010, an updated version of *Economic Impact of International Education in Canada* estimated even higher economic benefits to Canada from the increase in IS, stating that IS spent in excess of $7.7 billion on tuition, accommodation, and discretionary spending; created over 81,000 jobs; and generated more than $445 million in government revenue (Kunin and Associates 2012). With such data-driven evidence of the direct – and increasing – economic value of IS, the government legitimized not only its policy discourse but also its power in shaping IS policy to meet its broader national (economic) objectives. IE and IS were now central to the government's economic plans. Not only did the government's 2011

Economic Action Plan allocate funding for the development of an IE strategy, but the 2013 Global Markets Action Plan 1 also identified IE as one of the Canadian economy's twenty-two priority sectors.

In 2014, Minister of International Trade Ed Fast announced Canada's first-ever IE strategy by stating that "international education is critical to Canada's success ... International education is at the very heart of our current and future prosperity" (DFATD 2014, 4). The contributions of IS to the Canadian economy were estimated to be $8.5 billion, with the creation of over 86,570 jobs in addition to more than $455 million in generated tax revenues (DFATD 2014). The strategy's goals include doubling IS numbers in Canada by 2022 and "increasing the number of international students choosing to remain in Canada as Permanent Residents after graduation" (DFATD 2014, 17). By 2014, IE had become synonymous with recruiting more IS. In the words of one interviewee, there was "really strong recognition ... *that international students are actually golden,* because they are the ones who will go in, get a Canadian education, and be ready for a Canadian workforce experience" (Personal Interview, 18 May 2011; emphasis added).

To facilitate this policy imperative, CIC started issuing IS study permits with automatic off-campus work authorization as of June 2014. On 1 January 2015, however, CIC introduced the Express Entry program, a new electronic application management system that places IS immigration applications alongside other rank-ordered immigrants (CIC 2015). This change in the processing of immigration applications has initiated a debate as to whether it "hinders [IS] access to permanent residency instead of promoting it" (Keung 2015, para. 1), and if in fact it contradicts one of the main "selling features for Canada's international education" – that is, "the opportunity for foreign students to immigrate and stay in Canada after earning their Canadian experience" (Keung 2015, para. 21–2). The new Express Entry program reflects the Canadian government's more targeted approach to immigration as a way to address the needs of the Canadian labour market. Whereas IS, given their personal and educational attributes and their potential to contribute positively to the Canadian labour market, are still envisioned as a valuable pool of talent, the new program favours immigration applicants, including IS, who have job offers supported by a Labour Market Impact Assessment or provincial/territorial nomination, and who can thus immediately contribute to the labour market and the broader economy.[3]

---

3 Express Entry is an electronic application management system that applies to most of the immigration routes: Federal Skilled Worker Program (FSWP); Federal Skilled Trades Program (FSTP); Canadian Experience Class (CEC); and a portion of the Provincial Nominee Program (PNP) (CIC 2015). Under the new Express Entry system (introduced

A summary of the policy changes made during the 2002–15 period that enabled the federal government to meet its dual interest of recruiting IS and retaining them as permanent residents is provided in Table 2.1.

Table 2.1 CIC International Student Policy Changes, 2002–15

Year	Policy/Program	Description of Changes
2002	Immigration and Refugee Protection Act (IRPA)	Waived the study permit requirement for IS registered in a short-term course or program of six months or less.
2005	Study Permit (SP)	Streamlined the SP application process, enabling IS to obtain an SP valid for the full length of their intended period of study, and those in post-secondary studies to transfer between programs of study and institutions (public and private) without first making an application to CIC.
	Post-Graduation Work Permit (PGWP) Program	Enabled IS graduates from recognized Canadian educational institutions outside Montreal, Toronto, and Vancouver to work after graduation in Canada for an additional year (up to a total of two years).
2006	Off-Campus Work Permit (OCWP) Program	Enabled full-time IS at participating educational institutions to work off campus during their studies for up to twenty hours per week.
2008	PGWP Program	Allowed IS to obtain an open work permit (for up to three years), with no restrictions on the type of employment and no requirement of a job offer.
	Online Applications	Enabled IS in Canada to apply online for an off-campus work permit.
	Canadian Experience Class (CEC)	Introduced a new immigration stream that allows IS graduates with professional, managerial, and skilled work experience to immigrate, recognizing their education and work experience in Canada as key selection criteria for permanent residence.
2009	OCWP	Enabled IS to apply for OCWP processing through online applications.
	Provincial Nominee Program (PNP)	Introduced the International Student Category to facilitate IS conversion under provincial nomination targets.

Year	Policy/Program	Description of Changes
2013	International Student Program (ISP)	Enabled IS to stay in Canada for up to three years following graduation, giving them more time to gain Canadian work experience prior to applying for permanent residency.
		Reduced Canadian work experience requirement for residency from twenty-four to twelve months.
2014	ISP	Limited the issuance of study permits to applicants who will be studying at a designated learning institution.
		Required students to actively pursue their studies while in Canada
		Allowed full-time IS enrolled at designated institutions in certain programs to work part-time off campus and full-time during scheduled school breaks without a work permit.
	Bill C-35	Excluded both IE agents, as well as IS advisers employed by Canadian institutions, from advising students on immigration matters unless they completed training and certification as a Regulated Canadian Immigration Consultant (RCIC) with the Immigration Consultants of Canada Regulatory Council (ICCRC).
2015	Express Entry	Introduced the Express Entry program as a new electronic application management system that applies to most of the immigration routes: Federal Skilled Worker Program (FSWP); Federal Skilled Trades Program (FSTP); Canadian Experience Class (CEC); and a portion of the Provincial Nominee Program (PNP)
		IS with secured job offers from a Canadian employer are favoured; however, they do not get extra points for their education in Canada.
2016	Express Entry (amendments)	Introduced amendments to Express Entry according to which IS are advantaged by earning extra points for their education in Canada. Points depend on the duration of the program that the IS is enrolled in (IS enrolled in programs that last three years or longer earn more points than those whose program duration is one to two years).

Note: sections of this table adapted from Citizenship and Immigration Canada, 2010.

Canada in the Context of International Trends

While, as noted above, the federal government has been engaged in IS and IE policy, a distinctive feature of the Canadian case is that, unlike other international jurisdictions, formal policy and funding allocations for IS recruitment in Canada emerged primarily at the institutional and provincial levels rather than at the national level (Shubert, Jones, and Trilokekar 2009). Canada's unique federal structure, in which education is solely a provincial responsibility, is partly the reason for this anomaly. Given the jurisdictional divide, Canadian provinces have historically resisted federal initiatives deemed "educational," including the development of any national IS policy (Allison 1999; Trilokekar 2007). In 2006, when the federal government attempted to establish an educational brand for Canada, there was tremendous pushback from the provinces, who felt that education did not fall under federal jurisdiction, and that the provinces should represent Canadian education nationally (Trilokekar 2007). Provincial sentiment against formal recognition of any federal role in education was so strong that the Council of Ministers of Education Canada (CMEC[4]) participated only as an observer at DFAIT meetings, refusing to engage as a provincial representative with the federal government on education-related matters (Trilokekar 2007, 2009). In fact, several provinces had established IE policies long before the launch of the federal government's strategy, and Canadian universities have been at the forefront of IS recruitment strategies, some even investing far more via budget allocations for IS recruitment than the federal government (DFAIT 2012).

With an increased sense of global competition, however, these traditional policy dichotomies seem to have changed. For example, in the Government of Ontario's *Rae Report*, the province made a call for greater collaboration with other partners, including the federal government, to present "the whole [education] sector to the world" (Ontario 2005, 11). Similarly, in its 2011 IE marketing plan, the CMEC recognized that a multilaterally coordinated government action to promote

---

on 1 January 2015), IS immigration applications are processed and ranked alongside other immigrants using the Comprehensive Ranking System (CRS), which is "a scoring mechanism tied to best predictors of economic success." For more details, see: http://www.cic.gc.ca/english/pdf/pub/Express_Entry_Technical_Briefing.pdf

4 The CMEC is an intergovernmental body founded in 1967 by the provincial ministers of education to provide leadership in education at the pan-Canadian and international levels.

its education systems abroad would benefit all stakeholders; it therefore addressed the need to work in partnership with the federal government, even "call[ing] upon the federal government to exercise greater leadership in this area" (Council of the Federation Secretariat 2011, 10) – an extraordinary move within the context of Canadian higher education. The provinces came together under the auspices of the CMEC in 2011 to advance their first collaborative international education marketing plan (Council of the Federation Secretariat 2011; DFATD 2012). This culminated with the publication of federal government's first-ever formal IE policy in 2014, *Harnessing Our Knowledge Advantage to Drive Innovation and Prosperity.*

As most provincial policies have identified the recruitment and retention of IS as their top priority, it was essential for the provinces to work in close cooperation with the federal government to enhance the retention of IS as permanent residents. Thus, over time there has been greater policy alignment and coordination between the provincial and federal governments on IS policy. As Guhr, Mondino, and Lundberg (2011) rightly observe, "the shifting demographic balance and current and predicted labour market challenges across Canada's provinces result in close alignment of economic and immigration policy between the provinces and the provincial and federal governments" (68). Furthermore, the provinces are equally concerned with "retaining more of the talented students who come to Canada to study ... through developing more integrated use of the PNPs[5] [Provincial Nominee Programs] and of innovative initiatives under immigration agreements" (Council of the Federation Secretariat 2011, 17).

IE and IS policies in Canada thus exhibit trends that diverge from those in other international jurisdictions. For example, both the UK and Australian governments invested large sums of money in national-level recruitment initiatives resulting in aggressive strategies both at the national and institutional levels (Ortiz, Chang, and Fang 2015, Trilokekar and Kizilbash 2013). Countries like France, the United States, the United Kingdom, and Germany have a well-developed national infrastructure for promoting IS cultural and educational exchanges. Unlike these countries, Canada did not develop a top-down approach; that is, the federal government was not the first to initiate a policy, which then had subsequent implications/impact at the provincial and

---

5 PNPs are provincially run immigration streams. Provinces and territories may recruit immigrants under an agreement with the federal government.

institutional levels. Rather, the institutional, provincial, and federal policy approaches have worked mostly independently, though at times there has been some cooperation. Canada's overarching approach to IS does, however, exhibit many overlaps with global trends. The title of the 2010 World Education Services (WES)[6] symposium – International Students: The New Skilled Migrants – speaks to the study-migration pathway as a growing global phenomenon (Lowe 2010). Contributing to this need for an educated labour force is the new global knowledge economy, in which "a nation's 'knowledge advantage' in cultivating a well-educated, highly skilled and flexible workforce has been recognized as the most critical asset for economic prosperity" (She and Wotherspoon 2013, 1). Germany has recently made a dramatic shift in immigration policy, and is now promoting a "culture of remaining" (Morris-Lange and Brands 2015, 44); indeed, Germany now has some of the most liberal IS transition policies in the world. It not only offers tuition-free higher education to IS, it also provides excellent examples of expanding post-study work/residency options, non-restrictive labour regulations, and pilot initiatives supporting the transition and entry of IS into the labour market (Morris-Lange and Brands 2015). Along with New Zealand, France, and Japan, Germany's increasingly competitive approach to IS recruitment is resulting in a diminishing global market share for the four key players – the United States, the United Kingdom, Australia, and Canada (Choudaha, Li, and Kono 2013).

Canada recognizes this heightened international competition for the same pool of highly educated and skilled potential immigrants. It is partly in response to this increased sense of global competition that the federal and provincial governments are addressing the need for national approaches, a unique occurrence in the Canadian context. The rhetoric adopted by the Canadian government speaks to its desire to attract and retain "top talent" to address the skilled labour shortage, which is becoming "desperate, [thereby] threatening our ability to keep up in a global, knowledge-based economy" (DFATD 2014, 9). This is in keeping with the rhetoric used by other countries, which alludes to a "global race for talent" in a "global knowledge/talent war" (Douglass and Edelstein 2009; Hawthorne 2008a, 2008b; She and Wotherspoon 2013; Wildavsky 2010; Ziguras and Law 2006). This sense of global competition is perhaps most clearly captured in the following statement:

---

6 WES is a non-profit international education organization specializing in international credential evaluation services. It hosted the referenced conference in November 2010.

You don't compare yourself to the guy down the street. You've got to say, "Who's doing this best anywhere in the world, and how do we match that?" That's got to be the new standard ... The basis of the comparison has to be, "Is Canada doing as good of a job as Australia and the Brits?" If not, why not and how do we improve? Who's doing it best? (Interview with Bob Rae, 27 May 2011)

Despite the increased number of IS in Canada, the federal government argues that, as a relatively late starter in the race for IS recruitment and retention, Canada needs to more aggressively "seize [its] share" (DFAIT 2012, xii) of the market. Through a "robust international education strategy," the Canadian government therefore aims to "seiz[e] the moment" by ensuring that a good proportion of the 6.4 million IS expected by 2025 are attracted to study in Canada (DFATD 2014, 9). As a result of this approach, Canada hosted 353,000 IS in 2015 – a 92 per cent increase since 2008 (CBIE 2016). In the spirit of competition, the Government of Canada claims to take advantage of the decreased share of the international student market of countries such as Australia and the United Kingdom (She and Wotherspoon 2013) and the dysfunctional US immigration system (Burgmann 2014). As Jason Kenney, former federal employment minister, stated, "Stalled immigration reforms in the United States are an opportunity for Canada to scoop up a wealth of young, 'brilliant' foreign nationals and direct them into burgeoning tech-sector employment ... We're seeking very deliberately to benefit from the dysfunctional American immigration system. I make no bones about it" (Quoted in Burgmann 2014, paras. 1 and 3). Such aggressive and highly competitive rhetoric is not common within the Canadian context, but it is very much in keeping with the global concern that countries can no longer take increased inflows of IS for granted and the sense that most nations have to be making continuous efforts to better and more competitively recruit, attract, and support IS (Becker and Kolster 2012). In the case of Canada, the argument that policy convergence is determined by forces of globalization may seem convincing. However, we argue that a closer examination of the historical, economic, and political context suggests that the forces of globalization are not deterministic, but rather reflect a conscious choice on the part of the state. Canadian government policymakers borrow selectively from the global policy discourse to suit the specifics of the Canadian context, adapting things to protect their own interests (Wells 2005, 111). We elaborate our position further in the next section.

Discussion

This chapter set out to examine the changing IE policy context and approaches to IS in Canada via a historical policy analysis to ascertain whether Canadian policy converges, diverges, and/or represents a hybrid policy formation in relation to global trends.

In reviewing the federal government's approach to IE and IS recruitment over time, we noted a considerable shift over the 1960–2015 period (Table 2.2). During this time, Canada's policy orientation shifted from an outward focus on IE as an instrument to strengthen Canada's place in the world and its relationships with the international community to an inward focus where IE became an instrument to meet national and local economic and human capital needs. Below is a brief synopsis of these changing policy directions.

In outlining the federal government's policy orientation towards IS, four distinct policy approaches can be identified, reflecting broader changes in policy priorities. In the first phase, Canada's IS policy was part of its foreign policy – namely as a form of international development

Table 2.2 Summary of Federal IE and IS Approaches

Timeframe	Policy Driver	Policy Direction
1960s–1970s	**Post–Second World War Period**	**Overseas Development Assistance program**
	Soft power/cultural diplomacy	Funding IS to study in Canada
1980s	**Domestication of Foreign Policy**	**Linking IE and IS recruitment with international trade**
	Priority to benefits for Canadian economy	Expanding fee-paying model for IS across Canada
1990s	**International Trade as Foreign Policy**	**IE marketization and branding initiatives**
	Education as international trade	Intensifying IS recruitment initiatives; IS immigration friendly policies
2000s	**Domestic Labour Market and Immigration Needs**	**IS immigration-friendly policies to retain as future immigrants**
	IE/IS as both revenue generation venue and human capital pool	Branding Canadian education abroad, increased IS recruitment

assistance; the second phase also approached IS recruitment in terms of foreign policy, as it related to projecting the Canadian image abroad and meeting Canadian domestic interests. In the third phase, IS policy was again framed as a matter of foreign policy, in this case primarily dictated by international trade priorities, while in the fourth phase, IS policy was not shaped by foreign policy, but by immigration policy and human resource/labour market imperatives.

Are these four distinctive policy orientations simply reflective of global trends?

Canada's initial IS policy was directly linked with its post–Second World War foreign policy. Identifying as a middle power, Canada was committed to world peace and "humane internationalism" – that is, "an acceptance that the citizens and governments of the industrialized world have ethical responsibilities towards those beyond their borders who are suffering severely and who live in abject poverty" (Morrison 1998, 2). This foreign policy translated into investments in international development assistance, which led Canada to be identified as "one of the more generous donors among industrialized countries" (Morrison 1998, 1). Canada's interest in IS in the 1960s and 1970s had to do primarily with training and developing the infrastructure and human resource base of the developing world.[7] Indeed, as Dolby (2011) suggests, this was a period when internationalization paradigms were anchored in principles of humanitarianism and the fostering of world peace and international cooperation. To this end, several Western countries embarked on IE exchange programs, with the United States' flagship Fulbright and Peace Corps programs and Germany's large-scale investments in cultural and educational diplomacy serving as prime examples (Trilokekar 2007). While the Canadian approach was certainly well within this international ethos, the country nonetheless positioned itself as a "non-colonial" middle power distinct from countries such as the United States or Britain (Trilokekar 2010). This positioning translated into a particular policy discourse that legitimized the federal government's role in IE in a way that was distinct from that of other Western nations. For example, the United States centred its policy rhetoric around national security in the Cold War period (Ruther 2002, 60), and Germany focused on building trust and regaining its position in the post-Nazi period (Trilokekar 2007). Canada, by contrast, did not have same global political agenda

---

7 Canada's Commonwealth ties influence its preference for specific countries.

during this period, hence it did not invest in international education as a form of international diplomacy.

In the 1970s, however Canada's policy rationale for hosting IS shifted dramatically, paralleling a major transition in Canadian foreign policy. The impetus for Canada to "domesticate" its foreign policy resulted from a need to differentiate itself from its powerful US neighbour and concentrate on serving Canadian interests (Trilokekar 2007). We would argue that this policy shift was largely a result of regional geopolitics – specifically, Canada's fear of over-reliance on the United States for its economic development, as well as its social and cultural capital (Wright 2004). The policy shift enacted in this period opened Canada's doors to new markets in the Asia-Pacific region, which in turn drew policymakers' attention to Australia's highly successful policy outreach approaches within the region. These new priorities ultimately pushed the Canadian government to make what we note as a third shift in policy.

This shift was most visible in the 1980s with the amalgamation into a single body of the Departments of Foreign Affairs and International Trade and the federal government's exclusive focus on promoting trade as the most crucial element of Canada's foreign policy. With this emphasis on trade, such rhetoric as "education is trade" received immediate support from the federal government. The ultimate test of this new policy orientation was a shift in Canada's International Development Assistance program, whereby the Canadian International Development Agency (CIDA) began funding Canadian Education Centres in developing countries to "market [Canadian] educational products and services" (Trilokekar 2007, 224). In many ways, this IE-as-trade and IS-as-commodity discourse could be considered international in scope. In the 1990s, this discourse was legitimized when the General Agreement on Trade in Services (GATS) included a discussion on education. For Canada, however, Australia's tremendous success in recruiting IS was of particular interest and served as an excellent policy rationale for its own strategic approach. The Government of Canada recognizes the many similarities between the two countries (Trilokekar and Kizilbash 2013) and sees the Asia-Pacific region, where Australia's IS recruitment efforts has been most active, as a lucrative market for Canadian educational services.

These global trends, while influencing Canadian policy, did not force the Canadian government into "blind imitation or pressure to conform." Rather, we argue, they enabled the Canadian government to legitimize a policy orientation that had already taken form within its foreign policy. The government's approach was much more reflective of a "conscious adaptation" (Stromquist quoted in Wells 2005, 110) or a strategic choice to engage the global policy discourse to maximize its own policy agenda.

To make our case, we refer to the Australian context, where the implementation of high differential tuition fees for IS and the resultant push to increase the recruitment and enrolment of IS was a direct result of a shift in domestic educational policy – namely the Jackson and Dawkins policy reforms – which in turn steered Australian universities to a set of market-like behaviours (Trilokekar and Kizilbash 2013). IS recruitment was a by-product of these policy shifts, although the Australian government did provide universities with several direct incentives to further develop IE promotional and marketing activities. The Canadian context was different. IS recruitment was initiated by the federal government primarily as an international trade activity; however, given its restricted jurisdictional authority on educational matters, the Canadian government was not in a position to announce a formalized IE strategy, nor was able to directly steer institutional policy approaches and outcomes. Rather, it had to battle with the provinces to establish its legitimacy in the arena of education policy. So while on the surface, the Canadian and Australian policy approaches may seem similar, their respective contexts in which they were developed created differences in the location, rate, and nature of their impact on the higher education sector. We therefore concur with Marginson and Sawir (2005) when they suggest that

> while tendencies to converge are obvious, when we look more closely for difference as well as similarity we find the global transformations are not identical by time and place. Rather, they are constituted in each place by an amalgam of global, national and local factors in complex ways. (289)

At the provincial level, one could argue that there is increased alignment between government policy and commonly associated globalization practices – namely decreased public-sector funding, increased marketization, greater accountability, and the establishment of an audit culture (Dolby 2011). However, even at the provincial level, these policies have been adopted in local contexts. For example, Quebec's IS policy differentiates between francophone and non-francophone IS, so that francophone IS from select countries are exempt from paying the IS fee differential (Picard and Mills 2009). Such a strategy is clearly in keeping with Quebec's international relations and cultural policies, and is not based on a purely economic rationale. Similarly, Newfoundland and Labrador has frozen IS fees (as well as domestic tuition) and, given its specific local challenges, has "decided to swim against the nationwide tide" (Taber 2013). These specific cases lend further credence to Marginson's and Rhoades's (2002) "gloconal" heuristic, which argues that the global, local, and national flows are "simultaneous and multidimensional" (Dolby 2011, 4).

The fourth shift in IS policy orientation is linked to broader national economic returns, as the former Ontario premier notes:

> [International education] is not just about education. This is about the economy, immigration, our innovation, and our overall capacity to succeed as an economy. So it isn't just about education. (Interview with Bob Rae, 27 May 2011)

This policy discourse continues the earlier narrative on IE as an important national economic strategy, given that IS bring in large revenues to the host country; indeed, it extends it further. IS are important in terms of both their short- and long-term contributions to the economy, first as fee-paying IS, then as workers in the labour market, and then as employed, tax-paying permanent residents. IS and IE are framed as being critical to "Canada's success" and "long-term economic security," and as contributing to "a more prosperous, more innovative, and more competitive Canada" (DFATD 2014, 4). This policy orientation in many ways marks a radical shift from Canada's ideological stance in the 1960s of building expert knowledge within developing countries and restricting the so-called brain drain of talent from the developed world, to one that aggressively seeks to attract talent (brain gain) from these very same countries. With the current policy discourse, the government has steered away from terms such as "brain drain," adopting instead the terminology of "brain circulation" or the "global race for talent" to legitimize its particular policy approach.

The global policy rhetoric on the knowledge economy and its revalidation of human capital theory has certainly been brought to bear on the Canadian government's policy discourse, in a way that is similar to several other countries. However, the framing of IS policy as an immediate domestic imperative holds a lot more currency in the Canadian context. We propose that this precise interest in IS as future permanent residents to meet domestic labour market needs, given Canada's aging population and increasing dependence on immigration, served as the primary policy lever for the Harper government to launch its first IE strategy. No

Canadian government before had declared a federal IE strategy, despite an interest in recruiting IS.

We identify specific national contexts that enable the IS-as-new-immigrants policy direction. First, Canada is expressly reliant on immigration to meet its labour market/economic needs. It is one of the few countries where immigration is expected to count for 100 per cent of net workforce growth (DFATD 2014; Hawthorne 2008a, 2008b). Second, Canada already has an immigration policy that gives preference to those entering through the economic pathway (62 per cent). The emphasis placed on economic immigration and a traditional foreign policy focus on international trade creates a policy environment within Canada where the different policy discourses – IE, foreign policy, and immigration – reinforce one another, creating a powerful, convergent, and seemingly normative policy discourse on IS.

Canada's past challenges in integrating new immigrants into its labour force serves as a third factor supporting the IS-as-new-immigrants policy. In Canada, there has been concern over the reliance on economic immigrants given that their credentials and work experience are often not recognized in the Canadian labour market, resulting in subsequent loss of revenue and poor economic impact on Canadian society (Hawthorne 2008a, 2008b; Reitz 2005). In addition, the notion of attracting the "right" people has been an object of constant debate in Canadian immigration policy (Li 2003). Given this context, a policy that profiles IS as ideal immigrants who have proven their "economic worth" by paying high IS fees and spending on housing, food, transportation, and travel (Abu-Laban 1988 quoted in Sakamoto et.al 2013, 6), earning Canadian credentials, developing proficiency in at least one official language, and building familiarity with Canadian social customs and Canadian work experience is one that holds merit at both the federal and provincial levels. IS as Simmons's "ideal" or "designer immigrants" (quoted in Chira 2013, 7) are easily accepted as "home-grown," and therefore a "palatable option" (Hawthorne 2012, 432). They represent a low financial risk/burden for government and are therefore seen as an efficient, cost-effective means to meet immigration targets. In addition, as a group that has self-funded their education to meet Canadian employer requirements (Hawthorne 2012, 422), IS are considered a "prized ... human capital resource" (Hawthorne 2012, 417). The framing of IE/IS policy as linked to the labour market and immigration also serves to further legitimize the role of the federal government, given that the labour market and immigration (unlike education) are commonly accepted to be federal responsibilities.

Using a US example, we make our final point to illustrate Canada's unique context and approach. The United States is often recognized as a country that originally spearheaded the acquisition of global talent (Hawthorne 2010; 2008a, 2008b). Its approach has been to enroll mostly graduate-level IS in the engineering and science disciplines, a rationale linked directly to its innovation and research agendas (Tremblay 2005). A similar trend has been followed by countries such as the Netherlands, Germany, Switzerland, and the United Kingdom, who also put a strong emphasis on the recruitment of IS at the master's and doctoral levels, some through a wide range of national government scholarships targeted at these levels of study (Becker and Kolster 2012). In particular, several countries – including the four listed above – strongly emphasize the recruitment of IS in the STEM (science, technology, engineering, and mathematics) fields. In fact, the United Kingdom is noted to have had 13.7 per cent annual growth in the number of international graduate students in STEM (She and Wotherspoon 2013). IS are considered a vital source of enrollments for these fields in the United States, with more than one in three IS enrolled in a STEM field (Ortiz, Chang, and Fang 2015). Canada's approach has focused primarily on the recruitment of fee-paying undergraduate students, not necessarily concentrated in STEM. This recruitment strategy aligns more with domestic labour market and immigration policies and the economic imperative for increased trade than with enhancing the nation's innovation or research agenda as part of a global knowledge economy. Thus, as She and Wotherspoon (2013) note, while Canada has demonstrated its potential in attracting IS – the country has had the fastest growth in IS enrolment over the past decade with its major advantage being its channels to permanent residency – it remains relatively disadvantaged when compared to countries such as the United States and the United Kingdom because of its low stock of IS and the low proportion of IS in post-graduate programs.

Conclusion

Gale's policy historiography approach enables us to study specific policy domains across different time periods to examine the "possible relationships between the socio-educational present and the socio-educational past" (Kincheloe quoted in Gale 2001, 385). In investigating Canada's IS policy, one notes a dramatic shift in policy orientation over five decades, though each shift was in alignment with the government's broader political and/or economic imperatives of that time. In the present context, IS policy is in alignment with Canada's rising economic criteria within its immigration policy. With the new Express Entry program, IS policies, immigration, and the labour market are more tightly linked. The government's approach to immigration is more targeted and this has major implications in that it leads to more targeted services for IS and a greater need for collaboration between universities, potential employers, and CIC. IS policy is synonymous with immigration policy and as such is affected by economic imperatives, a far cry from its historical origins in international development.

As Codd (1988) has written, "policies produced by and for the state are obvious instances in which language serves a political purpose, constructing particular meanings and signs that work to mask social conflict and foster commitment to the notion of a universal public interest" (237). She and Wotherspoon (2013) rightly suggest that "managing IS policy as part of the strategy to manage highly skilled migration goes beyond merely a matter of skill formation and in fact represents specific social relations and power struggles in each host nation" (12). "The management of IS mobility, among other national strategies aiming at the high skill economy, never exists simply as an economic issue of productivity, but embraces a collective goal of national interests. Host countries' governments in fact seek to balance the concerns of different stakeholders in order to sustain and strengthen the government's authority and legitimacy" (She and Wotherspoon 2013, 11–12). The Canadian government has engaged in various legitimization strategies to sanction its role and particular policy approach while giving credence to some voices and largely suppressing the formation of any counter-discourse. In framing its policy discourse, we agree that the Canadian government has privileged specific international agendas and that "these agendas become hegemonic through international (global, supranational) discourse among the myriad of actors and organizations that are involved in their development and education" (Monkman and Baird quoted in Wells 2005, 116). Thus, the growing economic rationale and global policy discourse on higher education as instrumental, neo-liberal, and market-orientated has been privileged. Comparisons to other OECD countries such as the United Kingdom, Australia, and New Zealand, which share similar policy objectives as Canada, have served as a tool of consensus to normalize these dominant policy discourses. The voices of IS themselves, or the sending countries, or for that matter interest groups such as the Canadian Federation of Students, to cite a few examples, are largely missing in the 2014 federal IE policy. Similarly, government investments in academic exchanges and/or research collaborations, such as the US government's 100,000 strong educational exchange initiatives, the UK government's India Education and Research Initiative (UKIERI), or Germany's investments in the German Houses of Science and Innovation (DWIHs), are overlooked as legitimate approaches to IE and the engagement of IS (Becker and Kolster 2012).

Thus, we conclude that while globalization and internationalization will continue to shape global policy rhetoric and discourse, it is ultimately a nation's particular historical, geopolitical, economic, and cultural context that will determine the borrowing of the global policy discourse, its adaptation to national/local interests, and its final outcomes. In short, we assert that the nation state matters. In the case of Canada, its unique system of federalism, its domestic demographic challenges, its geopolitical location vis-à-vis the United States, and a growing conservatism within its society are just a few characteristics that will continue to differentiate how and what aspects of the global policy rhetoric the country chooses to engage with. We agree with Drezner (2001) when he states that

> an approach that concedes the significance of globalization but also asks how states try to maximize their relative advantage in such a world is fruitful ... [because] globalization is not deterministic; there is no single predicted location for policy convergence. The ability of states to cooperate and their ability to agree on norms of governance determine the extent of policy convergence. (78)

References

Allison, John Daniel. 1999. *Federalism, Diplomacy and Education: Canada's Role in Education-Related International Activities, 1960–1984.* PhD dissertation, University of Toronto.

Altbach, Philip G., and Jane Knight. 2007. "The Internationalization of Higher Education: Motivations and Realities." *Journal of Studies in International Education* 11 (3–4): 274–90.

Altbach, Philip, Liz Reisberg, and Laura Rumbley. 2009. *Trends in Global Higher Education: Tracking an Academic Revolution. A Report Prepared for the UNESCO 2009 World Conference on Higher Education.* Paris: UNESCO.

Association of Universities and Colleges of Canada (AUCC). 2014. *Canada's Universities in the World AUCC Internationalization Survey.* https://www.univcan.ca/wp-content/uploads/2015/07/internationalization-survey-2014.pdf.

Becker, Rosa, and Renze Kolster. 2012. *International Student Recruitment: Policies and Development in Selected Countries.* The Hague: Netherlands Organisation for International Cooperation in Higher Education. https://www.nuffic.nl/en/publications/find-a-publication/international-student-recruitment.pdf.

Beine, Michel, Anna Boucher, Brian Burgoon, Mary Crock, Justin Gest, Michael Hiscox, Patrick McGovern, Hillel Rapoport, Joep Schaper, and Eiko Thielemann. 2015. "Comparing Immigration Policies: An Overview from the IMPALA Database." *International Migration Review* 50 (4): 827–63. https://doi.org/10.1111/imre.12169.

Bond, Sheryl L., and Jean-Pierre Lemasson. 1999. *A New World of Knowledge: Canadian Universities and Globalization.* Ottawa: IDRC.

Burgmann, Tamsyn. 2014. "Jason Kenney: 'Dysfunctional' U.S. Immigration System a Boost to Canada." *Canadian Press,* 6 August. http://www.huffingtonpost.ca/2014/08/07/jason-kenney-immigration-canada-us_n_5656589.html.

Canadian Bureau for International Education. 2016. *Facts and Figures: Canada's Performance and Potential in International Education 2016.* http://cbie.ca/media/facts-and-figures/).

Canadian Federation of Students. 2015. "International Students." http://cfs-fcee.ca/the-issues/international-students/.

Chaloff, Jonathan, and Georges Lemaître. 2009. *Managing Highly-Skilled Labour Migration: A Comparative Analysis of Migration Policies and Challenges in OECD Countries.* Paris: OECD Social Employment and Migration Working Papers No. 79. http://www.oecd.org/els/mig/46656535.pdf.https://doi.org/10.1787/1815199x.

Chignal, Selina. 2015. "Foreign student enrolment in Canada rising." *IPolitics,* 30 November. http://ipolitics.ca/2015/11/30/foreign-student-enrolment-in-canada-rising/.

Chira, Sinziana. 2013. *Dreaming Big, Coming Up Short: The Challenging Realities of International Students and Graduates in Atlantic Canada.* Halifax, NS: Atlantic Metropolis Centre.

Choudaha, Rahul, Li Chang, and Yoko Kono. 2013. "International Student Mobility Trends 2013: Towards Responsive Recruitment Strategies." *World Education News and Reviews,* 1 March. https://wenr.wes.org/2013/03/wenr-march-2013-international-student-mobility-trends-2013-towards-responsive-recruitment-strategies.

Citizen and Immigration Canada (CIC). 2010. *Evaluation of the International Student Program.* Ottawa: CIC Evaluation Division. https://www.canada.ca/content/dam/ircc/migration/ircc/english/pdf/research-stats/2010-eval-isp-e.pdf.

– 2015. "Express Entry System: Technical Briefing." http://www.cic.gc.ca/english/pdf/pub/Express_Entry_Technical_Briefing.pdf.

Codd, John A. 1988. "The Construction and Deconstruction of Educational Policy Documents." *Journal of Education Policy* 3 (3): 235–47. https://doi.org/10.1080/0268093880030303.

Cornelius, Wayne A., and Takeyuki Tsuda. 2004. "Controlling Immigration: The Limits of Government Intervention." In *Controlling Immigration: A Global Perspective*, 2nd ed., ed. Wayne A. Cornelius, Takeyuki Tsuda, Philip Martin, and John Hollifield, 3–50. Chicago: Stanford University Press.

Council of the Federation Secretariat. 2011. *Bringing Education in Canada to the World, Bringing the World to Canada: An International Education Marketing Action Plan for Provinces and Territories.* http://www.cmec.ca/Publications/Lists/Publications/Attachments/264/COF_Bringing_Ed_to_Canada_Eng_final.pdf.

Currie, Janice, and Janice Newson. 1998. *Universities and Globalization: Critical Perspectives.* Thousand Oaks, CA: Sage Publications.

de Wit, Hans. 2011. "International Students and Immigration: The Netherlands Case in a European Context." *Canadian Diversity* 8 (5): 61–5.

Dennison, John D., and Hans G. Schuetze. 2004. "Extending Access, Choice, and the Reign of the Market: Higher Education Reforms in British Columbia, 1989–2004." *Canadian Journal of Higher Education* 34 (3): 13–38.

Department of Foreign Affairs and International Trade (DFAIT). 1988. "Academic Relations Program: An Historical Perspective." *Academic Relations.* File 55–11. acc no. 219557. vol. 2.

– 2012. "Advisory Panel on Canada's International Education Strategy Final Report – International Education: A Key Driver of Canada's Future Prosperity." http://www.international.gc.ca/education/advisory-consultation.aspx?view=d.

Dolby, Nadine. 2011. *Internationalizing Higher Education in South Africa and the United States: Policy and Practice in Global, National, and Local Perspective.* http://files.eric.ed.gov/fulltext/ED523150.pdf.

Douglass, John A., and Richard Edelstein. 2009. "The Global Competition for Talent. The Rapidly Changing Market for IIS and the Need for a Strategic Approach in the U.S. Center for Studies in Higher Education, Research & Occasional Papers Series." Berkeley, CA: Center for Studies in Higher Education Research & Occasional Paper Series. https://globalhighered.files.wordpress.com/2009/10/rops-jd-re-globaltalent-9-25-09.pdf.

Drezner, Daniel W. 2001. "Globalization and Policy Convergence." *International Studies Review* 3 (1): 53–78. https://doi.org/10.1111/1521-9488.00225.

Enders, Jürgen, and Oliver Fulton (eds). 2002. *Higher Education in a Globalising World.* Dordrecht, NL: Kluwer Academic Publishers. https://doi .org/10.1007/978-94-010-0579-1.

Foreign Affairs Trade and Development Canada (DFATD). 2012. "Advisory Panel on Canada's International Education Strategy Final Report – International Education: A Key Driver of Canada's Future Prosperity." http:// www.international.gc.ca/education/advisory-consultation.aspx?view=d.

– 2014. "Canada's International Education Strategy: Harnessing our Knowledge Advantage to Drive Innovation and Prosperity." http:// international.gc.ca/global-markets-marches-mondiaux/assets/pdfs/ overview-apercu-eng.pdf.

Gale, Trevor. 2001. "Critical Policy Sociology: Historiography, Archaeology and Genealogy as Methods of Policy analysis." *Journal of Education Policy* 16 (5): 379–93. https://doi.org/10.1080/02680930110071002.

Gribble, Cate, and Jill Blackmore. 2012. "Re-Positioning Australia's International Education in Global Knowledge Economies: Implications of Shifts in Skilled Migration Policies for Universities." *Journal of Higher Education Policy and Management* 34 (4): 341–54. https://doi.org/10.1080/136 0080X.2012.689181.

Guhr, Daniel, Mauro Mondino, and Alexander Lundberg. 2011. *Canada's Capacity for International Student Enrollment.* San Carlos, CA: Illuminate Consulting Group (ICG).

Hawthorne, Lesleyanne. 2008a. *The Growing Global Demand for Students as Skilled Migrants.* Washington, DC: Migration Policy Institute.

– 2008b. "The Impact of Economic Selection Policy on Labor Market Outcomes for Degree Qualified Migrants in Canada and Australia." *IRPP Choices* 14:1–50.

– 2010. "How Valuable is 'Two-Step Migration'? Labour Market Outcomes for International Student Migrants to Australia." *Asian and Pacific Migration Journal* 19 (1): 5–36. https://doi.org/10.1177/011719681001900102.

– 2012. "Designer Immigrants? International Students and Two-Step Migration." In *The SAGE Handbook of International Higher Education*, ed. Darla K. Deardorff, Hans de Wit, John D. Heyl, and Tony Adams, 419–35. Thousand Oaks, CA: Sage Publications.

ICEF Monitor. 2013. "Canada's International Student Enrolment Up 94% Over Past Decade." http://monitor.icef.com/2013/11/ canadas-international-student-enrolment-up-94-over-past-decade/.

Johnstone, Marjorie, and Eunjung Lee. 2014. "Branded: International Education and 21st Century Canadian Immigration, Education Policy and the Welfare State." *International Social Work* 57 (3): 209–21. https://doi .org/10.1177/0020872813508572.

Joyal, S. 1994. *International Cultural Affairs, Higher Education and Scientific Cooperation. Refocusing Canada's International Cultural Policy in the Nineties: Issues and Solutions. Report to the Minister of Foreign Affairs.* Ottawa: Department of Foreign Affairs and International Trade.

Keung, Nicholas. 2015. "Foreign Students Left Behind in New Express Entry Immigration Program." *Toronto Star,* 21 March. http://www.thestar.com/ news/immigration/2015/03/21/foreign-students-left-behind-in-new -express-entry-immigration-program.html

Knight, Jane. 2008. *Higher Education in Turmoil: The Changing World of Internationalization.* Rotterdam: Sense Publisher.

Kunin, Roslyn, and Associates. Inc. 2012. *Economic Impact of International Education in Canada—An Update.* http://www.international.gc.ca/education/ assets/pdfs/economic_impact_en.pdf.

Li, Peter. 2003. *Destination Canada: Immigration Debates and Issues.* Don Mills, ON: Oxford University Press.

Lowe, S. 2010. "International Students: The New Skilled Migrants." Paper presented at World Education Services Symposium Program, Toronto ON, 4 November. http://www.wes.org/ewenr/10dec/feature.htm.

Marginson, Simon. 2011. "It's a Long Way Down: The Underlying Tensions in the Education Export Industry." *Australian Universities Review* 53 (2): 21–33.

Marginson, Simon, and Gary Rhoades. 2002. "Beyond National States, Markets, and Systems of Higher Education: A Gloconal Agency Heuristic." *Higher Education* 43 (3): 281–309. https://doi.org/10.1023/A:101469960 5875.

Marginson, Simon, and Erlenawati Sawir. 2005. "Interrogating Global Flows in Higher Education." *Globalisation, Societies and Education* 3 (3): 281–309. https://doi.org/10.1080/14767720500166878.

Morris-Lange, Simon, and Florinda Brands. 2015. *Train and Retain: Career Support for International Students in Canada, Germany, the Netherlands, and Sweden.* Berlin: Expert Council of German Foundations on Integration and Migration.

Morrison, David R. 1998. *Aid and Ebb Tide: A History of CIDA and Canadian Development Assistance.* Waterloo, ON: Wilfred Laurier University Press.

Ontario. 2005. *Ontario: A Leader in Learning: Report & Recommendations, February 2005.* Toronto: Ministry of Training, Colleges and Universities. http://www .collegesontario.org/research/research_reports/EXT_RAE_REPORT.pdf.

Organisation for Economic Co-operation and Development (OECD). 2015. *Education at a Glance 2015: OECD Indicators*. Paris: OECD Publishing.

Ortiz, Alejandro, Li Chang, and Yuanyuan Fang. 2015. *International Student Mobility Trends 2015: An Economic Perspective*. World Education News and Reviews, 2 February. https://wenr.wes.org/2015/02/international-student-mobility-trends-2015-an-economic-perspective.

Pécoud, Antoine. 2013. "Introduction: Disciplining the Transnational Mobility of People." In *Disciplining the Transnational Mobility of People*, ed. Martin Geiger and Antoine Pécoud, 1–14. New York: Palgrave Macmillan. https://doi.org/10.1057/9781137263070_1.

Picard, France, and D. Mills. 2009. "The Internationalization of Quebec Universities: From Public Policies to Concrete Measures." In *Canada's Universities Go Global*, ed. Roopa Desai Trilokekar, Glen A. Jones, and Adrian Shubert, 134–53. Toronto: James Lorimer and Company.

Reitz, Jeffrey. 2005. "Tapping Immigrants' Skills: New Directions for Immigration Policy in the Knowledge Economy." *Law and Business Review of the Americas* 11 (3). https://scholar.smu.edu/lbra/vol11/iss3/6/.

Riaño, Yvonne, and Etienne Piguet. 2016. "International Student Migration." In *Oxford Bibliography in Geography*, ed. Barney Warf, 1–24. New York: Oxford University Press.

Rizvi, Fazal. 2011. "Theorizing Student Mobility in an Era of Globalization." *Teachers and Teaching* 17 (6): 693–701. https://doi.org/10.1080/13540602.2011.625145.

Ruther, Nancy L. 2002. *Barely There, Powerfully Present: Thirty Years of U.S. Policy on International Higher Education*. New York: Routledge Falmer.

Sá, Creso, and Emma Sabzalieva. 2016. *Public Policy and the Attraction of International Students*. Toronto: Centre for the Study of Canadian and International Higher Education, OISE University of Toronto.

Sakamoto, Izumi, Daphne Jeyapal, Rupaleem Bhuyan, Jane Ku, Lin Fang, Heidi Zhang, and Flavia Genovese. 2013. *An Overview of Discourses of Skilled Immigrants and "Canadian Experience": An English –Language Print Media Analysis*. CERIS Working Paper No. 98. https://tspace.library.utoronto.ca/bitstream/1807/78816/1/Sakamoto%20Bhuyan%20discourses%20of%20skilled%20immigrants%20and%20Canadian%20experience.pdf.

Santiago, Paulo, Karine Tremblay, Ester Basri, and Elena Arnal. 2008. *Tertiary Education for the Knowledge Society*, vol. 2. Paris: OECD Publishing. http://www.oecd.org/education/skills-beyond-school/41266759.pdf.

She, Qianru. 2011. "International Student Mobility and Highly Skilled Migration: A Comparative Study of Canada, the United States and the United Kingdom." MA thesis, University of Saskatchewan.

She, Qianru, and Terry Wotherspoon. 2013. "International Student Mobility and Highly Skilled Migration: A Comparative Study of Canada, the United States, and the United Kingdom." *SpringerPlus* 2 (1). https://doi.org/10.1186/2193-1801-2-132. Medline:23667802

Shubert, Adrian, Glen A. Jones, and Roopa Desai Trilokekar. 2009. "Introduction." In *Canada's Universities Go Global*, ed. Roopa Desai Trilokekar, Glen A. Jones, and Adrian Shubert, 6–15. Toronto: James Lorimer and Company.

Statistics Canada. 2010. "Definition of 'International Students.'" http://www.statcan.gc.ca/pub/81-004-x/2010005/def/intlstudent-etudiantetranger-eng.htm.

Stromquist, Nelly. 2013. "Globalization and 'Policyscapes': Ruptures and Continuities in Higher Education." In *Making Policy in Turbulent Times: Challenges and Prospects for Higher Education*, ed. Paul Axelrod, Roopa Desai Trilokekar, Richard Wellen, and Theresa Shanahan, 221–48. Montreal and Kingston: McGill-Queens University Press.

Suter, Brigitte, and Michael Jandl. 2006. *Comparative Study on Policies Towards Foreign Graduates: Study on Admission and Retention Policies Towards Foreign Students in Industrialized Countries*. Vienna: International Center for Migration Policy Development (ICMPD). http://www.net4you.com/jandlftp/Students_Final.pdf.

Taber, Jane. 2013. "Newfoundland Reaps Rewards of Low-tuition Strategy." *Globe and Mail* (Toronto), 13 September. http://www.theglobeandmail.com/news/national/newfoundland-reaps-rewards-of-low-tuition-strategy/article14324686/.

Taylor, Sandra. 1997. "Critical Policy Analysis: Exploring Contexts, Texts and Consequences." *Discourse (Abingdon)* 18 (1): 23–35. https://doi.org/10.1080/0159630970180102.

Tremblay, Karine. 2005. "Academic Mobility and Immigration." *Journal of Studies in International Education* 9 (3): 196–228. https://doi.org/10.1177/1028315305277618.

Trilokekar, Roopa Desai. 2007. "Federalism, Foreign Policy and the Internationalization of Higher Education: A Case Study of the Department of Foreign Affairs (FAC), Canada." PhD dissertation, University of Toronto.

– 2009. "The Department of Foreign Affairs and International Trade (DEFAIT), Canada: Providing Leadership in the Internationalization of Canadian Higher Education?" In *Canada's Universities Go Global*, ed. Roopa Desai Trilokekar, Glen A. Jones, and Adrian Shubert, 355–69. Toronto: James Lorimer and Company.

– 2010. "International Education as Soft Power? The Contributions and Challenges of Canadian Foreign Policy to the Internationalization of

Higher Education." *Higher Education* 59 (2): 131–47. https://doi.org/10.1007/s10734-009-9240-y.

Trilokekar, Roopa Desai, and Zainab Kizilbash. 2013. "Imagine: Canada as a Leader in International Education. How Can Canada Benefit from the Australian Experience?" *Canadian Journal of Higher Education* 43 (2): 1–26.

Verbik, Line, and Veronica Lasanowski. 2007. *International Student Mobility: Patterns and Trends.* London, UK: Observatory on Borderless Higher Education.

Wells, Traci. 2005. "Educational Policy Networks and their Role in Policy Discourse, Action and Implementation." *Comparative Education Review* 49 (1): 109–17. https://doi.org/10.1086/426163.

Wildavsky, Ben. 2010. The Great Brain Race: How Global Universities are Reshaping the World. Princeton, NJ: Princeton University Press.

Wright, Gerald. 2004. "Mitchell Sharp: Legacy of a Foreign Policy Icon." *International Journal: Canada's Journal of Global Policy* 59 (3): 597.

Ziguras, Christopher, and Siew-Fang Law. 2006. "Recruiting International Students as Skilled migrants: The Global 'Skills Race' as Viewed from Australia and Malaysia." *Globalisation, Societies and Education* 4 (1): 59–76. https://doi.org/10.1080/14767720600555087.

3 Explaining International Student Mobility to Canada: A Review

ANN H. KIM AND GUNJAN SONDHI

This chapter examines key themes and findings from existing research to identify explanations of international student mobility (ISM) to Canada. We define the ISM literature broadly to include studies of international students, foreign students, visa students, study abroad students, sojourning students, and unaccompanied minors for educational purposes – terms that refer to education migrants. We include literature on students at all educational levels regardless of legal (i.e., migration) status. Perspectives are drawn from across the social sciences to bring into focus the various structural, social, and cultural contexts that shape ISM to Canada. In our review, which includes academic and grey literature on Canada published from 1973 to August 2014,[1] we follow Findlay's (2011) framing of ISM theories into two strands: demand-side and supply-side perspectives. Demand-side explanations of ISM flows address the motivations of students and their parents, as well as the influence of social capital and class. On the other hand, studies emphasizing supply-side practices highlight the role of states and institutions in driving student migration flows and patterns.

The text of this chapter was adapted from sections of the "Bridging the Literature on Education Migration" report, funded by Western University's Population Change and Lifecourse Cluster and the York Centre for Asian Research.

1 We limit the literature review period to 2014 to give sufficient time to examine literature published during the period immediately after the launch of Canada's marketing brand in 2007, and to distinguish it from the post-2014 period, which saw regulatory changes to Canada's International Student Program (CIC 2015).

Demand-Side Explanations: Choice and Social Class, Push and Pull

Studies emphasizing the demand for cross-border education carried an underlying assumption that students, and their parents, made choices about where to go for their international education. Some studies conceptualized this behavioural model within a framework of social class and capital (Findlay 2011). Under this demand-side approach, which is also commonly used in studies of other types of migration, push and pull motivations explain geographic patterns of mobility, and international students and their families tend to be the subjects of investigation.

The literature on international mobility to Canada shows that student motivations have not shifted over time. A range of factors, including individual characteristics, along with social, cultural, institutional, economic, and political factors, have shaped individual decisions to go abroad for university. Studies published before 1990 on student motivations for tertiary level study in Canada (Chandras 1974; Glaser and Habers 1974; Holdaway, Bryan, and Allan 1988; Neice 1977) report findings similar to those of their successors.

Push and pull factors relate to both the home and the host country. Push factors motivating students to leave home included political, ethnic, or linguistic tensions, as well as lack of economic and educational opportunities (Chandras 1974; Glaser and Habers 1974; Mickle 1985; Neice 1977). Pull factors making it difficult for students to leave home included ties to family and friends and financial considerations, while a push factor keeping students away from destination countries was their apprehensiveness about educational programs, which usually reflected language concerns (Glaser and Habers 1974). Finally, pull factors drawing students towards destinations were academic quality and reputation, academic benefits, employment experience, and perceptions within the home country of the prestige and value of an overseas education; for some, the possibility of permanent migration was an added incentive (Chandras 1974; Glaser and Habers 1974; Holdaway, Bryan, and Allan 1988; Neice 1977).

Further investigation of the foregoing broad, but informative, factors revealed differences in motivation across subgroups within the international student population – namely by degree level (undergraduate versus graduate), region, and social class. For example, Holdaway, Bryan, and Allan (1988) found that undergraduate students at the University of Alberta considered the relative costs of the school compared to other universities, as well as its proximity to friends and family. Graduate students, on the other hand, focused more on research facilities and faculty reputation. Chandras (1974) emphasized differences by social class background, noting that the opportunity to obtain an advanced degree attracted international students from upper-class East Indian backgrounds. In contrast, lower- and middle-class students felt pushed out of India by the lack of economic opportunities and pulled to Canada by financial support (77 per cent of lower-class students from India received a scholarship, assistantship, fellowship, or grant, compared to 67 per cent of upper-class students).

More recent studies have pointed to similar push and pull factors (Canadian Bureau for International Education 2009; Chen 2006, 2007; Chira, Barber, and Belkhodja 2013; Li, DiPetta, and Woloshyn 2012; Madgett and Bélanger 2008; Massey and Burrow 2012). Another push factor not acknowledged in earlier studies was the influence of parents who pressure their children to attend universities abroad, as described in Li, DiPetta, and Woloshyn's (2012) study of female Chinese MA students at an undisclosed university in Ontario. Additional pull factors to Canada were multiculturalism and Canada's openness to international students, the environment, safety and security, professional development and other career-related reasons, and language-related reasons (Canadian Bureau for International Education 2009; Chen 2006, 2007; Li, DiPetta, and Woloshyn 2012; Liu 2007; Madgett and Bélanger 2008; Massey and Burrow 2012). Also highlighted were visa-related considerations, such as ease and speed of approval and work permits for self and spouse. The issue of visa approvals was particularly salient for students whose first choice of destination was not Canada (Chen 2006, 2007). Those themes related to border policies as well as institution-side decisions regarding admissions would be more suited to a supply-side perspective, which we discuss in the following section.

From this body of work, we also learn that there is a hierarchy of motivations, or a "decision hierarchy" (Neice 1977), and that priorities in the recent period are also likely to vary by level and type of study, as shown by Holdaway, Bryan, and Allan (1988), as well as by region (Canadian Bureau for International Education 2009; Chen 2006, 2007; Madgett and Bélanger 2008; Massey and Burrow 2012). In her study of East Asian graduate students at the University of Toronto and York University in 2003–4, Chen (2006, 2007) identified academic and program considerations to be of primary importance, followed by institution and country factors, multicultural diversity, and a safe environment. Consistent with Chen's findings, Madgett and Bélanger's (2008) Canada-wide online survey found that academic environment and schooling costs were more important considerations for graduate students than for undergraduates. For incoming study abroad students at an undisclosed medium-sized university in Ontario, however, the cross-cultural dimension was the most valued, followed by academics (Massey and Burrow 2012).

In addition to differences among study abroad, undergraduate, and graduate students, there were some differences between college and university students, as well as among students in different regions (Canadian Bureau for International Education 2009), although these factors were likely to be confounding. In any case, college students cited safety, quality of education, language-related reasons, and work opportunities as very important considerations in choosing Canada. University students most frequently cited quality of education, safety, language-related reasons, and prestige. University students were also less likely than college students to identify visa- and immigration-related reasons. Across all regions, the quality of education was the most common reason for coming to Canada. For students from Africa, Asia, and Central and South America, the perception of safety was the second most common reason. For those from Europe, North America, and places like New Zealand and Australia, the availability of programs offered in English or French was another top-rated reason, indicating that students from these regions likely prefer countries linguistically and culturally similar to their own, just as Canadian students tend to prefer studying in places such as the United Kingdom, Australia, France, Germany, and the United States (Association of Universities and Colleges in Canada 2014).

The foregoing studies included only tertiary-level students in their analyses, and very few researchers examined the motivations of younger students and their families. Centred on Chinese, Taiwanese, or Korean transnational families and/or unaccompanied youth, and often using parent samples, the published research on primary- and elementary-level students and their families revealed that these younger students were influenced by a slightly different emphasis on push and pull factors, although, they also shared many motivations with their tertiary-level counterparts.

The education systems of home and host countries, along with the desire to learn English, were the strongest push and pull factors for families with primary- and secondary-school-aged children who migrated to Canada as temporary residents (Chiang 2008; Irving, Benjamin, and Tsang 1999; Kim, Yun, Park, and Noh 2013; Shin 2013, 2014; Waters 2003a, 2003b) – although some arrived with permanent status or transitioned to permanent status during their stay, making this population somewhat difficult to demarcate. In this body of work, researchers pointed to the class basis of education migration and the perceived value of a Western education in enabling youth to circumvent the limitations and fears of failure in an overly competitive education system back home.

The transnational family strategy – where one parent stays with children or children remain alone to attend schools in destination settings – permitted children to accumulate cultural capital that was expected to expand opportunities for higher education, and to be transferable in the highly skilled labour market in their places of origin (Kim et al. 2013; Shin 2013, 2014; Waters 2003a, 2003b, 2006a, 2009). In this way, families have the best chance at reproducing their class positions as children engaged in this strategy often begin at the higher end of the socioeconomic hierarchy in terms of wealth and parents' education, much like their older counterparts (Irving, Benjamin, and Tsang 1999; Kim et al. 2013; Lu, Zong, and Schissel 2009).

Regardless of the students' education level, the strategy for social mobility through international education is not without its problems, pitfalls, and contradictions, as we see in the discussion of experiences below. Moreover, as Chiang (2008) argues, transnational family migration is more than a strategy to ensure class reproduction: social factors are also at play. In addition to education-related reasons, mothers in Chiang's study alluded to health, Taiwanese military conscription, lack of employment opportunities for spouses in Canada, and their children's age as factors shaping their migration decisions. Irving, Benjamin, and Tsang (1999) also found family linkages in Canada to be another important pull factor. These and other studies point to the importance of understanding migration decisions as complex and nuanced, and irreducible to a single explanation (Chiang 2008; Irving, Benjamin, and Tsang 1999; Kim et al. 2013; Ghosh and Wang 2003). Rather, some students contemplated migration decisions over a longer period and in multiple life stages (Beck 2009; Ghosh and Wang 2003).

Contextualizing the micro-level push-pull model of ISM are the broader structural conditions and changes that influence the demand for education abroad. These include the unmet need for higher education in domestic education systems (Gattoo and Gattoo 2013; Mickle 1985), decolonization (Cameron 2006), the end of the Cold War (Picard and Mills 2009), and growth of a middle class in newly industrializing economies, particularly in Asia (Kim 2015). Such macro conditions that shape the demand for higher education are important considerations in demand-side perspectives. We now turn to supply-side explanations.

Supply-Side Explanations: Globalization and the Internationalization of Education

It is interesting, but perhaps not surprising, to learn that some newly emerging pull factors, according to international students and their families, are Canada's multicultural environment and its safety and security, which are reflective of the global Canadian international education narrative. As the mission statement of the Imagine Education au/in Canada brand states, "Canada's educational institutions are committed to providing a wide range of world-class programs and an academic environment that is welcoming, stimulating and safe and in which tolerance and celebration of cultural and educational diversity are paramount."[2] Launched in 2007, and rebranded in 2015, the initiative serves as a marketing tool to recruit international students (Trilokekar and Kizilbash 2013).

The reality that students list ease of obtaining visas as one of the top reasons for coming to Canada shows the fuzziness and limitations of the push-pull model. While policies and practices at both state and institutional levels may be perceived as driving students' "choices," students' decision-making power is restrained by forces that are clearly out of their control. National governments, national-level non-governmental organizations, and academic institutions are key players in shaping internationalization (Knight 2004). Such supply-side perspectives that relate to governments and institutions, Findlay (2011) argues, have not received sufficient attention in the literature. However, the literature on Canada demonstrates that this is not so, with numerous journal articles, reports, and a 2009 edited collection investigating supply-side questions. The importance of this supply-side aspect of ISM in shaping the asymmetric patterns and compositions of student flows cannot be overstated. The current engagement with internationalization is a collaborative effort on the parts of the federal, provincial, and municipal levels of government, non-governmental agencies such as the Canadian Bureau for International Education (CBIE), the Association of Universities and Colleges of Canada (AUCC), and the Colleges and Institutes Canada (CICan,

---

2 The webpage for Imagine Education au/in Canada was imagine.cmed.ca/en/. It was rebranded in 2016 after the 2015 federal election and subsequent change in government, with a new web page titled EduCanada: A World of Possibilities, available at http://educanada.ca/index.aspx?lang=eng.

formerly the Association of Canadian Community Colleges), and educational institutions, including local school boards.

The literature that speaks to supply-side issues focuses on three areas: national government/sector policies and programs; provincial governments and educational institutions; and international education services firms, or the export education industry. National government policy goals and actual flow volumes of ISM were often provided as rationales or context for research. Although very few research materials were published on international students in Canada prior to 1990, there has been a noticeable shift since then in what are highlighted as international student policy goals.

National Governments and Shifting Priorities

As official discourse, policy-setting, targets, funding and resource allocation, marketing, bilateral and subnational relations and agreements, and border control are tools that make the state an important player in influencing the direction and volume of international student flows (see Trilokekar and El Masri in this volume). In Canada, the state has long recognized the value of ISM, but there have been important shifts, which have resulted in changing numbers and composition. Cameron (2006), Gue and Holdaway (1973), Trilokekar and Kizilbash (2013), and Zelmer and Johnson (1988) demonstrate the centrality of development cooperation, international aid, social development, and leadership in an earlier system. Although Cameron (2006) and Yoo (2002) show that the connection between international students and development began well before the 1950s, Trilokekar and Kizilbash (2013) identify the 1950s as the key period of official interest. This period ended with budget cuts to the Canadian International Development Agency (CIDA, now the Department of Foreign Affairs, Trade and Development) in the 1970s, which shifted policy attention to fee-paying international students. Cameron (2006) noted this shift as well, highlighting the increasing number of overseas students (versus sponsored students) beginning in the mid-1970s, which coincided with the implementation of differential tuition fees for international students in Ontario and Alberta in 1977.

The 1986 report *Independence and Internationalism: Report of the Special Joint Committee on Canada's International Relations* included a section on international students in its chapter on international development (as opposed to its chapter on trade). In that section, the committee explained that the declining numbers of international students in the mid-1980s was caused by differential fees. It also noted that differential fees, by that point established in seven provinces, had been implemented for the purpose of cost recovery after the increase in foreign student numbers from the mid-1970s and the lack of accompanying increases in per capita educational transfers from the federal government. The practice of differential fees for international students was the most extreme in Ontario and Quebec, which had the highest fees, and was entirely absent in Manitoba, Saskatchewan, and Newfoundland (Special Joint Committee of the Senate and of the House of Commons on Canada's International Relations 1986). The committee also recognized Canada's role in educating students from developing countries and the need for those countries to develop their own institutions of higher education. In this period, the benefits to Canada of hosting international students were framed in terms of trade opportunities, cultural contacts, and foreign policy, and as a means of enhancing Canada's soft power on a global scale (Trilokekar 2009).

However, the mandate and motivation for that engagement has shifted from a political and cultural rationale to the current position of economic advancement in response to globalization. Still, there are remnants of these earlier values today. Indeed, Lehr (2008) argues that the contemporary Canadian international education system is now characterized by mixed messages and conflicting goals. On the one hand, Canada offers development assistance and capacity-building in development contexts, primarily through CIDA scholarships, while also promoting a nation-building agenda through an increasingly market-driven international education system and by facilitating the permanent migration of international students. "Global citizenship," often lauded as a benefit of international education, may be consistent with both goals, but according to Lehr, the present policy fails to ask, "Global citizenship to what end?" In her view, Canada presently follows the paradigm of global citizenship for capital markets, whereas the alternative approach – she uses Cuba as an example – pursues global citizenship for social justice (Lehr 2008).

This paradigm of international education for capital markets is evident in recent government reports and in the increasingly (and paradoxically) inward focus of Canada's internationalization goals. Current documents clearly frame the benefits of international students to Canada in economic terms, often by making reference to a study reporting that 265,000 international students spent $8.4 billion in 2012, while helping sustain 86,570 jobs, and generating $455 million in federal and provincial tax revenues (Foreign Affairs, Trade and Development Canada 2014).

Despite the shift in paradigm and the call to expand international-ization efforts, the decentralization of Canada's education system chal-lenges the federal government's ability to establish a national policy on international education (Trilokekar 2009; Trilokekar and El Masri in this volume). Nevertheless, the federal government has found a role to play at the nexus of international education and human resource develop-ment (Trilokekar 2009). This can be observed in the claims of a loom-ing crisis of a skilled labour shortage, which has been contested as a social construction (Barnetson and Foster 2014) and as a mismatch of the skills of workers and the skills required by employers, as well as a geographic mismatch (McQuillan 2013). Yet, in accordance with the human resource approach to internationalization, scholars have pointed to changes to immigration policy with respect to international students, who were previously expected to leave after their studies but are now given options to stay.

ISM can be a form of highly skilled migration and a pathway to skilled migration (Tremblay 2005), but national governments vary in how they manage student migration and opportunities to enter the labour mar-ket (She and Wotherspoon 2013; Tremblay 2005). In her comparative study, Tremblay explored the degree to which seven countries' respec-tive immigration policies gave international students special consider-ation for permanent residence. She found a trend towards immigration policies with specific schemes favouring former students. Interestingly, a separate scheme for international students had not been developed in Canada at the time of her writing, but one – the Canadian Experience Class program – has been implemented and discontinued since. She and Wotherspoon (2013) also compared Canada with the United States and the United Kingdom and found that all three countries attempted to achieve a balance between opening borders and controlling long-term settlement. They argue that, in keeping with Canada's historic pattern of nation-building through selective migration, there is presently a high degree of openness as concerns the entry of international students and a low degree of control over their settlement, including opportunities to work. These studies point to national-level policy frameworks that shape student mobilities.

But ISM, like other forms of migration, are also shaped by the poli-cies of other countries within a migration system. Both She and Woth-erspoon (2013) and Mueller (2009), explain that the demand for a Canadian education is influenced by the border policies of the United States. Mueller (2009) illustrated this linkage using data on students from predominantly Muslim countries entering Canada and the United States after 9/11. He found that after the events of 9/11, the number of students from predominantly Muslim countries going to the United States fell while the number of students from other countries stabilized. In contrast, students going to Canada from non-Muslim countries slightly decreased, while those from predominantly Muslim countries increased. Chen's (2006) study (described above) of Chinese students whose first choice was the United States but who "chose" Canada due to visa issues provides further evidence of this linkage. The cost and availability of work permits and avenues to permanent residence were also considerations for many international students (Chira, Barber, and Belkhodja 2013; Holdaway, Bryan, and Allan 1988; Li, DiPetta, and Woloshyn 2012; Madgett and Bélanger 2008), further showing the nature of an ISM system.

Regional Governments and Educational Institutions

Provincial governments and educational institutions serve as other important gatekeepers on the supply side of the equation. Provincial governments, which have jurisdictional authority over education, shape ISM through their respective internationalization strategies, policies, and regulations (Leyton-Brown 2008), including those related to immigration through the Provincial Nominee Program (PNP) (She and Wotherspoon 2013). The provinces and territories, through separate agreements with the federal government, operate immigration programs targeted to particular migrants, including students. Chira and Belkhodja (2012), in their study of international students in the Atlantic provinces, explored the settlement services and practices of organizations and found that, with the exception of New Brunswick, the three other Atlantic provincial governments – Nova Scotia, Prince Edward Island, and Newfoundland and Labrador – offered recent graduates a pathway to permanent settlement through their PNPs, particularly for those with offers of employment. However, a more recent study showed that at least two of these PNPs were discontinued, highlighting issues of duplication with federal immigration programs such as the Canadian Experience Class (Chira, Barber, and Belkhodja 2013).

Beyond immigration and settlement, the provinces' support for and regulation of internationalization activities is characterized by their varied histories and target populations. Manitoba's involvement began in 1999 and focused primarily on post-secondary students, while Alberta's involvement began with the primary and secondary student populations but has now shifted to post-secondary students (Savage 2009). Quebec also has a longer history with international students and appears to focus on the post-secondary population (Picard and Mills 2009). In general, provinces' internationalization activities include strategic planning, funding, scholarships and programming (e.g., offshore schools, study abroad programs), the setting of fees, promotional and marketing activities, and coordination. Provinces clearly vary in the roles they play in the supply side of international education. However, like the federal government, they also need the participation and engagement of educational institutions – including universities, community colleges, and local school boards – for any degree of international education activity.

The former AUCC (now Universities Canada), an umbrella organization of over ninety universities, periodically conducted surveys of its membership. The 2014 survey covered a range of internationalization activities: institutional planning; institutional partnerships and activities abroad; student mobility; teaching, learning, and faculty engagement; and international collaboration and research (Association of Universities and Colleges of Canada 2014). The AUCC found that more than 95 per cent of the seventy-eight responding universities reported their planning included internationalization, with nearly half of them engaged at a high or very high level, and with a focus on undergraduate student recruitment from China, followed by India, the United States, Saudi Arabia, Brazil, and Nigeria. As such, the concentrated flows of particular students from particular places is as much a result of priority-setting by states and institutions as it is the result of the aggregated decisions of individual students and their families.

The 2014 report also showed that most universities actively engaged in recruitment activities aimed at both undergraduate and graduate students using websites, printed promotional materials, recruitment fairs, visits to overseas schools, and overseas recruiters or agents. A large percentage of universities offered scholarships, financial aid, and, at the graduate level, stipends or tuition waivers. And the push for expansion is noticeable. Total international full-time undergraduate and graduate enrolments have increased since 2000 to comprise 11 per cent of full-time undergraduates, or 89,000 students, and 28 per cent of graduate students, or 44,000 students (Association of Universities and Colleges of Canada 2014). Students come from two hundred countries but were concentrated among the top five (China, France, the United States, India, and Saudi Arabia), which represented over half of all international students in Canada.

Compared to the federal government, universities expressed their reasons for internationalizing less in economic terms, although revenue generation was often found among the top five reasons. Universities hoped to prepare internationally and interculturally competent graduates and to increase enrolment in specific programs; they also hoped to build strategic alliances and partnerships with institutions abroad, promote an internationalized campus, and increase the institution's global profile (Association of Universities and Colleges of Canada 2014). In terms of funding internationalization activities, international students on campus appeared to receive very little support from the institutions' overall budgets, although many universities offered orientation programs, individualized academic support and advising, ongoing counselling and settlement services, and language support and mentoring programs. Very few offered immigration assistance and even fewer offered support for dependents.

The nationally representative AUCC survey is the most comprehensive examination of the goals and practices of universities. Its findings are similar to those of other studies on higher education institutions as regards overall support for internationalization (Knight 1997), ranges of activities (Taylor 2004) – including social media (Bélanger, Bali, and Longden 2014) – and reasons for internationalizing, such as increasing revenues (Burnett and Huisman 2010; Cudmore 2005; Knight 1997) and preparing graduates (Knight 1997). An inward shift is also apparent among universities. While social change in Canada and abroad was a common rationale for internationalizing among educational institutions in the past (Knight 1997), the issue is not identified in more recent studies.

Extending these general results, a number of studies have shown that the role of institutions varies by individual institution and locality, and that institutional and geographic factors shape the ability to attract and recruit students. A shortcoming of the AUCC report, then, is the lack of explanation for variations in internationalization practices across institutions. Burnett and Huisman (2010) fill this gap in their study of four universities by revealing how a university's culture may play an important role in shaping its response to globalization. They found that an enterprising university – one with an explicit mission and planning for the global dimension, a supportive organizational culture, administrative and financial supports, and a strong commitment to the university community – tended to be strategic and initiate more responses to opportunities. The AUCC report also neglected to look at the impact of internationalization on universities and local communities, though we know that internationalization can clearly have an impact on these communities through the student body and the international student centre, and by attracting future permanent migrants (Walton-Roberts 2011). This recent study of Kitchener-Waterloo is of particular interest here because it shows how smaller cities that receive fewer immigrants may seek to attract more students through their local educational institutions as a way of achieving economic goals, and social and cultural diversity.

The International Education Services Sector

In addition to the initiatives of the federal and provincial governments and of universities and colleges aimed at shaping international migration flows, there is a much wider field that encompasses many different kinds of institutions. This field includes local school boards, which often have their own internationalization initiatives (Kwak 2013; Waters 2006b), employers (Knight 1997; Schell et al. 1986), and participants in the international education services sector, or export education industry (Kwak 2004, 2013). Participants in the international education economy include educational migration agents, recruiters, and brokers, travel agencies, tutoring/ESL schools, immigration lawyers, employers, and food and accommodation services (e.g., homestays). Kwak and Hiebert (2010) argue that, by way of the regulated and unregulated work of these participants in the education industry, internationalization also takes shape from the bottom up. The importance of the local international education services sector and the local economy for broader internationalization efforts was revealed in the official reactions to attacks on Asian female international students in Vancouver in the early 2000s, when local officials engaged in damage control to contain the potential harm to Asian investments in the city (Park 2010).

Discussion

In this chapter, we reviewed the literature explaining ISM to Canada, specifically limiting the review up to 2014. This covered the early literature in the 1970s to the seven years following the launching of the official Canadian brand of international education in 2007. We explored what Findlay (2011) refers to as demand- and supply-side perspectives in order to understand the multilayered factors shaping student flows, from individuals and families to institutions and regional governments and states. We found that past research explained ISM using a neo-classical economic approach, considering factors related to family, political economy, and institutions. Our review reveals that, in general, we have a good understanding of why students (and their families) choose Canadian institutions and that these reasons have been relatively stable since the 1970s, with changes reflecting the shift from the individual to the family as the unit of analysis.

The literature on Canada also confirms that a focus on motivations alone misses the broader context in which international student flows occur. More so now than in the past, scholars account for the local, regional, and national contexts for ISM, from national governments to local institutions, from immigration policy and national targets to the food and accommodation services that cater to international students. These institutional factors can facilitate or inhibit international student flows as well as shape the demand for international education.

Finally, the review revealed a few gaps. In particular, we could benefit from studies examining bilateral agreements between institutions and between governments, as well as the role and interests of sending states with large flows of students to Canada. This is one area where the literature on Canada is weak. Moreover, future work on the mechanisms that bridge demand and supply, such as social networks, social capital, and the role of social media, will provide a more complete understanding of ISM to Canada. To fill some of these gaps, we require some shifts in our conceptualization of migration to examine countries and individuals in terms of networks. As the next chapter will show, how we conceptualize social phenomena such as ISM and the data we produce shape our knowledge. And in the case of international students, there is very little representative data.

References

Association of Universities and Colleges of Canada (AUCC). 2014. *Canada's Universities in the World: AUCC Internationalization Survey.* Ottawa: Association of Universities and Colleges of Canada 2a. https://www.univcan.ca/wp-content/uploads/2015/07/internationalization-survey-2014.pdf.

Barnetson, Bob, and Jason Foster. 2014. "The Political Justification of Migrant Workers in Alberta, Canada." *Journal of International Migration and Integration* 15 (2): 349–70. https://doi.org/10.1007/s12134-013-0292-6.

Beck, Kumari. 2009. "Questioning the Emperor's New Clothes: Towards Ethical Practices in Internationalization." In *Canada's Universities Go Global,* ed. Roopa Desai Trilokekar, Glen A. Jones, and Adrian Shubert, 307–66. Toronto: James Lorimer and Company.

Bélanger, Charles H., Suchita Bali, and Bernard Longden. 2014. "How Canadian Universities Use Social Media to Brand Themselves." *Tertiary Education and Management* 20 (1): 14–29. https://doi.org/10.1080/13583883.2013.852237.

Burnett, Sally-Ann, and Jeroen Huisman. 2010. "Universities' Responses to Globalisation: The Influence of Organisational Culture." *Journal of Studies in International Education* 14 (2): 117–42. https://doi.org/10.1177/1028315309350717.

Cameron, James D. 2006. "International Student Integration into the Canadian University: A Post-World War Two Historical Case Study." *History of Intellectual Culture* 6 (1). http://www.ucalgary.ca/hic/issues/vol6/1.

Canadian Bureau for International Education. 2009. *Canada First: The 2009 Survey of International Students.* Ottawa, ON: Canadian Bureau for International Education.

Chandras, Kananur V. 1974. *The Adjustment and Attitudes of East Indian Students in Canada.* Fort Valley, GA: R.D. Reed.

Chen, Liang-Hsuan. 2006. "Attracting East Asian Students to Canadian Graduate Schools." *Canadian Journal of Higher Education* 36 (2): 77–105.

– 2007. "Choosing Canadian Graduate Schools from Afar: East Asian Students' Perspectives." *Higher Education* 54 (5): 759–80. https://doi.org/10.1007/s10734-006-9022-8.

Chiang, Lan-Hung Nora. 2008. "'Astronaut Families': Transnational Lives of Middle-class Taiwanese Married Women in Canada." *Social & Cultural Geography* 9 (5): 505–18. https://doi.org/10.1080/14649360802175709.

Chira, Sinziana, Pauline Barber, and Chedly Belkhodja. 2013. *Dreaming Big, Coming up Short: The Challenging Realities of International Students and Graduates in Atlantic Canada.* Atlantic Metropolis Centre's Working Paper Series 47–2013. http://community.smu.ca/atlantic/documents/ChiraDreamingbigcomingupshort_000.pdf.

Chira, Sinziana, and Chedly Belkhodja. 2012. *Best Practices for the Integration of International Students in Atlantic Canada: Findings and Recommendations. A Study of the Policies and Practices Surrounding the Settlement of International Students in the Atlantic Provinces.* Halifax, NS: Atlantic Metropolis Centre. http://smu.ca/webfiles/Best-Practices-in-the-Integration-of-International-Students-in-Atlantic-Canada.pdf.

Citizenship and Immigration Canada. 2015. "Evaluation of the International Student Program. Report: Evaluation Division." https://www.canada.ca/content/dam/ircc/migration/ircc/english/resources/evaluation/isp/2015/e3-2013-isp.pdf.

Cudmore, Geoffrey. 2005. "Globalization, Internationalization, and the Recruitment of International Students in Higher Education, and in the Ontario Colleges of Applied Arts and Technology." *Canadian Journal of Higher Education* 35 (1): 37–60.

Findlay, Allan M. 2011. "An Assessment of Supply and Demand-Side Theorizations of International Student Mobility." *International Migration (Geneva, Switzerland)* 49 (2): 162–90. https://doi.org/10.1111/j.1468 -2435.2010.00643.x.

Foreign Affairs, Trade and Development Canada. 2014. "Canada's International Education Strategy: Harnessing Our Knowledge Advantage to Drive Innovation and Prosperity." http://international.gc.ca/global-markets -marches-mondiaux/education/index.aspx?lang=eng.

Gattoo, Muneeb Hussaid, and Mujeeb Hussain Gattoo. 2013. "Internationalization of Higher Education and Its Effects on Student Mobility." *International Journal of Research in Commerce, Economics and Management* 3 (10): 126–31.

Ghosh, Sutama, and Lu Wang. 2003. "Transnationalism and Identity: A Tale of Two Faces and Multiple Lives." *Canadian Geographer. Geographe Canadien* 47 (3): 269–82. https://doi.org/10.1111/1541-0064.00022.

Glaser, William A., and G. Christopher Habers. 1974. "The Migration and Return of Professionals." *International Migration Review* 8 (2): 227–44. https://doi.org/10.2307/3002782.

Gue, Leslie R., and Edward A. Holdaway. 1973. "English Proficiency Tests as Predictors of Success in Graduate Studies in Education." *Language Learning* 23 (1): 89–103. https://doi.org/10.1111/j.1467-1770.1973.tb00099.x.

Holdaway, Edward A., Wendy M. Bryan, and Wilfred H. Allan. 1988. "International University Students in Canada: Obtaining the Information Needed for Policy Making." *Canadian Journal of Higher Education* 18 (3): 13–29.

Irving, Howard H., Michael Benjamin, and A.K. Tat Tsang. 1999. "Hong Kong Satellite Children in Canada: An Exploratory Study of Their Experience." *Hong Kong Journal of Social Work* 33 (01n02): 1–21. https://doi.org/10.1142/ S0219246299000029.

Kim, Ann H. 2015. "Structuring Transnationalism: The Mothering Discourse and the Educational Project." In *Engendering Transnational Voices Studies in Families, Work, and Identities*, ed. Guida Man and Rina Cohen, 235–54. Waterloo, ON: Wilfrid Laurier University Press.

Kim, Ann H., Sung Hyun Yun, Wansoo Park, and Samuel Noh. 2013. "Explaining the Migration Strategy: Comparing Transnational and Intact Migration Families from South Korea to Canada." In *Koreans in North America: Their Experiences in the Twenty-First Century*, ed. Pyong Gap Min, 103–20. Lanham, MD: Lexington Books.

Knight, Jane. 1997. "A Shared Vision? Stakeholders' Perspectives on the Internationalization of Higher Education in Canada." *Journal of Studies in International Education* 1 (1): 27–44. https://doi.org/10.1177/102831539700100105.
– 2004. "Internationalization Remodeled: Definition, Approaches, and Rationales." *Journal of Studies in International Education* 8 (1): 5–31. https://doi.org/10.1177/1028315303260832.
Kwak, Min-Jung. 2004. *An Exploration of the Korean-Canadian Community in Vancouver.* Vancouver: Research on Immigration and Integration in the Metropolis Working Paper Series.
– 2013. "Rethinking the Neoliberal Nexus of Education, Migration, and Institutions." *Environment & Planning A* 45 (8): 1858–72. https://doi.org/10.1068/a43493.
Kwak, Min-Jung, and Daniel Hiebert. 2010. "Globalizing Canadian Education from Below: A Case Study of Transnational Immigrant Entrepreneurship between Seoul, Korea and Vancouver Canada." *Journal of International Migration and Integration/Revue de l'integration et de la migration internationale* 11 (2): 131–53. http://doi.org/10.1007/s12134-010-0130-z.
Lehr, Sabine. 2008. "Ethical Dilemmas in Individual and Collective Rights-Based Approaches to Tertiary Education Scholarships: The Cases of Canada and Cuba." *Comparative Education* 44 (4): 425–44. https://doi.org/10.1080/03050060802481454.
Leyton-Brown, David. 2008. "Social and Legal Aspects of Doctoral Training in Canada: Criteria and Consequences of Admission." *Higher Education in Europe* 33 (1): 111–23. https://doi.org/10.1080/03797720802228241.
Li, Xiaobin, Tony DiPetta, and Vera Woloshyn. 2012. "Why Do Chinese Study for a Master of Education Degree in Canada? What Are Their Experiences?" *Canadian Journal of Education* 35 (3): 149–63.
Liu, Chun Ge. 2007. "Adult Learning and Change: An Autobiographical Portrait of a Chinese Woman in Canada." *Canadian Journal of University Continuing Education* 33 (1): 107–25.
Lu, Yixi, Li Zong, and Bernard Schissel. 2009. "To Stay or Return: Migration Intentions of Students from People's Republic of China in Saskatchewan, Canada." *Journal of International Migration and Integration* 10 (3): 283–310. https://doi.org/10.1007/s12134-009-0103-2.
Madgett, Paul J., and Charles Bélanger. 2008. "International Students: The Canadian Experience." *Tertiary Education and Management* 14 (3): 191–207. https://doi.org/10.1080/13583880802228182.
Massey, Jennifer, and Jeff Burrow. 2012. "Coming to Canada to Study: Factors That Influence Students' Decisions to Participate in International

Exchange." *Journal of Student Affairs Research and Practice* 49 (1): 83–100. https://doi.org/10.1515/jsarp-2012-6177.

McQuillan, Kevin. 2013. *All the Workers We Need: Debunking Canada's Labour-Shortage Fallacy.* Rochester, NY: Social Science Research Network. http://papers.ssrn.com/abstract=2262529.

Mickle, Kathryn. 1985. *The Adaptation of Hong Kong Students to Canada.* Toronto: University of Toronto-York University Joint Centre on Modern East Asia.

Mueller, Richard E. 2009. "Does the Statue of Liberty Still Face Out? The Diversion of Foreign Students from the United States to Canada in the Post 9/11 Period." *Canadian Journal of Higher Education* 39 (1): 15–43. http://journals.sfu.ca/cjhe/index.php/cjhe/article/view/492.

Neice, David C. 1977. *A Patron for the World?* Toronto: Survey Research Centre, Institute for Behavioural Research, York University.

Park, Hijin. 2010. "The Stranger That Is Welcomed: Female Foreign Students from Asia, the English Language Industry, and the Ambivalence of 'Asia Rising' in British Columbia, Canada." *Gender, Place and Culture* 17 (3): 337–55. https://doi.org/10.1080/09663691003737603.

Picard, France, and D. Mills. 2009. "Provincial Internationalization Efforts: Programs, Policies and Plans in Manitoba and Alberta." In *Canada's Universities Go Global,* ed. Roopa Desai Trilokekar, Glen A. Jones, and Adrian Shubert, 134–53. Toronto: James Lorimer and Company.

Savage, Christine. 2009. "Provincial Internationalization Efforts: Programs, Policies and Plans in Manitoba and Alberta." In *Canada's Universities Go Global,* ed. Roopa Desai Trilokekar, Glen A. Jones, and Adrian Shubert, 119–33. Toronto: James Lorimer and Company.

Schell, Bernadette, Helen Sherritt, Mark Lewis, and Paul Mansfield. 1986. "An Investigation of Worldmindedness, Satisfaction and Commitment for Hirers of Foreign Student Exchanges." *Psychological Reports* 59 (2): 911–20. https://doi.org/10.2466/pr0.1986.59.2.911.

She, Qianru, and Terry Wotherspoon. 2013. "International Student Mobility and Highly Skilled Migration: A Comparative Study of Canada, the United States, and the United Kingdom." *SpringerPlus* 2 (1): 132–45. https://doi.org/10.1186/2193-1801-2-132. Medline:23667802.

Shin, Hyunjung. 2013. "Ambivalent Calculations in Toronto: Negotiating the Meaning of Success among Early Study Abroad High School Students." *Asian and Pacific Migration Journal* 22 (4): 527–46. https://doi.org/10.1177/011719681302200404.

– 2014. "Social Class, Habitus, and Language Learning: The Case of Korean Early Study-Abroad Students." *Journal of Language, Identity, and Education* 13 (2): 99–103. https://doi.org/10.1080/15348458.2014.901821.

Special Joint Committee of the Senate and of the House of Commons on
Canada's International Relations. 1986. *Independence and Internationalism:
Report of the Special Joint Committee of the Senate and of the House of Commons on
Canada's International Relations.* Ottawa: Queen's Printer for Canada.

Taylor, John. 2004. "Toward a Strategy for Internationalisation: Lessons and
Practice from Four Universities." *Journal of Studies in International Education*
8 (2): 149–71. https://doi.org/10.1177/1028315303260827.

Tremblay, Karine. 2005. "Academic Mobility and Immigration." *Journal of
Studies in International Education* 9 (3): 196–228. https://doi.org/
10.1177/1028315305277618.

Trilokekar, Roopa Desai. 2009. "The Department of Foreign Affairs and
International Trade (DFAIT), Canada: Providing Leadership in the
Internationalization of Canadian Higher Education?" In *Canada's
Universities Go Global*, ed. Roopa Desai Trilokekar, Glen A. Jones, and Adrian
Shubert, 355–69. Toronto: James Lorimer and Company.

Trilokekar, Roopa Desai, and Zainab Kizilbash. 2013. "IMAGINE: Canada as
a Leader in International Education. How Can Canada Benefit from the
Australian Experience?" *Canadian Journal of Higher Education* 43 (2): 1–26.

Walton-Roberts, Margaret W. 2011. "Immigration, the University and
the Welcoming Second Tier City." *Journal of International Migration and
Integration* 12 (4): 453–73.

Waters, Johanna L. 2003a. "Flexible Citizens? Transnationalism and
Citizenship amongst Economic Immigrants in Vancouver." *Canadian
Geographer. Geographe Canadien* 47 (3): 219–34. https://doi.org/
10.1111/1541-0064.00019.

– 2003b. "'Satellite Kids' in Vancouver." In *Asian Migrants and Education:
The Tensions of Education in Immigrant Societies and Among Migrant Groups*,
ed. Michael W. Charney, Brenda Yeoh, and Tong Chee Kiong, 165–84.
Dordrecht, NL: Kluwer Academic Publishers. https://doi.org/
10.1007/978-94-017-0117-4_13.

– 2006a. "Geographies of Cultural Capital: Education, International
Migration and Family Strategies between Hong Kong and Canada."
Transactions of the Institute of British Geographers 31 (2): 179–92. https://doi
.org/10.1111/j.1475-5661.2006.00202.x.

– 2006b. "Emergent Geographies of International Education
and Social Exclusion." *Antipode* 38 (5): 1046–68. https://doi.
org/10.1111/j.1467-8330.2006.00492.x.

– 2009. "Transnational Geographies of Academic Distinction: The Role of
Social Capital in the Recognition and Evaluation of 'overseas' Credentials."
Globalisation, Societies and Education 7 (2): 113–29. https://doi.org/10.1080/
14767720902907895.

Yoo, Young-sik. 2002. "Canada and Korea: A Shared History." In *Canada and Korea: Perspectives 2000,* ed. R.W.L. Guisso and Young-sik Yoo. Toronto: Centre for Korean Studies, University of Toronto.

Zelmer, Amy E., and Neil A. Johnson. 1988. "International Students in Higher Education: A Follow-up Study of University Graduates." *Canadian Journal of Higher Education* 18 (3): 31–50.

4 Barriers to Knowledge on International Students and a Potential Opportunity

ANN H. KIM, REEM ATTIEH, AND TIMOTHY OWEN

Introduction

With the significant increase in the number of temporary migrants over the past decade resulting from labour and immigration policy changes, our need to recognize the unique social location of various temporary resident groups has intensified. However, developing high-quality data on the experiences of temporary migrants, such as international students, is a low priority for a host country like Canada, which bases its policies and programs on a predominantly permanent migration model. Consequently, as observed in the previous chapter, this lack of attention to data gaps limits our knowledge about a growing segment of migrants.

This chapter describes Canada's national-level data sources on international students, and discusses their limitations and potential opportunities. We focus our review on selected national microdata sources and ask to what extent they can address questions related to immigration status. We examine how the temporary migrant population is operationalized in the questionnaires, paying particular attention to international students. Our review highlights serious gaps in our knowledge of international students created by the lack of nationally representative microdata, and we propose an alternative approach for addressing some of the gaps using a case study from the Agency Data on Migration (ADMIG) project.

Statistics in Context

From the time of Thomas Robert Malthus's (1798) *An Essay in the Principle of Population* to W.E.B. Du Bois's (1899) *The Philadelphia Negro* to the present, quantitative data has helped to elucidate social processes and the conditions of social groups in society. Influenced by the natural sciences, social researchers in the early nineteenth century began to collect large volumes of data to study correlations and causal patterns. Conducted under a positivist paradigm, these social studies were often used to influence government policies. Yet much of the analysis and framing of the causal relations were based on moral judgments rather than empirical evidence (Tonkiss 2004). As Tonkiss (2004) notes, in the late nineteenth and early twentieth century, studies on poverty in both England and the United States paved the way for the development of social survey research methods, including the systematic collection and analysis of data.

Recognizing the important role of statistics in shedding light on social, demographic, and economic conditions and in establishing sound policies and planning, the United Nations declared 20 October 2010 the first World Statistics Day. The then UN secretary general Ban Ki-moon stressed that statistics could offer insights into trends and forces that affect people's lives and were "a vital tool for economic and social development" that could also promote peace and democracy (United Nations 2010). Ironically, earlier that same year, the Government of Canada, led at the time by Stephen Harper's Conservative Party, cancelled the compulsory long-form census and replaced it with a voluntary household survey, stimulating significant debate, criticism, and outcry. Liberal MP Ted Hsu's attempt to reinstate the long-form census with the introduction of a private member's bill (Bill C-626) in the fall of 2014 was defeated by the majority Conservative government in February 2015. However, in November 2015, the newly elected federal government led by Justin Trudeau's Liberal Party reinstated the long-form census for 2016.

In spite of these political shifts, analyses of data from censuses and nationally representative surveys in Canada, along with more localized quantitative and qualitative research, have contributed to our understanding of immigrant integration and settlement so that we now have a fairly solid appreciation of the factors shaping immigrants' social, economic, and political lives and well-being. Yet, studies that rely only on large-scale, nationally representative microdata are limited to migrants who have more or less permanently settled in Canada. While this empirical focus on permanent residents is consistent with the nation-building paradigm that has characterized much of Canada's development over the past two centuries, it neglects the growing trend towards temporary migration (Goldring and Landolt 2012; Vosko, Preston, and Latham

2014). Below, we take stock of the data presently available on temporary migrants, highlighting the (lack of) data on international students.

The Two Main Agencies in Canada for Microdata on International Students

As early as 1905, the need for accurate and timely labour market statistics resulted in the Census and Statistics Act, which established the Office of Census and Statistics and coordinated the data-collection process across the provinces. In addition to conducting the periodic census, the Office of Census and Statistics also had a mandate to develop statistical programs on various subjects (Worton 1998).

Renamed Statistics Canada in 1971, the now centralized federal agency is Canada's national statistical agency under Industry Canada – itself a federal agency – and its mandate is outlined in the Statistics Act of 1985. The agency conducts the quinquennial census as well as other nationally representative surveys and also houses some administrative data. Various forms of data are available: some are publicly available online (http://www.statcan.gc.ca/, typically in the form of tabulations); others are available through a cost-recovery program or on university campuses through the Statistics Canada Data Liberation Initiative (DLI), a partnership between 78 post-secondary institutions and Statistics Canada to increase usage of data; and still other data are available by special permission on-site in Ottawa or by collaborating with Statistics Canada analysts. At the time of writing, Statistics Canada listed 354 active and 341 inactive surveys and statistical programs on their website. Most of the Statistics Canada microdata sources reviewed in this chapter are available to researchers via the DLI.

Along with data products, Statistics Canada also houses administrative records that provide valuable information on specific programs and segments of the population. Immigration, Refugees and Citizenship Canada (formerly Citizenship and Immigration Canada) is the federal department responsible for setting immigration policy, programs, and targets, and processing applications for permanent residence and temporary visas. The department reports to Parliament on the number of immigrants admitted into the country under the various programs. This information is publicly available in the form of aggregated tables by year (www.cic.gc.ca). Selected microdata are also available to researchers through the Statistics Canada DLI.

Data Source Selection

Statistics Canada conducts national surveys, both cross-sectional and longitudinal, on a variety of issues and topics on an ongoing basis; there are hundreds of active surveys and statistical programs at any given time. From the full list of active and inactive data sources at Statistics Canada available at the start of our review, along with several additional sources outside this list, we selected twenty-five population-based surveys and databases based on sociological relevance, relevance to immigration, and a review of the immigration literature. Several data sources followed repeated cross-sectional or panel designs, in which case we examined the most recent questionnaire available at the time of writing.

Given our interest in assessing whether publicly available national microdata sources could be used to gain an understanding of the international student experience and student trajectories over time, our review was guided by two sets of questions: 1) Does the data source capture immigration status? If so, how? What is measured in terms of immigration status? 2) Does the data source capture transitions in status, or "switchers"? Does it measure whether the respondent was a temporary migrant (and if so, which type) before becoming a landed immigrant?

The Visibility of Permanence and the Invisibility of Temporariness

Of the 25 data sources reviewed, 19 included questions to establish nativity, length of residence, landed immigrant status (permanent or non-permanent residence), and/or legal citizenship. Some surveys focused on a specific subset of the population, while other data were obtained from a broad target population of those living in Canada. Questionnaires contained one or more questions regarding nativity, landed immigrant status, year of arrival, and citizenship, but no questions on class of entry or the specific temporary resident class of those who were not landed immigrants. In Table 4.1, we list 11 data sources according to their immigration-related variables; the remaining eight sources are discussed in detail in the next section as they offer greater possibilities for understanding the experience of migrants based on immigration status.

More specifically, in sources with information on landed immigrant status (top two rows of Table 4.1), questions on nativity were typically

Table 4.1 Data Sources Containing Standard Immigration-Related Variables

Variables	Data sources
Nativity	Census Long-Form 2006
Landed immigrant status	National Household Survey 2011
Year of landing	National Longitudinal Survey of Children and Youth 2009
Citizenship	Ethnic Diversity Survey 2002
Nativity	Survey of Labour and Income Dynamics 2011
Landed immigrant status	Canadian Income Survey 2012
Year of landing	Labour Force Survey 2012
	Canadian Health Measures Survey 2013
	GSS Cycle 27 – Giving, Volunteering and Participating 2013
Nativity	Canadian Community Health Survey 2014
Year of arrival	
Citizenship	
Nativity	World Values Survey 2005
Year of arrival	

followed by two questions to identify landed status (or permanent residence) and the length of residence for landed immigrants: Is this person now, or has this person ever been, a landed immigrant? And, In what year did this person first become a landed immigrant? Where data are available with sufficient sample sizes, researchers can make comparisons among non-immigrants, landed immigrants, and non-permanent residents; between citizens and non-citizens; and among immigrant cohorts. However, there are no further follow-up questions.

Consequently, we are unable to distinguish among the landed immigrant groups (i.e., by class of entry) or among the non-permanent resident groups, the three main segments being international students, temporary foreign workers, and refugee claimants. We also do not know whether they were in Canada previously. For non-permanent residents, we are also unable to determine, in contrast to permanent residents, how long they have been living in Canada. This leaves a significant knowledge gap, as length of residence (or exposure to a host society) is an important determinant of migrant outcomes. Finally, among those sources that do not ask about landed status (bottom two rows of Table 4.1), we are unable to differentiate between non-permanent and permanent. This variable lumping of migrants renders their distinctive experiences invisible.

The data sources in this review clearly reveal that Statistics Canada, in consultation with its advisory groups of researchers, policymakers, and stakeholders, gives great weight and importance to permanent residents. Yet, unlike the questions about language, religion, visible minority status, and ethnic origins, which generate some debate (Bourhis 2003), critical conceptual and methodological questions related to immigrant status and citizenship are noticeably absent. Perhaps this is due to the overly simplistic way in which the issue of status is conceptualized, measured, and defined – one is either born in Canada or not; one is either a card-carrying citizen or not. Yet, as the Canadian families of those born overseas will attest, even these measures are not precise.

In this chapter, we argue that the exclusion of, or failure to recognize, particular groups of migrants by Canada's official statistics agency denies the social reality that there is a growing presence and diversity of temporary residents, that increasingly permanent residents will have had some prior experience of temporariness, and that the migration program at entry can be important for shaping future outcomes (Goldring and Landolt 2012; see also Lu and Hou in this volume). Although the census and other data-gathering instruments can be perceived as tools of the state to regulate and control the population – or as, Anderson (2006) argues, an institution of power (163) – for others, the political nature of census-making in contemporary democracies leaves space for individual and collective self-knowledge (McDaniel and MacDonald 2012). In pursuit of such self-knowledge, we investigate in greater detail some relevant data sources below and ask what they reveal about Canada in terms of the temporary resident population and, in particular, international students.

Some Developments on Immigration Status and Trajectories

Statistics Canada Sources

In this section, we examine four surveys that show progress in acknowledging the non-permanent resident population: the Longitudinal Survey of Immigrants to Canada (LSIC); the General Social Survey on Social Identity (GSS-Social Identity); the Longitudinal and International Study of Adults (LISA); and the National Graduates Survey (NGS).

The purpose of the LSIC was to understand the settlement and integration experience of recent immigrants. A panel study of the 20,300 permanent migrants who arrived between 1 October 2000 and 30 September 2001, it consisted of three post-arrival waves: a six-month wave (Wave 1, 2001, 12,000 respondents); a two-year wave (Wave 2, 2003, 9,300 respondents); and a four-year wave (Wave 3, 2005, 7,716 respondents). In accordance with the LSIC sample criteria, only those who had applied for and received their permanent resident permits abroad were selected to participate in the survey. As we will see, this criterion did not exclude those who had previously been in Canada on a temporary visa before applying for permanent residence from abroad, but it did eliminate those who transitioned from temporary to permanent status without leaving Canada.

Nevertheless, the LSIC was one of the first surveys to recognize that immigrants may have had prior exposure to Canada by asking the following question: "Did you ever live in Canada before coming here? Was that ... on a work visa ... on a student visa ... as a refugee claimant?" Respondents were able to choose more than one answer. They were also asked the duration of past stays in total, excluding tourist visits. This set of questions permits us to identify respondents with past status as a temporary resident and to compare them to immigrants without such prior Canadian experience. Furthermore, it allows us to examine how particular kinds of prior experience – i.e., as international students – may shape integration outcomes. However, there are limitations to this approach, as there is no timeline for respondents' prior stays and there is no comparison group of non-immigrants. Moreover, this survey has been discontinued, leaving us with no new or recent data.

The GSS-Social Identity (Cycle 27, 2013) module is part of the General Social Survey program, which began in 1985. It is a series of annual cross-sectional surveys on various topics that are repeated approximately every five years. In 2013, two GSS modules were conducted, one on social identity (SI), which had a sample size of 27,695 respondents, and the other on giving, volunteering, and participating (GVP), which had a sample size of about 47,100 households. Although GSS modules typically confined to questions on nativity, landed status, and year of landing, the SI module, which focused on respondents' social identity and sense of belonging, also had a question on Canadian citizenship. In addition, a section called "Landed Immigrant Programs (LIP)" expanded on questions related to immigrant background, asking, "Under which of the following broad immigration programs did you become a landed immigrant in Canada?" The three main response categories were the refugee program, the program of reunification with a family member already in Canada, and the points system (skilled workers and professionals, investors, entrepreneurs, and self-employed persons). Those who arrived under the points system were also asked whether they or another family member had been the main applicant.

The inclusion of a question to differentiate among landed immigrant classes in the GSS-SI module demonstrates an appreciation of the importance of migration pathways in shaping opportunities. However, the absence of questions for migrants without landed status clearly shows that the concern for permanent residents predominates. This is the case with the LISA as well.

LISA, a computer-assisted personal interviewing panel survey with a focus on education, employment, training, and social services, began with Wave 1 in 2012 and a sample of 30,000 individuals within selected households (Heisz 2013). This first wave was integrated with the Program for International Assessment of Adult Competencies (PIAAC), also known as the International Study of Adults (ISA). Wave 2 of LISA took place in 2014 and was not yet released at the time of writing. Similar to the GSS-SI, LISA contained questions about nativity, landed status, year of landing, and landed immigrant program, but not citizenship, and cases were linked to administrative tax files. Interestingly, LISA also goes beyond the GSS-SI LIP by asking respondents who landed under the family reunification program or the points system the following question: "When you first came to Canada, were you a refugee?" This is followed by a question to all those born outside of Canada: "How old were you when you first came to Canada to live or in which year did you come? You may have first come to live in Canada on a work or study permit or as a refugee claimant." Finally, the section ends with a question about total years in Canada.

We now have growing evidence that the particular program (e.g., skilled worker, family class, business class, refugee, etc.) under the permanent migration stream is being recognized as a meaningful concept in official statistics, but there continues to be little interest in differentiating among non-permanent residents. Time in Canada also appears to be more salient than the particular immigration program for non-permanent migrants. Nevertheless, statistical programs are beginning to catch up to the reality of immigration experiences.

Finally, the last Statistics Canada survey presented here is the most promising for the study of international student outcomes, but it is limited in scope and conducted on an irregular basis. The National Graduates Survey (NGS) of 2013, consisting of a sample of 38,500 individuals, examined employment-related topics for those graduating from a Canadian post-secondary institution in 2009–10. Graduates living in Canada and the United States were interviewed. Going beyond the data sources reviewed earlier in this chapter, and giving hope to research on international students, the NGS included several questions that make it possible to examine transitions in immigration status, albeit without timing and duration data. As with other Statistics Canada surveys, respondents were asked about nativity, year of first arrival, landed status, year of landing, and citizenship. However, exceeding the data gathered in other surveys, the NGS also asked those born outside of Canada about past visa or foreign student status as well as current status as visa holder or foreign student.

Data from the NGS can reveal the extent to which respondents transition from foreign student to landed immigrant to citizen. However, those transitions cannot be traced by the specific landed immigrant program, by other non-permanent programs, or by time. Another limitation of the NGS is that the timing and location of data collection – after students have graduated and only respondents in Canada and the United States – omits students who have moved to other countries or returned to places of origin. Nevertheless, through the NGS data, we now have an opportunity to compare international students and domestic students on a range of education and employment outcomes.

Citizenship and Immigration Canada Records

Government administrative records contain a wealth of information on population groups and changes over time. Three sources of data are of particular interest to migration researchers. The first source consists of the Permanent Resident Data System (PRDS), also known as Permanent Resident Landing File (PRLF), and its temporary resident counterpart, the Temporary Residents Data System (TRDS). Both are microdata sources derived from administrative records collected by Citizenship and Immigration Canada (CIC). The PRDS, once available to member researchers as part of the Metropolis Project, contained landing data along with information on age, gender, marital status, mother tongue, knowledge of official language(s), country of birth, last permanent residence, citizenship, intended destination, educational attainment, intended occupation, and class of entry (or landed immigrant program). It is now available as part of the Longitudinal Immigration Database (IMDB) described below. The TRDS is not widely available to researchers but it contains useful information on foreign students by educational level, foreign workers, refugee claimants and humanitarian cases, and temporary to permanent transitions. Aggregate tables from the TRDS can be found in CIC's annual *Facts and Figures: Immigration Overview – Permanent and Temporary Residents* report.

Two additional data sources that include CIC records from the PRDS are now available at Statistics Canada. The first microdata source is the IMDB and the second is the Longitudinal Administrative Databank (LAD), which adds 20 per cent of the tax-filing population as a whole to a 20 per cent sample of the IMDB. The IMDB on its own permits the investigation of economic outcomes for immigrants who have arrived since 1980 by linking PRDS data with tax return information from 1982 on. Landing data, which are referred to as "tombstone" or static data, do not change; they are set and can form the basis for comparative studies. The tax files provide researchers with information on income level as well as residential mobility within Canada. New cases are added to the database each year as either new immigrants or as older immigrants who have filed taxes or were linked to landing data for the first time. Although this data file permits the examination of immigrant characteristics at landing and economic outcomes among permanent residents, it does not capture those permanent migrants who do not file taxes; it also excludes non-permanent residents as well as non-immigrants.

The addition of tax files from the general population permits a comparison between immigrants and non-immigrants on economic measures, and new cases are added annually. However, both sources carry the same limitations: only those who arrived as permanent residents can be identified; landing records do not contain information on past status; and non-permanent residents who file taxes may be in the sample but they cannot be identified. Thus, there is no mechanism to compare the multiple groups of migrants and as well, no opportunity to understand the transitions some international students might make from temporary to permanent status to citizen, or how such transitions may be linked to integration experiences. As such, neither source can be used for the study of international students. The TRDS could be used to examine transitions from international student status to permanent residence or to other temporary statuses, which is more likely as students are generally required to obtain a temporary work visa prior to applying for permanent residence. However, these microdata omit important social and economic measures and the data file is not readily available to researchers. Moreover, recent changes in how temporary resident data are reported by CIC complicate the analysis and comparisons over time. To address some of these important gaps in our understanding of international students and temporary residents more generally, it would make sense to integrate TRDS data with LAD and IMDB data.

The Third Sector as Knowledge Agent

The Canadian Bureau for International Education

The Canadian Bureau for International Education (CBIE) is a non-profit organization that promotes international education in Canada and abroad. Established in 1966, the organization administers periodic surveys on international students in Canada. Topics covered on the now web-based survey, with samples in the range of 6,000 students, include reasons for decision to study in Canada, experiences with Canadian officials and academic institutions, satisfaction, work experience, and future plans. In addition, there are questions about age, gender, marital status, grades, living arrangements, country of origin, length of residence in Canada, home language, and family background.

CBIE directly contacts universities and colleges across Canada to participate in the survey. Notably, CIC (one of the funders) requested the inclusion of additional questions in the recent survey. Results published by CBIE focus on a comparison between university and college students (Prairie Research Associates 2009); but, despite lacking a domestic comparison group, the CBIE data could produce a number of additional studies that would contribute significantly to our understanding of international students.

A Third-Sector Case Study: World Education Services and the ADMIG Pilot Project

Without a repository of non-government surveys and data files in Canada, an awareness of potential data sources is only possible through word of mouth and professional networks. And even then, gaining access to the data is highly unlikely. As a result, researchers tend to rely on Statistics Canada for national-level data. However, as shown in the example above, there may be opportunities in the non-profit sector to develop research partnerships and exchange data and knowledge. For example, frontline agencies serving international students and other migrant groups routinely collect basic demographic information and other details on their clients as part of their daily administrative process. This information is rarely, if ever, used for any purpose beyond the head counts mandated by funding bodies. Yet, notwithstanding issues of representativeness and quality, the data collected could provide a wealth of information on segments of the population omitted from or rendered invisible by traditional data sources. In other words, these data could give insight to important issues facing marginalized groups. This premise was the basis for the Agency Data on Migration Pilot Project, or ADMIG.

ADMIG was an academic-community research partnership involving Access Alliance Multicultural Health and Community Services, the Ontario Council of Agencies Serving Immigrants (OCASI), Social Planning Toronto (SPT), World Education Services (WES), and researchers at Ryerson University and York University. Based in Toronto, the three-year pilot study explored the feasibility of data sharing and coordination among frontline agencies to address knowledge gaps on temporary and permanent migrants. In phase 2 of the pilot study, we explored potential opportunities for research on temporary migrants using data from two agencies. We show one example here using data from WES, a well-known agency now designated by CIC to provide assessments of educational credentials earned outside Canada. WES collects information on clients through its application form, and like many other organizations, it also conducts surveys.

For our analysis, we were fortunate to obtain anonymized client records from December 2010 to October 2011 linked with 560 cases from the organization's 2012 Credential Impact Survey. The administrative data file contained information on age, gender, country of residence at the time of application, purpose of credential evaluation, country of education, and educational attainment. The survey data had a number of additional variables, including immigration status, language ability, goals of credential evaluation, and barriers. Cases were selected if the respondent lived in Canada at the time of the survey and was aged eighteen years and older.

Although the WES data do not address many of the limitations inherent in national-level data – such as issues around longitudinal, transition, and duration analyses, timing, and prior status and experience – they do permit comparisons of different status groups and their connections to social issues. In addition, the key benefits of administrative data more generally are that data systems can be modified to collect relevant information, agencies can conduct trend analysis (longitudinal analyses for repeat clients), and data are recent. In the following analysis, we acknowledge the limitations and recognize that these data were collected to evaluate services rather than to conduct research on international student experiences.

Among the valid cases in the linked WES data, 60 per cent were female, 44 per cent were in their thirties, over 41 per cent had their origins in Asia, 80 per cent were fluent in English, and over 90 per cent had a bachelor's degree or higher. Although a range of disciplines were represented, business and management, health professions, and engineering were observed more frequently than others. In terms of immigration status, the majority of respondents (63 per cent) were permanent residents at the time of the survey, 27.3 per cent were Canadian citizens, 4.5 per cent were temporary workers, and 3.4 per cent were international students. By far, the largest group of respondents (44.5 per cent) obtained credential evaluation for the purposes of education, while 28.4 per cent and 20.9 per cent sought evaluations for employment and licensing reasons, respectively.

The survey asked respondents to select up to three barriers encountered while pursuing educational/career goals. Interestingly, responses to this question reflect many of the issues raised by recent immigrants. As Table 4.2 shows, the most common barriers were insufficient work experience in Canada, lack of recognition of foreign education, and a difficult job market.

Table 4.2 Perceived Barriers of WES Clients (up to three were selected)

	Per cent
Not enough work experience in Canada	50.0
Foreign education is not recognized	44.3
Difficult job market	44.3
Foreign licence is not recognized	23.2
Lack of information about jobs/academic institutions	17.7
Insufficient English-language skills	13.4
Discrimination	12.5
Not enough education/training	10.4

Note: n = 560 for each item

Although the sample of international students in the data is too small for a robust analysis, an examination of the perceived barriers by immigration status suggests that the top three barriers for the entire sample were also the top three among international students. However, compared to the other groups (i.e., Canadian citizens, permanent residents, and temporary foreign workers), international students were more likely to identify a lack of information about jobs and/or academic institutions, insufficient English-language skills, and not enough education/training as barriers to pursuing their goals. While these findings must be interpreted with caution, they do suggest that the barriers faced by international students in pursuing educational and economic goals may differ from those of other immigrant groups.

Discussion

An examination of nineteen national-level microdata sources reveals substantial limitations in the data on immigration, immigrant trajectories and transitions, and permanent and temporary residence. It is clear that current knowledge on immigrants is based on existing data sources developed to answer questions about permanent residents. It will take time for data and measures to capture the increasingly complex nature of human mobility – or hypermobility – but we have begun to see movement in this direction. Current discussions in policy circles and recent work (see Lu and Hou in this volume) inform us that initiatives are underway to address the gaps in data and, hence, in knowledge; but these advancements, as of yet, are not readily accessible to researchers. Without wider access, limitations and restrictions hinder, and even eliminate, the possibility for in-depth and independent research on particular segments of the migrant population in Canada – namely temporary migrants such as refugee claimants, temporary foreign workers, and international students.

In this chapter, we explored the potential benefits of using data collected by community organizations and non-profit agencies to learn about marginalized populations not captured in traditional data sources. Although agency records also have limitations and restrictions regarding access, there are numerous benefits to partnering with agencies to modify their data systems to integrate and achieve research objectives. The development of agency records for research purposes is an avenue worth pursuing.

Appendix: Data Sources Examined

1. Census 2006
2. National Household Survey 2011
3. National Longitudinal Survey of Children and Youth 2009
4. Ethnic Diversity Survey 2002
5. Survey of Labour and Income Dynamics 2011
6. Canadian Income Survey
7. Labour Force Survey 2012
8. Canadian Community Health Survey 2014
9. Canadian Health Measures Survey 2013
10. World Values Survey 2005
11. Longitudinal Survey of Immigrants to Canada (LSIC)
12. GSS-Social Identity (SI) 2013
13. GSS-Giving, Volunteering and Participating (GVP) 2013
14. Longitudinal and International Study of Adults (LISA)
15. Program for the International Assessment of Adult Competencies (PIAAC)
16. National Graduates Survey
17. Longitudinal Immigration Database (IMDB)
18. Longitudinal Administrative Databank (LAD)
19. Permanent Resident Data System (PRDS)/Temporary Resident Data System (TRDS)

References

Anderson, Benedict. 2006. *Imagined Communities: Reflections on the Origin and Spread of Nationalism.* New York: Verso.

Bourhis, Richard Y. 2003. "Measuring Ethnocultural Diversity using the Canadian Census." *Canadian Ethnic Studies* 35 (1): 9–32.

Du Bois, W.E.B. 1899. *The Philadelphia Negro: A Social Study.* Philadelphia: Published for the University Philadelphia.

Goldring, Luin, and Patricia Landolt. 2012. *The Impact of Legal Status on Immigrants' Economic Outcomes.* Ottawa: Institute for Research on Public Policy.

Heisz, Andrew. 2013. "LISA: CRDCN Pre-Conference Workshop." Presented at the CRDCN Pre-Conference Workshop, Waterloo, ON, 2 October 2013. http://www.rdc-cdr.ca/sites/default/files/workshop_longitudinal_and_international_study_of_adults_lisa.pdf.

Malthus, Thomas Robert. (1798) 2004. *An Essay on the Principle of Population.* New York: Norton.

McDaniel, Susan, and Heidi MacDonald. 2012. "To Know Ourselves – Not." *Canadian Journal of Sociology* 37 (3): 253–71.

Prairie Research Associates. 2009. *Canada First: The 2009 Survey of International Students.* Prepared for the Canadian Bureau for International Education. http://files.eric.ed.gov/fulltext/ED549797.pdf.

Tonkiss, Fran. 2004. "The History of the Social Survey." In *Researching Society and Culture,* ed. Clive Seale, 85–98. London: Sage Publications.

United Nations. 2010. "UN Secretary-General's Message on World Statistics Day." http://www.un.org/sg/statements/?nid=4865.

Vosko, Leah F., Valerie Preston, and Robert Latham, eds. 2014. *Liberating Temporariness: Migration, Work, and Citizenship in an Age of Insecurity in Canada.* Kingston, ON: McGill-Queen's University Press.

Worton, David. 1998. *The Dominion Bureau of Statistics: A History of Canada's Central Statistics Office and its Antecedents, 1841–1972.* Kingston, ON: McGill-Queen's University Press.

PART II

Integration and Adjustment in Educational Institutions

5 The International Undergraduate Experience through the Lens of Developmental Psychology

MAXINE GALLANDER WINTRE, STELLA DENTAKOS, SAEID CHAVOSHI, ABIRAMI R. KANDASAMY, AND LORNA WRIGHT

By 2025, the number of post-secondary students studying outside their country of citizenship is projected to reach a record-breaking 7.2 million (OECD 2013). By 2015 the number was already estimated to have surpassed 5 million (OECD 2015). This upsurge in international student mobility can be attributed to a number of factors, varying from the individual's perceived value of obtaining a post-secondary degree abroad to institutional and government-related initiatives, such as the development and implementation of extensive marketing and recruitment efforts (OECD 2013). In 2015, Canada was ranked by UNESCO as the eighth most-popular international student destination (WEF 2015), welcoming over 353,000 international students (Canadian Bureau for International Education 2016; for more on international student flows see the introduction to this volume).

Given these figures, as well as the economic, social, immigration, and foreign policy importance of international students (as demonstrated throughout this book), it seems ironic that the international undergraduate university experience has not been comprehensively examined through the lens of developmental psychology. International students are often seen as either migrants or students, but rarely as developing human beings at the brink of adulthood. Our research grew out of this need to consider international students from a dynamic developmental psychology perspective, simultaneously addressing international students' roles as university students, sojourning migrants, and emerging adults.

This chapter summarizes both the qualitative and quantitative empirical research conducted with a sample of undergraduate students attending York University, a large, multi-ethnic university in Toronto, Canada, where a significant portion of the students come from abroad. To put York in context, Canada outperforms the OECD average in percentage of international students in tertiary education in general (10 per cent versus 6 per cent) and undergraduate education in particular (8 per cent versus 7 per cent) (OECD 2015, 2016a, 2016b) and York outperforms the Canadian average for undergraduate students at 12 per cent (York University 2016).

The results of our research address the appropriateness of viewing international students as emerging adults undergoing a life course transition common among individuals living in Western industrialized countries, and they demonstrate international students' development related to education, financial independence via vocation and employment, and partnership/marriage (cf., Arnett 2000, 2013). The influences of different ecological/relational systems, as well as the compounding relationships between family, peers, school, and home and host culture on international students' cross-cultural experiences are also emphasized (Bronfenbrenner 1979; Lerner 2004; Sameroff 1995). Once we established the validity and reliability to the international sample of the Student Adaptation to College Questionnaire (SACQ) (Baker and Siryk 1986), a widely used research measure of domestic student university adjustment, we applied a Developmental Sequence Model to examine international students' adjustment to university. The model accounted for 60 per cent of the explained variance. Taken together, our findings help elucidate a better understanding of how to recruit, support, and ultimately enhance international students' experience abroad.

Historical and Theoretical Beginnings

Prior to this study, Dr. Wintre and her graduate students had been conducting research focusing on undergraduate students for a number of reasons. The first was the fact that many psychology researchers were using first-year psychology students as a sample of convenience for adult subjects. From a developmental perspective, Wintre, North, and Sugar (2001) questioned the appropriateness of this research, given that first-year students, as a young age group, were not representative of the adult population in many respects, such as marital status, settled vocation, financial independence, and so forth. Arnett (2000; 2013) has also made a strong case for introducing a new developmental stage for ages eighteen to twenty-nine, which he labelled "Emerging Adulthood." He presented this stage as a Western, industrial phenomenon, arising out of the need for higher education, and resulting in longer financial dependence on parents, increased individual exploration, delayed vocational decisions, and postponed decisions to marry and start families.

A second reason the Wintre lab investigated the undergraduate experience was the American Editor's Consortium (1996) statement regarding race and ethnicity, which required articles published in refereed psychology journals in the future to describe the racial and ethnic composition (i.e., African American, Hispanic, non-Hispanic, White, Native American, Asian-Pacific, and other) of participants. Wintre, Sugar, Yaffe, and Costin (2000) challenged the meaningfulness of such categories on the following grounds: 1) there are different ethnic populations in different countries (e.g., the terms "African American" and "Native American" are not as meaningful outside the United States); 2) overgeneralization (e.g., Hong Kong, China, Vietnam, Japan, Philippines, and Indonesia were all included in the Asian-Pacific category); 3) questions regarding how to assign students from mixed-race families; and 4) most importantly, these categories failed to consider the significant differences between generational statuses – that is, between immigrants, children of immigrants, and second- and third-generation citizens (and beyond). The research of Wintre et al. (2000) demonstrated significant differences between students of these different generations. More specifically, students who were immigrants or children of immigrants, when compared to students who were second-generation immigrants (and higher), were more likely to view their parents as authoritarian (i.e., more demanding, less nurturing, less communicative) (cf., Baumrind 1989) and less enabling of independence. Moreover, the immigrant students were less likely to have reciprocal relations with their parents, were less autonomous, and more likely to experience stress (Wintre et al. 2000). This research showed generational status was therefore a more meaningful way to summarize a racially, ethnically, and culturally diverse population (Wintre et al. 2000). And international students are definitely a unique subset of the newly arrived "migrant" population.

A third rationale for research on student populations was to examine the undergraduate university experience from a developmental perspective in order to empirically determine which variables enhance students' perceptions of their university adjustment. To this end, after considering the theories of sociologists (Chickering and Reisser 1993; Weidman

1989; Tinto 1975, 1993), the research took a dynamic developmental systems approach (Bronfenbrenner 1979; Sameroff 1995), emphasizing individual variables, environmental variables, and the interaction of individual and environmental variables as ongoing dynamic processes. The Wintre lab expanded individual student characteristics such as age, gender, grade point average (GPA), parenting styles, and generational status, to also include age-related changes in perceived reciprocity with parents (related to previous parenting styles), residence status, and personality variables (Wintre and Yaffe 2000; Wintre and Sugar 2000). The research described the beginnings of a developmental model of student adaptation and achievement (Wintre and Yaffe 2000), which helped delineate which students graduate (Wintre and Bowers 2007), as well as which students maintain their high school averages in post-secondary settings (Wintre et al. 2011).

Ultimately, the research from the developmental perspective became a multisite project including principal co-investigators from other Canadian universities (i.e., Wilfrid Laurier University, University of Toronto, University of Guelph, and Memorial University) in order to examine some of the environmental variables, such as size of host city, size of student population, ethnic diversity on campus, and percentage of students in college residence. The multisite research team also examined the interactions experienced between students and their university, including such things as social support provisions. They developed new measures to examine these individual by environment interactions, such as students' perception of the fit between their needs and the university environment (Student University Match [SUM]) (Wintre et al. 2008), and the students' perception of university support and structure (Student Perception of University Support and Structure [SPUSS]) (Wintre et al. 2009). These three groups of variables – individual, environmental, and their interactions – ranged from developmentally distal variables (i.e., existing prior to university) to more proximal variables (i.e., related to current perceptions while attending university).

When we began our research with the international students, we had several driving questions. First, we wondered whether the concept of emerging adulthood would be relevant to international students coming from different countries – especially non-Western and non-industrialized countries (Arnett 2000). Second, we questioned whether the validity of the SACQ, which was the gold standard measure of student adjustment for North American students, would be applicable to international

students. Third, we were curious as to whether there were other variables related to international students' success that had not been considered or were not relevant to domestic students, such as migrant-related
factors.

And finally, there was the need to determine if our developmental
model could identify significant predictors of international student
adjustment to inform recruiters and enhance the selection process
of potential international students, as well as to suggest to the university potential programs to support and facilitate international student
success.

The Method

International students were recruited through the York University International Office during the spring and summer of 2011 to complete an
online questionnaire and consider a follow-up interview. Only students
who had no previous education in Canada prior to attending university
were included in the final data sets. Among the 266 international students who completed the online questionnaire, 70 volunteered to complete the interview.

The questionnaire included demographic information such as age,
gender, country of origin, family income, parents' education, current
place of residence, GPA, standardized English-language scores from the
Test of English as a Foreign Language (TOEFL) and the International
English Language Testing System (IELTS), as well as self-perceived rat-
ings of English competence. Established scales included in the question-
naire were as follows: the Student Adjustment to College Questionnaire
(SACQ) (Baker and Siryk 1986); the Acculturation Motivation Scale
(AMS) (Chirkov et al. 2007); the Revised UCLA Loneliness Scale
(R-UCLALS) (Russell, Peplau, and Cutrona 1980); the Perceived Stress
Scale (PSS) (Cohen 1983); the Social Provisions Scale (SPS) (Cutrona
and Russell 1987); the Perception of Parental Reciprocity Scale (POPRS)
(Wintre, Yaffe, and Crowley 1995); the Student–University Match (SUM)
(Wintre et al. 2008);and the Student Perception of University Support
and Structure (Wintre et al. 2009).

The in-depth, semi-structured interview addressed issues such as
rationale for studying abroad, fulfilment of pre-migration expectations,
challenges and adjustment, group relations, perceptions of university,
perceptions of home and host country, and future immigration plans.
All interviews were conducted in English, with audio recorded and

transcribed verbatim into written text prior to coding. Inter-rater reliability was established for a variety of different categories (Wintre et al. 2015).

The Sample and Initial Descriptive Data

The overall sample consisted of 266 undergraduate international students between the ages of 18 and 29. The mean age was 22 years, and 36.1 per cent were male. Just over a quarter of the students (27.4 per cent) were in first year, followed by 30.5 per cent in second year, 24.8 per cent in third year, and 17.3 per cent in their final year (see Table 5.1).

Table 5.1 Socio-demographic Descriptors of Current Sample

	N	%
Sex		
Female	170	63.90
Male	96	36.10
Academic year		
1	73	27.40
2	81	30.50
3	66	24.80
4 or more	46	17.30
Marital status		
Single	204	76.70
In a relationship	50	18.80
Married/common law	11	4.10
Other	1	0.04
Region of origin		
China	98	36.80
South Asia	41	15.40
East Asia	38	14.30
Caribbean	23	8.60
Africa	21	7.90
Middle East	13	4.90
Other	21	7.90
South America	11	4.10

	N	%
Current academic average		
50%–59%	11	4.10
60%–69%	80	30.10
70%–79%	123	46.20
80%–100%	52	19.50
Family income		
Below average	17	6.40
Average	113	42.50
Above average	117	44.00
Well above average	19	7.10
Current place of residence		
Roommates, off-campus housing	71	26.70
Alone, off-campus housing	54	30.30
Relative or other family friend	47	17.70
Alone, university residence	57	21.40
Other	19	7.10
Roommates, university residence	16	6.00
Parent(s)	2	0.80

Table 5.2 Breakdown of Countries of Origin Included in Each Category

Region	Countries Included
China	China, Hong Kong, Taiwan
South Asia	India, Pakistan, Sri Lanka, Bangladesh
East Asia	Thailand, Vietnam, Japan, South Korea, Indonesia, Singapore, Philippines, Malaysia, Cambodia, Republic of Korea
Caribbean	Bahamas, Jamaica, Cayman Islands, Barbados, St. Lucia, Trinidad and Tobago, St. Vincent
Africa	Kenya, Nigeria, Tanzania, Ghana, Egypt, Ethiopia, Malawi, Swaziland, Democratic Republic of Congo
Middle East	Syria, Lebanon, Turkey, Yemen, United Arab Emirates, Kuwait, Iran, Saudi Arabia, Qatar, Kuwait
Latin America	Chile, Colombia, Venezuela, Peru, Brazil, Mexico, Nicaragua
Other	Denmark, Greece, France, Italy, Israel, Kazakhstan, Russia, Croatia, United Sates of America, Azerbaijan, Mauritius

The majority of students reported that they were unmarried (95.5 per cent) and tuition was being primarily covered by their parents (87.1 per cent) (see Table 5.1). Family income was self-perceived as mainly average (42.5 per cent) or above average (44.0 per cent), with only 6.4 per cent reporting family income as below average. As shown in Table 5.2, the sample originated from 60 countries, which were grouped into the following categories: China (48.8 per cent), South Asia (15.4 per cent), East Asia (14.3 per cent), Caribbean (8.6 per cent), Africa (7.9 per cent), Middle East (4.9 per cent), Latin America (4.1 per cent), and other (7.9 per cent). We can see that York's top three source regions track UNESCO's statistics on the top three countries sending students abroad – China, India, and the Republic of Korea (WEF 2015).

Students were asked about their current living situation, and we found that 27.4 per cent of the international students lived in on-campus residence, either alone or with a roommate, whereas 57 per cent lived off-campus, either alone or with a roommate, and an additional 17.7 per cent lived with relatives (see Figure 5.1).

Friendship Networks

When asked with whom they socialized, 61.4 per cent of international students responded that they socialized most with other international students, followed by 24.3 per cent reporting equal ties with both international and domestic students, and 11.4 per cent reporting friendships with domestic students only. Despite the fact that the majority of international students described their primary social network as an international one, 80.0 per cent of students also reported that they had one or more Canadian friend(s). These two findings support the original bimodal model of international student friendship patterns described by Bochner, McLeod, and Lin's (1977), which suggests that even though international students mainly develop friendships with other international students, they also report having ties with domestic students. However, Bochner, McLeod, and Lin (1977) also caution that it is important to distinguish between quality and quantity of friendships: international students may report ties with local students, yet the quality of these relationships may be more superficial compared to the friendship quality they maintain with other international students (Chan and Birman 2009). International students from our sample seemed to rely on other international students for support, despite the majority having at least one connection with local domestic students (c.f., Grayson 2008). Note that this low frequency of domestic student friends was not related to any perceived discrimination, as 79.0 per cent of the students responded that they had never felt discriminated against while in Canada.

Family Ties

Beyond preferred social networks, our data also explored both family connections in Canada as well as the maintenance of family relationships abroad. First, close to half of international students cited having a relative in Toronto (48.6 per cent). For the majority of these students, having a relative in Toronto was a consideration in choosing to attend a university in the city (85.3 per cent). Indeed, 39.4 per cent of those with relatives in Toronto also began their sojourn by living with them, or they were still living with their relatives. These findings suggest that some international students gravitate toward a university in a city where they have at least one relative. This has implications for future recruitment efforts, such that institutions may want to partner with local immigration and settlement agencies in order to encourage and/or facilitate the recruitment of immigrants' families and friends from abroad.

A second finding that caught our attention was how frequently international students communicated with their parents abroad (Chavoshi, Wintre, and Wright 2011) (see Figures 5.1 and 5.2). In particular we were interested in information about the frequency of international students' interactions with their parents and the use of various long-distance communication systems (e.g., email, Facebook/Twitter, Skype/Google Talk, Blackberry Messenger/smart phone apps versus letters). The results showed that male students communicated with their mothers on average twice a week and with their fathers a bit less, while female students communicated with their parents significantly more than the males – 2.5 times a week with mothers and almost twice a week with fathers. We also observed that students from South and East Asia communicated more with both parents than students from the other regions. Students reported their top three preferred communication mediums to be phone calls, Internet video calling options such as Skype or Google Hangouts, and email (see Figure 5.2).

We also investigated whether frequency of communication was related to the Perception of Parents Reciprocity Scale (Wintre, Yaffe, and Crowley 1995), which has subscales for each parent. This scale measures a developmental transformation in the student's relations with parents that begins in adolescence and continues through emerging adulthood. The transformation (originally described by Youniss [1980] and Youniss and Smollar [1985]) involves using relations with peers as a template to develop a more symmetrical, reciprocal, and trusting relationship with parents than the asymmetrical relationship of childhood. Data revealed that frequency of communication with mothers was positively associated with better perceptions of feelings, mutual trust, and reciprocity. Similarly, frequency of communication with fathers was positively related to greater feelings of trust and reciprocity.

Figure 5.1. International Students' Rate of Communication with Their Parents by Gender

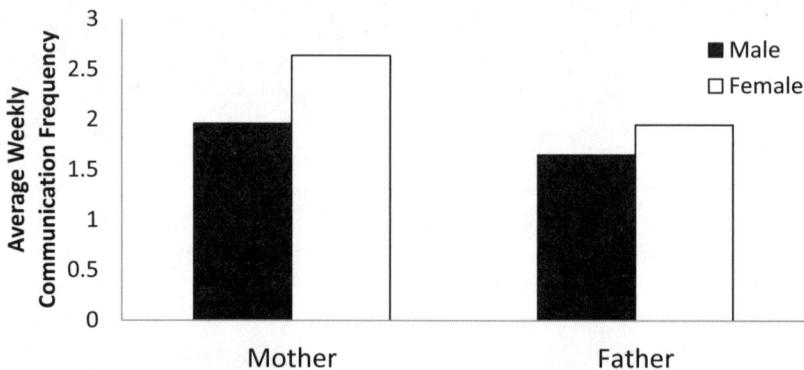

Figure 5.2. Differences in Preference and Use of Communication Mediums When Interacting with Parents

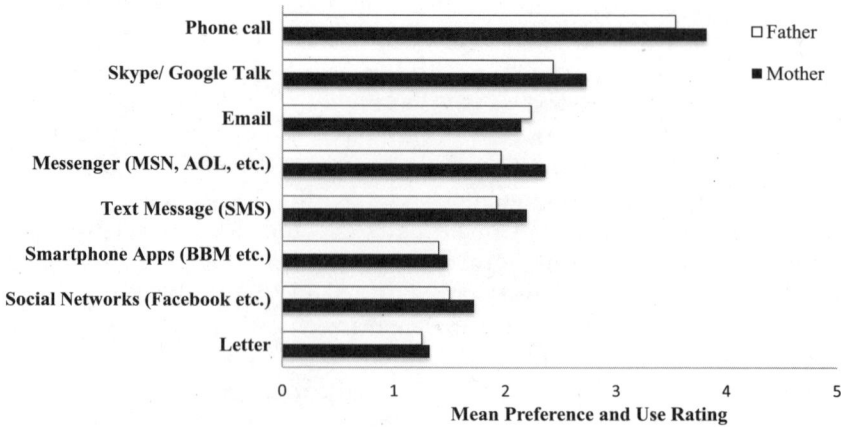

So, although international students may feel isolated and removed from their families, our data suggest that twenty-first-century international students remain in contact with their family and friends at home.

Are International Students Emerging Adults?

Despite the recent recognition of the emerging adulthood life stage, it has been debated whether this stage is a universally experienced phenomenon or, in contrast, a cultural construction of Western and industrialized countries (Nelson, Badger, and Wu 2004). For example, emerging adulthood may be less pronounced or non-existent in non-Western cultures where education is limited and transitions to adulthood occur earlier, such that individuals forego this "in between" period (Arnett 2013; Walsh et al. 2005). Yet, international students who take part in a sojourn abroad typically have postponed engaging in permanent adult roles in order to pursue higher levels of education, a key developmental feature that likens them to their Western emerging adult peers. We therefore considered whether international students fit the emerging adult demographic.

To explore this question, we examined international students' motivations, goals, and expectations in studying abroad (Wintre et al. 2015). A thematic analysis of interview responses revealed that students' motivations could be grouped in the following eight themes: (1) education/learning experience; (2) friends/relatives in Canada; (3) new experiences; (4) country characteristics (home and host); (5) future prospects of career/immigration; (6) location; (7) qualities of the university; and (8) financial reasons. Following this thematic grouping, we investigated whether the derived themes from our study mapped onto Arnett's (2000) five features of emerging adulthood.

The first two features of Arnett's (2000) emerging adulthood life stage are "identity exploration" and "self-focus." While "identity exploration" typifies emerging adults' efforts to determine who they are in terms of work, school, and relationships, "self-focus" represents their ability to explore these areas without the constraints of marriage, children, and career (Arnett 2000). Arnett's features of "identity exploration" and "self-focus" correspond well with our themes of "education/learning experience" and "new experiences," which were captured in international students' descriptions of studying abroad as an opportunity for self-discovery and improvement.

The next feature of Arnett's emerging adulthood is that of "instability." This feature reflects the period in which emerging adults may attend university, change residences frequently, and either live alone, with friends, or with a romantic partner (Arnett 2000). The feature of "instability" corresponds well with our theme of "location." Furthermore, international students, by definition, have left their family homes in order to live abroad. Given that their return to their home countries is uncertain, the feature of "instability" is particularly fitting with such a population.

The fourth feature of emerging adulthood is "feeling in-between." This feature reflects the semi-autonomous time in which emerging adults take responsibility for themselves while being partially dependent on family (Arnett 2000). The feature of "feeling in-between" corresponds with our theme of "financial reasons." Even though students considered themselves to be independent and autonomous, in the present sample of international students, their parents were primarily responsible for their tuition (87.1 per cent).

Finally, the fifth feature of emerging adulthood is "possibilities/optimism," which reflects emerging adults' optimistic views and hopes for the future (Arnett 2000). This feature corresponds well with our theme of "future prospects of career/immigration," whereby international students view studying abroad as the key to a better quality of life.

Overall, our qualitative exploration of international students' motives and expectations for studying abroad revealed many emerging adulthood themes, such as desire for change, increased opportunities, independence, and autonomy, the ability to explore majors and possible vocations, concerns for a better future, and experiencing different lifestyles. Example excerpts highlighting these themes include the following:

Q. Why did you decide to study abroad?
A. ... my sister has been here for 7 years and I have other relatives here. They told me about Canada's education level, the system, so I was very much impressed. That encouraged me to come here. (Male, Pakistan)
A. One, the experience, two, the life, three, better opportunity. (Female, St. Lucia)
Q. What were your goals and/or expectations for studying abroad?
A. Studying abroad can help me improve my English and help me become more independent. And maybe I can practice my social skills, and maybe it can help me learn more things, because if I stayed home, there are things that I'm familiar with – there are things that are limited in your perspective and I think that's the reason. (Female, China)
Q. Why did you decide to study in Canada specifically?

A. Actually, I had relatives here – that's why I pick here. And my parents feel comfortable if I stay with my aunt and someone can help me. (Female, China)

Considering the aforementioned findings, the data supported the inclusion of international students within the emerging adulthood demographic. However, the findings also highlighted features unique to the international student experience. These include challenges with being away from home, language difficulties, lack of job opportunities, and integration concerns. The following interview excerpts exemplify these concerns:

Q. Is there an obstacle, challenge or problem that you still face today?
A. I think it's the English problems and they cause, that I can't talk with them (domestic students) very well with speaking and with listening and maybe they say something very funny or we talk about something I don't know and I can't join with them. It was harder to make friends. (Male, China)
Q. What were some of the earliest problems or challenges you faced?
A. Earliest problem was for academic – listening problem. I can read stuff in textbook or blackboard, on the slides. But I always have problem in listening … I always feel they speak too quickly or I only catch a few words, a few simple words. I don't understand almost 50 percent of what professor says during lecture. That's a big problem. (Female, Pakistan)

Thus, for international students, as for domestic students, the transition to university includes not only having to become independent and self-sufficient, but unlike domestic students, international students also have to manage these developmental demands in a foreign language, within a foreign culture and country. International students are therefore simultaneously confronted by a novel developmental experience as well as a novel cultural experience. We concluded that international students should be considered part of the emerging adulthood demographic, but also a unique subset of this demographic.

Student Adaptation to College Questionnaire: Validity and Reliability

Having placed international students within the emerging adult framework, the next step was to build and test an overall developmental model of international student adjustment. Yet, to investigate variables that predict international student adjustment, we first needed to determine an appropriate measure of international student adjustment. Baker and Siryk (1999) developed the SACQ based on a multifaceted view of student adjustment. The SACQ is a sixty-seven-item survey that yields a total score indicative of overall adjustment, as well as four subscales measuring different dimensions of adaptation to university: (1) academic adjustment; (2) social adjustment; (3) personal-emotional adjustment; and (4) institutional attachment and affiliation. Although the SACQ is a widely used global measure of student adjustment primarily employed with domestic student populations, we first established that it was valid and reliable with our international student sample (statistical results available upon request to authors). With the confidence of a reliable measure of international student adjustment, we could then investigate which factors – individual, environmental, or an interaction – predict international student adjustment.

Individual Predictors of International Student Adjustment

Within the existing international student literature, demographic characteristics, academic variables, and host country language abilities tend to be the most commonly used individual predictors of international student adjustment. However, empirical evidence has been mixed on whether such variables actually do play a role in international students' cross-cultural success (Berry et al. 1987; Neto 2002; Poyrazli et al. 2004; Yeh and Inose 2003). For example, empirical studies have both supported (e.g., Berry et al. 1987) and failed to find support for (e.g., Neto 2002; Poyrazli et al. 2004; Yeh and Inose 2003) the roles played by age, gender, and GPA on acculturative stress and international student adjustment. Findings on the role of host country language abilities have also been variable. That is, international students' actual English-language abilities as represented by scores on standardized English-language measures (i.e., TOEFL and/or IELTS) have been found to not predict international student adjustment, while student's *perceptions* of their English-language abilities have been found to predict adjustment (e.g., Lewthwaite 1996). Similarly, using the present data from the 150 international students who provided either TOEFL or IELTS scores, we found that standardized English test scores were not predictive of current GPA, student adjustment as measured by the SACQ, or with the SACQ subscales.

Given these overall findings, we decided that age, gender, country of origin, and self-perceived English-language abilities should be included as individual predictors within our model. However, given the lack of support for standardized English-language scores we opted to exclude them.

In addition to choosing individual variables from the existing literature, we wanted to examine alternative variables of international student adjustment that had yet to be considered. In particular, we found it peculiar that most studies have ignored the basic fact that international students are not just students, but also sojourning migrants. That is, international students' initial relocation is for a specific purpose (i.e., to obtain a post-secondary degree) and for a specific time frame (i.e., duration of degree). International students must therefore not only become accustomed to a novel cultural environment, but must do so not knowing the odds of an eventual return to their home countries. As a result of the possible impermanence of their stay, sojourning migrants may be less likely to value learning about or adapting to the host country environment (e.g., "What's the point? I'm only here for four years anyways ..." [Kim 2001]). Given how this temporality impacts the way in which students view integration, Chirkov et al. (2007) have suggested that when exploring international student outcomes, it is important to consider students' motivation to acculturate. Acculturation motivation is defined as the willingness to learn about the host culture, to develop friendships with citizens of the host country, and to explore the host country's social and cultural environments (Chirkov et al. 2007, 2008). Past research on the role of acculturation motivation has shown that there is a relationship between level of motivation and host county involvement in which greater motivation to acculturate is associated with greater host country interactions (Kim 2001; Chirkov et al. 2007, 2008; Selltiz, Christ, Havel, and Cook 1963). Similarly, we questioned whether greater motivation to acculturate could also be associated with greater overall adjustment. To test this, we conducted a mixed-methods study using both the international student interview and the questionnaires, including the Acculturation Motivations Scale (AMS; Chirkov et al. 2007) and the SACQ (Dentakos et al. 2016). The main purpose of this mixed-method study was to explore whether international students with differing levels of acculturation motivation would report qualitatively and quantitatively different adjustment experiences in Canada. Both our qualitative and quantitative results supported the role of acculturation motivation as an individual predictor of international student adjustment, demonstrating that greater levels of acculturation motivation were associated with the reporting of positive experiences in Canada, better adjustment outcomes, and the desire to pursue permanent Canadian residency. For example, one international student with high acculturation motivation made the following statement:

> I've had the most amazing experience. I love York so much – I've learned so much. It's been great. I've had some amazing professors, and I am very much satisfied with the academic side of everything … and there is like so much social life and so much to do and so many different events, and a lot of which are free. And it is so easy to make friends. You can meet people from all over the world, and it is really, really incredible. (Female, twenty-four, Kazakhstan)

In contrast, lower levels of acculturation motivation were associated with the reporting of negative experiences in Canada, poorer adjustment outcomes, and wanting to return to the home country. For example, one international student with low acculturation motivation made the following statement:

> I would tell them [friends who are contemplating studying abroad] it's really not easy to study abroad … It's definitely harder than studying in China, because you're studying very professional knowledge in another language. And not just academic challenges, but also personal ones. (Female, twenty-one, China)

Overall, these findings support acculturation motivation as an individual predictor of international student adjustment, therefore warranting its inclusion within our overall developmental model of international student adjustment.

Putting It All Together: A Developmental Sequence Model to University Adjustment

Having delineated which individual variables would be included in our developmental model of international student adjustment, it was time to develop and test this model (see Figure 5.3). In addition to the individual variables mentioned above, both environmental and individual by environment process variables were considered, including students' perception of their social support, the level of support and structure perceived

Figure 5.3. Developmental Sequence Model to University Adjustment (variables in bold indicate statistically significant predictors of adjustment)

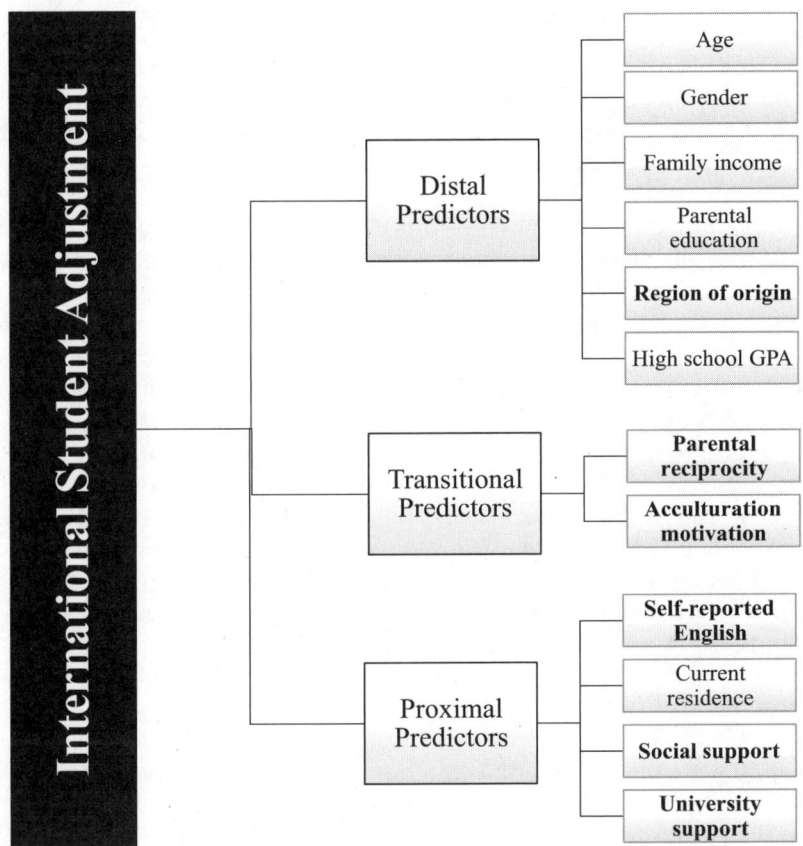

in the university, and the reciprocity within their parental relationship. Using hierarchical regression, our model explained 60.1 per cent of the variance in the international student adjustment scores as measured by the SACQ (Chavoshi, Wintre, and Wright 2017).

Results

Demographic variables such as age, gender, family income, and parental education were not significant predictors of student adjustment. And as mentioned previously, neither were high school GPA nor standardized English scores (TOEFL or IELTS).

In contrast, the region of origin (see Table 5.2) contributed significantly to explaining a modest portion of the variance. Students from the Caribbean and Africa had better adjustment scores than those from China and the Middle East; and those from China had better adjustment than those from the Middle East. These results suggest that each subgroup of international students might have unique needs arising from different cultural, linguistic, and institutional challenges. For instance, Tidwell and Hanassab (2007) found that within US institutions African and Asian international students reported the greatest number of needs. Southeast Asian students expressed the greatest need for career information and communication skills; African students for dealing with discrimination concerns, knowledge about immigration regulations and visa requirements, and acculturation challenges; and Asian students for dealing with psychological issues (Tidwell and Hanassab 2007).

Acculturation motivation was a positive predictor of international student adjustment. This suggests that international students' willingness to go beyond academic concerns and engage with the host country, its culture, language, and people is more likely to lead to a better transition and adjustment to university in comparison to students who approach their sojourn experience as essentially temporary with no interest in integration (Dentakos et al. 2016).

Three Main Players

Over 50 per cent of the variance in the adjustment scores was accounted for by three predictors: (1) perceived social support, as measured by the Social Provisions Scale; (2) perceived reciprocal child-parent relationship, as measured by the Perception of Parental Reciprocity Scale; and (3) perceived support of the student by the university, as measured by Student Perception of University's Support and Structure.

Social Support

Social support accounted for the greatest share of the variance in the social adjustment, personal-emotional adjustment, and institutional attachment subscales of the SACQ. These findings corroborate a number of previous studies showing the important role social support plays in the successful transition and adjustment of international students (Poyrazli et al. 2004; Ramsay, Jones, and Barker 2007; Yeh and Inose 2003). Other researchers also suggest that one of the biggest challenges faced by international students is experiencing a loss or lack of social support (Hayes and Lin 1994; Pedersen 1991). Given the importance of social support, one of the essential roles of an academic institution's international office must be to facilitate and encourage the development of international students' social networks.

Relationship with Parents

Perceived Reciprocity with Parents was a significant predictor not only for the main regression model on SACQ mean scores but also for all the subscales. This is noteworthy as it is the first study to investigate and establish the positive relationship of age-appropriate relations with parents and international student adjustment. Plus, this variable has been shown to be related both to past parenting styles (Wintre et al. 2000) and the frequency of the international students' communication with their parents in the present study.

International Student ↔ University Interaction

Student Perception of University Support and Structure accounted for the greatest share of the variance. SPUSS is rooted in a systems theory perspective (Lerner 2004; Sameroff 1995) and focuses on the dynamic and ongoing interactions between the student and university rather than static traits of the individual (Wintre et al. 2008; Wintre et al. 2009). The role of the relationship between the institution and adjustment of the international student is further highlighted by the relatively large effect size of SPUSS compared to all other factors in predicting positive student adaptation. High scores on SPUSS represent students' perceptions of the university experience as supportive, structured, and demanding (authoritative), as opposed to being overly punitive and demanding (authoritarian) or one that is neither supportive nor demanding (permissive or neglectful).

The overwhelming importance of the effect of ecological interaction on international students' adjustment, combined with the irrelevance of high school GPA and standardized English scores, demand a critical reappraisal of the current recruitment and admission process and a paradigm shift in how institutions view and invest in the transition and adjustment of their international students. Alongside the significance of the students' parental relationships, these measures point to the important role that ecological interactions play in the adjustment of international students over that of any fixed trait, characteristics, or attributes of the student.

Conclusion

This chapter presents a bird's eye view of a faculty collaboration to provide empirical evidence to inform a university about its international student population and how to enhance university efforts to recruit students for their programs and improve student experience and success. The orientation perspective of the research questions many past ideas, including the lack of a dynamic developmental theoretical approach. We found international students to be a subset within the emerging adult stage, but with additional unique challenges related to living within a new culture. The present data are from a sample of international students from a diverse group of home countries, but they are limited by the fact that those students all attend one large, multi-ethnic university in a large metropolitan city. Future research will hopefully address this limitation by including many university environment variables of the dynamic developmental model, such as ethnic diversity of the university, size of the student body, size and diversity of host city, percentage of students in residence, etc. Future research should also include comparisons of domestic students and international students over the undergraduate years – and of course, a longitudinal study at a variety of different university campuses, with English competence and perception of parental reciprocity scores at baseline, would be ideal. And needless to say, these findings will need to be replicated.

It is important that the study highlights the current ongoing dynamic transactions between international students and their parents, as well as between international students and the university environment. The ongoing transformation of perceived parental trust and reciprocity through continued contact with parents, as well as the perceived social support and perception of university support and structure, accounted for more variance than individual demographics, host country, or personal, trait-based variables put together.

Furthermore, the findings challenge and clarify many of the historical perceptions that have dominated the field, including the assumptions that students have limited contact with their parents and mostly live on campus, and more particularly that TOEFL and IELTS scores, as well as high school averages, are predictors of international students' future success. The present study also lays the foundation for future research by determining the validity and reliability of the SACQ, and establishing the multifaceted set of transactional predictors (i.e., POPRS, SUM, and SPUSS) that account for over 50 per cent of the variability of student adjustment. The research also identifies a number of variables for determining applicant success, including perceived English competence (not standardized English-language scores or high school average), perceived reciprocity with parents, relatives in the host country, and acculturation motivation. Finally, the study illuminates more proximal variables of consequence to students' success, many of which the university environment can address, such as students' perception of university support and structure and social support. A valuable suggestion for university implementation would be to provide incoming international students with support groups led by upper-level international and domestic students.

We believe this research provides a step forward in understanding the international student experience and providing both a research perspective for moving forward and practical applications of value to the students, the universities, and the host countries.

References

Arnett, Jeffrey Jensen. 2000. "Emerging adulthood. A theory of development from the late teens through the twenties." *American Psychologist* 55 (5): 469–80. https://doi.org/10.1037/0003-066X.55.5.469. Medline:10842426.
– 2013. *Human Development: A Cultural Approach.* Upper Saddle River, NJ: Pearson.
Baker, Robert W., and Bohdan Siryk. 1986. "Exploratory Intervention with a Scale Measuring Adjustment to College." *Journal of Counseling Psychology* 33 (1): 31–8. https://doi.org/10.1037/0022-0167.33.1.31.
– 1999. *SACQ: Student Adaptation to College Questionnaire: Manual.* Los Angeles, CA: Western Psychological Services.
Baumrind, Diana. 1989. "The Permanence of Change and the Impermanence of Stability." *Human Development* 32 (3–4): 187–95. https://doi.org/10.1159/000276467.
Berry, John W., Uichol Kim, Thomas Minde, and Doris Mok. 1987. "Comparative Studies of Acculturative Stress." *International Migration Review* 21 (3): 491–511. https://doi.org/10.2307/2546607.
Bochner, Stephen, Beverly M. McLeod, and Anli Lin. 1977. "Friendship Patterns of Overseas Students: A Functional Model." *International Journal of Psychology* 12 (4): 277–94. https://doi.org/10.1080/00207597708247396.

Bronfenbrenner, Urie. 1979. "Contexts of Child Rearing: Problems and Prospects." *American Psychologist* 34 (10): 844–50. https://doi.org/10.1037/0003-066X.34.10.844.

Canadian Bureau for International Education. 2016. *International Students in Canada 2016*. http://cbie.ca/wp-content/uploads/2016/11Infographic-Inbound_EN.pdf.

Chan, Wing Yi, and Dina Birman. 2009. "Cross- and Same-race Friendships of Vietnamese Immigrant Adolescents: A Focus on Acculturation and School Diversity." *International Journal of Intercultural Relations* 33 (4): 313–24. https://doi.org/10.1016/j.ijintrel.2009.05.003.

Chavoshi, Saeid, Maxine Gallander Wintre, and Lorna Wright. 2011. "Does Distance Make the Heart Grow Fonder? International Students' Communication and Perceived Reciprocity with Parents." Presentation at the Biannual Convention of the Society of the Study of Emerging Adulthood, Providence, RI, 27–28 October 2011.

– 2017. "A Developmental Sequence Model to University Adjustment of International Undergraduate Students (DSMUA)." *Journal of International Students* 7 (3): 703–27.

Chickering, Arthur W., and Linda Reisser. 1993. *Education and Identity. The Jossey-Bass Higher and Adult Education Series. San Francisco.* San Francisco: Jossey-Bass Inc.

Chirkov, Valery I., Saba Safdar, J. de Guzman, and K. Playford. 2008. "Further Examining the Role Motivation to Study Abroad Plays in the Adaptation of International Students in Canada." *International Journal of Intercultural Relations* 32 (5): 427–40. https://doi.org/10.1016/j.ijintrel.2007.12.001.

Chirkov, Valery, Maarten Vansteenkiste, Ran Tao, and Martin Lynch. 2007. "The Role of Self-Determined Motivation and Goals for Study Abroad in the Adaptation of International Students." *International Journal of Intercultural Relations* 31 (2): 199–222. https://doi.org/10.1016/j.ijintrel.2006.03.002.

Cohen, Sheldon, Tom Kamarck, and Robin Mermelstein. 1983. "A Global Measure of Perceived Stress." *Journal of Health and Social Behavior* 24 (4): 385–96.

Cutrona, Carolyn E., and Daniel Wayne Russell. 1987. "The Provision of Social Relationships and Adaptation to Stress." In *Advances in Personal Relationships*, Vol. 1, ed. W.H. Jones and D. Perlman, 37–67. Greenwich, CT: JAI.

Dentakos, Stella, Maxine Gallander Wintre, Saied Chavoshi, and Lorna Wright. 2016. "Acculturation Motivation in International Student Adjustment and Permanent Residency Intentions: A Mixed-Methods Approach." *Emerging Adulthood* 4:1–15.

Editors Consortium. 1996. "Statement by the Editors Consortium on development and psychopathology for reporting SES and race/ethnicity information." *Journal of Research on Adolescence* (6): 377–8.

Grayson, Paul J. 2008. "The Experiences and Outcomes of Domestic and International Students at Four Canadian Universities." *Higher Education Research & Development* 27 (3): 215–30. https://doi.org/10.1080/07294360802183788.

Hayes, Richard L., and Heng-Rue Lin. 1994. "Coming to America: Developing Social Support Systems for International Students." *Journal of Multicultural Counseling and Development* 22 (1): 7–16. https://doi.org/10.1002/j.2161-1912.1994.tb00238.x.

Kim, Young Yun. 2001. *Becoming Intercultural: An Integrative Theory of Communication and Cross-cultural Adaptation.* Thousand Oaks, CA: Sage.

Lerner, Richard M. 2004. "Diversity in Individual ↔ Context Relations as the Basis for Positive Development Across the Life Span: A Developmental Systems Perspective for Theory, Research, and Application (The 2004 Society for the Study of Human Development Presidential Address)." *Research in Human Development* 1 (4): 327–46. https://doi.org/10.1207/s15427617rhd0104_5.

Lewthwaite, Malcolm. 1996. "A Study of International Students' Perspectives on Cross-cultural Adaptation." *International Journal for the Advancement of Counseling* 19 (2): 167–85. https://doi.org/10.1007/BF00114787.

Nelson, Larry J., Sarah Badger, and Bo Wu. 2004. "The Influence of Culture in Emerging Adulthood: Perspectives of Chinese College Students." *International Journal of Behavioral Development* 28 (1): 26–36. https://doi.org/10.1080/01650250344000244.

Neto, Felix. 2002. "Social Adaptation Difficulties of Adolescents with Immigrant Backgrounds." *Social Behavior and Personality* 30 (4): 335–45. https://doi.org/10.2224/sbp.2002.30.4.335.

Organisation for Economic Co-operation and Development (OECD). 2013. "How is International Student Mobility Shaping Up?" *Education Indicators in Focus, No. 14.* Paris: OECD Publishing. https://doi.org/10.1787/5k43k8r4k821-en.

– 2015. *Education at a Glance 2015: OECD Indicators.* Paris: OECD Publishing.

– 2016a. "Canada." *Education at a Glance 2016: OECD Indicators.* Paris: OECD Publishing. https://doi.org/10.1787/eag-2016-45-en.

– 2016b. "Who Are the Bachelor's and Master's Graduates?" *Education Indicators in Focus, No. 37.* Paris: OECD Publishing. https://doi.org/10.1787/5jm5hl10rbtj-en.

Pedersen, Paul B. 1991. "Counseling International Students." *Counseling Psychologist* 19 (1): 10–58. https://doi.org/10.1177/0011000091191002.

Poyrazli, Senel, Philip R. Kavanaugh, Adria Baker, and Nada Al-Timimi. 2004. "Social support and demographic correlates of acculturative stress in international students." *Journal of College Counseling* 7 (1): 73–82. https://doi.org/10.1002/j.2161-1882.2004.tb00261.x.

Ramsay, Sheryl, Elizabeth Jones, and Michelle Barker. 2007. "Relationship between Adjustment and Support Types: Young and Mature-aged Local and International First Year University Students." *Higher Education* 54 (2): 247–65. https://doi.org/10.1007/s10734-006-9001-0.

Russell, Dan, Letitia A. Peplau, and Carolyn E. Cutrona. 1980. "The revised UCLA Loneliness Scale: Concurrent and discriminant validity evidence." *Journal of Personality and Social Psychology* 39 (3): 472–80. https://doi.org/10.1037/0022-3514.39.3.472. Medline:7431205

Sameroff, Arnold J. 1995. *General Systems Theories and Developmental Psychopathology.* In *Wiley Series on Personality Processes. Developmental Psychopathology, Vol. 1. Theory and Methods,* ed. Dante Cicchetti and Donald J. Cohen, 659–95. Oxford: John Wiley & Sons.

Selltiz, Claire, June R. Christ, Joan Havel, and Stuart W. Cook. 1963. *Attitudes and Social Relations of Foreign Students in the United States.* Minneapolis: University of Minnesota Press.

Tidwell, Romeria, and Shideh Hanassab. 2007. "New Challenges for Professional Counsellors: The Higher Education International Student Population." *Counselling Psychology Quarterly* 20 (4): 313–24. https://doi.org/10.1080/09515070701573927.

Tinto, Vincent. 1975. "Dropout from Higher Education: A Theoretical Synthesis of Recent Research." *Review of Educational Research* 45 (1): 89–125. https://doi.org/10.3102/00346543045001089.

– 1993. *Leaving College: Rethinking the Causes and Cures of Student Attrition.* Chicago: University of Chicago Press.

Walsh, Sophie, Shmuel Shulman, Benny Feldman, and Offer Maurer. 2005. "The Impact of Immigration on the Internal Processes and Developmental Tasks of Emerging Adulthood." *Journal of Youth and Adolescence* 34 (5): 413–26. https://doi.org/10.1007/s10964-005-7259-7.

Weidman, John. C. 1989. *Undergraduate Socialization: A Conceptual Approach. Higher Education. Handbook of Theory and Research. Volume V.* New York: Agathon Press.

Wintre, Maxine Gallander, and Colleen Dorothy Bowers. 2007. "Predictors of Persistence to Graduation: Extending a Model and Data on the Transition to University Model." *Canadian Journal of Behavioural Science / Revue*

Canadienne Des Sciences Du Comportement 39 (3): 220–34. https://doi
.org/10.1037/cjbs2007017.

Wintre, Maxine Gallander, Barry Dilouya, Mark S. Pancer, Michael W. Pratt,
Shelly Birnie-Lefcovitch, Janet Polivy, and Gerald Adams. 2011. "Academic
Achievement in First Year University: Who Maintains their High School
Average?" *Higher Education: The International Journal of Higher Education and
Educational Planning* 62 (4): 467–81. https://doi.org/10.1007/s10734-010-9399-2.

Wintre, Maxine Gallander, Shawn K.E. Gates, W. Mark Pancer, Michael S.
Pratt, Janet Polivy, Shelly Birnie-Lefcovitch, and Gerald Adams. 2009. "The
Student Perception of University Support and Structure Scale: Development
and Validation." *Journal of Youth Studies* 12 (3): 289–306. https://doi
.org/10.1080/13676260902775085.

Wintre, Maxine Gallander, Abirami R. Kandasamy, Saied Chavoshi, and
Lorna Wright. 2015. "Are International Undergraduate Students Emerging
Adults? Motivations for Studying Abroad." *Emerging Adulthood* 3 (4): 255–64.
https://doi.org/10.1177/2167696815571665.

Wintre, Maxine Gallander, Greg. M. Knoll, W. Mark Pancer, Michael S.
Pratt, Janet Polivy, Shelly Birnie-Lefcovitch, and Gerald R. Adams. 2008.
"The Transition to University: The Student-University Match (SUM)
Questionnaire." *Journal of Adolescent Research* 23 (6): 745–69. https://doi
.org/10.1177/0743558408325972.

Wintre, Maxine Gallander, Christopher North, and Lorne A. Sugar.
2001. "Psychologists' Response to Criticisms about Research Based on
Undergraduate Participants: A Developmental Perspective." *Canadian
Psychology* 42 (3): 216–25. https://doi.org/10.1037/h0086893.

Wintre, Maxine Gallander, and Lorne A. Sugar. 2000. "Relationships with
Parents, Personality, and the University Transition." *Journal of College Student
Development* 41 (2): 202–14.

Wintre, Maxine Gallander, L.A. Sugar, M. Yaffe, and D. Costin. 2000.
"Generational Status: A Canadian Response to the Editors' Consortium
Statement with Regard to Race/Ethnicity." *Canadian Psychology* 41
(4): 244–56. https://doi.org/10.1037/h0086872.

Wintre, Maxine Gallander, and Mordechai Yaffe. 2000. "First-Year Students'
Adjustment to University Life as a Function of Relationships with Parents."
Journal of Adolescent Research 15 (1): 9–37. https://doi.org/10.1177/
0743558400151002.

Wintre, Maxine Gallander, Marvin Yaffe, and Jeannine Crowley. 1995.
"Perception of Parental Reciprocity Scale (POPRS): Development and
Validation with Adolescents and Young Adults." *Social Development* 4 (2):
129–48. https://doi.org/10.1111/j.1467-9507.1995.tb00056.x.

World Economic Forum (WEF). 2015. "Which Countries are the Top
Destinations for Foreign Students?" https://www.weforum.org/
agenda/2015/07/which-countries-are-the-top-destinations-for-foreign
-students/.

Yeh, Christine J., and Mayuko Inose. 2003. "International Students' Reported
English Fluency, Social Support Satisfaction, and Social Connectedness as
Predictors of Acculturative Stress." *Counselling Psychology Quarterly* 16 (1):
15–28. https://doi.org/10.1080/0951507031000114058.

York University. 2016. *York University Factbook 2015–2016.* http://www.yorku.ca/
factbook/factbook/index.php?year=2015%20-%202016.

Youniss, James. 1980. *Parents and Peers in Social Development: A Sullivan-Piaget
Perspective.* Chicago: University of Chicago Press.

Youniss, James, and Jacqueline Smollar. 1985. *Adolescent Relations with Mothers,
Fathers, and Friends.* Chicago: University of Chicago Press.

6 Legal Status and School Experiences for Families with Young Students

ANN H. KIM, MIN-JUNG KWAK, EUNJUNG LEE, WANSOO PARK, AND SUNG HYUN YUN

Introduction

In most countries that receive international students, post-secondary students comprise the majority of the foreign student population, and our knowledge of international students is therefore concentrated at this level. While Canada fits into this general trend, it also receives a substantial contingent of students at the elementary and secondary levels ("younger students") about whom much less has been written and who deserve greater attention; as Resnik (2012) argues, "the expansion of international education ... in elementary and post-elementary schools ... point[s] to a new social phenomenon" (292). In Canada, 16 per cent of international students were elementary or secondary students in 2015, with the majority coming from China and South Korea (Knight-Grofe and Rauh 2016). South Korea, with 2,885 students in Canada's primary programs, was the largest source country of elementary students, and the second-largest source of secondary students, with 3,575 in secondary programs (Knight-Grofe and Rauh 2016). While the number of international students from South Korea may be falling at the post-secondary levels, it remains an important source country among younger students.

With the high numbers of temporary residents overall, including students, the impact of legal status on adjustment and integration has become one of the key migration issues of this decade. In this chapter, we compare younger foreign ("temporary") students from South Korea, as defined by legal status, with their more "permanent" peers to examine how students' experiences may or may not be shaped by their status. The analysis permits us to further examine the association between status and school-related experiences for newcomers.

Residents in the polity of Canada fall into four general status categories or classes of membership: undocumented, temporary, permanent, and citizen. These legal categories prescribe eligibility for political, social, and economic rights, benefits, and services. As such, legal status can have consequences for social and economic outcomes, with temporary and undocumented residents facing the greatest structural barriers to full participation. While there is limited research on the effects of legal status on migrant integration, the few studies on students that have examined the association between students' legal status and outcomes have highlighted the disadvantages for undocumented or temporary residents relative to their more permanent counterparts (Grayson 2008; Greenman and Hall 2013; see Kim and Attieh in this volume). However, these published studies tend to be limited to older students and leave open the question of how status affects the younger contingent.

There are institutional differences between institutions of higher learning and elementary and secondary schools: the latter are a public good held to principles of access, equity, and inclusion based on local residency. There are also differences in terms of mandates, applicable laws and regulations, organizational structures, services provided, curricula, relationships with students and their families, and other factors. Differences in classroom structure and pedagogical approach within these different institutional levels may also shape social dynamics, making it easier for younger international students to blend in and mix with domestic students, both native-born and immigrant.

Furthermore – and of particular importance to this study – the age of younger students and the involvement of parents and families may also be significant factors. An examination of younger students must consider how parents or caregivers, in addition to the students themselves, interact with educational institutions and institutional actors. School-related experiences also centre on key dimensions, such as academic outcomes, as well as those related to social experiences and psychosocial outcomes (Kim and Sondhi 2015). Although published research on the effects of immigration status on younger students (specifically, studies that compare children in various status categories) is lacking, there are several papers on other aspects of this segment of the international student population. Literature on these younger students, who are referred to as unaccompanied, transnational, or early study abroad students, suggests that they grapple with identity and feelings of acceptance (see Kwak et al. in this volume; Shin 2012).

To summarize, younger international students comprise a distinctive segment of the international student population due to their younger ages and earlier developmental stage; the interaction (or lack thereof) of caregivers with institutions and institutional actors; and institutional differences. Some research on younger students addresses the psychosocial aspects of studying in Canada, but research that compares this younger group with domestic students along various dimensions is lacking. Any effort to address this gap first raises the question of an adequate comparison group, and we argue that to isolate the effects of status beyond the effects of length of residence, language abilities, and the like, the most relevant reference group would be permanent migrant students from the same background. Fortunately, we have a unique data set on Korean families that allows us to make comparisons on school-related experiences, albeit with some limitations.

Toronto Korean Families Study – 2011 Survey

We use data from the Toronto Korean Families Study (TKFS) – 2011 Survey collected between May 2010 and May 2011 through in-person bilingual (Korean/English) interviews with recently arrived migrant families with school-aged children from South Korea living in the Greater Toronto Area. Data from this non-probability survey, which was designed to compare different types of migrant families, contains responses from 422 families (for further information on the survey, please see Kim, Yun, Park, and Noh 2013). One parent from each family completed the survey, which contained questions on migration and integration-related themes and questions about the family, including the first three children.

For the current analysis, we restricted the sample to parents and their first two children between 5 and 16 years of age who were living together (with at least one parent). Recognizing that parents and children may have different legal statuses, we considered investigating the effect of mixed-status families. However, upon closer examination, we found only five families with mixed statuses in our sample, and they were omitted. In the resulting sample of 215 families, the responding parent was usually a woman; approximately 9 per cent of the responding parents were men.

Ages of parents in the sample ranged from 31 to 57 years with a mean of 44 years. Length of residence in Canada ranged from 2 to 12 years with a mean of 5.4 years. In terms of legal immigration status, 20.5 per cent of parents were Canadian citizens, 47 per cent were permanent residents, and 32.6 per cent were temporary residents or visitors. The largest category of landed immigrants (i.e., permanent residents) was the skilled worker category, and visitors comprised the largest category in the temporary residents/visitors group.

A number of questions in the survey asked parents about their children. Some of the questions we examine in this chapter are related to parental contact with institutions and institutional actors as well as parents' perceptions of their children's experiences with such institutions. While there may be some issues around the validity of responses, particularly on children's experiences, due to the reliance on parent respondents, the survey design minimized the issue by focusing questions on topics that parents were most likely to know about; many questions also probed parents about their perspectives. At the same time, however, we are cautious in drawing firm conclusions about children's experiences, and all the more so since the survey was not drawn from a representative sample and also lacked information on the type of institution the children were attending. The variables we can explore, and which we interpret with caution, include academic performance, difficulties in school, parent-teacher relationships, perceived discrimination, and co-/extra-curricular involvement.

For the analysis, we disaggregated the sample by birth order into first children (which also includes only children) and second children, rather than pooling them together; this was done to avoid violating the statistical assumption of independent cases. Also, many studies have documented how birth order can affect educational outcomes (de Haan 2010; Fergusson, Horwood, and Boden 2006) and extra-curricular participation (Rees, Lopez, Averett, and Argys 2008). There were fewer first/only children (128) than second children (178) in our sample due to the age restriction of 5 to 16 years; many of the first-born children in the participating families were older than 16 years at the time of the survey, and they were therefore excluded.

Since our interest in this analysis is the association between legal status and school-related experiences, we further disaggregated each birth order sample by legal status. However, due to the small sample sizes, we grouped permanent residents and Canadian citizens into a single category (PR/CC) and temporary residents and visitors into a second category (TR/V). In practice, permanent residents and Canadian citizens have access to the same services and programs in Canada. The main differences lie in the rights to vote in elections and to access consular services while outside Canada. Differences between temporary residents and visitors may be greater in terms of access to programs and services, but Section 49.1 of the Ontario Education Act 1993 does not permit discrimination on grounds of immigration status, and some local school boards, such as the Toronto District School Board in 2007, have adopted a policy that entitles admission regardless of immigration status (TDSB n.d.). For both birth order samples, permanent residents comprised the majority in the PR/CC category and temporary residents comprised the majority in the TR/V status category.

First-Born Children: The Impact of Status on Difficulties in School and Activities

There were 128 children in the first/only child sample ranging in age from 8 to 16 years with a mean age of 12.9 years. Girls comprised 46.5 per cent and boys 53.5 per cent. Nearly two-thirds of the sample had PR/CC status (67.2 per cent) and less than a third had TR/V visas (32.8 per cent). The mean length of residence in Canada was 5 years.

Table 6.1 presents the results by immigration status and birth order. For each pool of children by birth order, we tested for statistical independence using the chi-square test between each variable of interest and immigration status. The first two columns of Table 6.1 contain the results for the first (or only) children sample. In general, we found substantive differences between status groups. When asked how the child's performance in school had changed since moving to Canada, the most common response was that it had remained the same. However, close to a quarter of parents in the TR/V group responded that their children's school performance had deteriorated, compared to less than 15 per cent of PR/CC parents.

There were similarities and differences in the difficulties children experienced in school. While most first children of both status groups did not experience academic difficulties, both groups did face challenges with language. Despite this pattern, TR/V students were more likely than PR/CC students to have difficulties with language (70.7 versus 51.8 per cent, respectively) and academics (14.6 versus 8.2 per cent, respectively).

All or most parents in the first children sample had met their child's teacher and were satisfied with the parent-teacher relationship, although TR/V parents were slightly less likely than PR/CC parents to have met their child's teacher. Over a third of parents of both status groups either felt their child had or were uncertain if their child had experienced discrimination or were treated unfairly at school. Finally, in co-curricular (at school) and extra-curricular (outside of school) activities, TR/V students were less likely to be participants. Nearly 55 per cent of TR/V students were not involved in co-curricular activities versus 41 per cent of PR/CC children; in the case of extra-curricular activities, the portions of uninvolved students were 24 per cent versus 17 per cent, respectively.

To summarize, these results tell us that status did not affect parents' access to teachers but it did affect first children's experiences at school and their participation in organized activities. However, despite some large substantive differences, we found that most of the associations were not statistically significant (p < .1). The one exception was language difficulty, but the effect disappeared when length of residence in Canada was controlled. In other words, the language difficulties of TR/V students appear to be related to the shorter period of time spent in Canada. We account for this later in the analysis (see Table 6.2).

Second-Born Children: The Impact of Status on Difficulties in School and Activities

Turning to the sample of 180 second children, the mean age of 12.2 years was slightly younger than in the first child sample. Ages in this sample ranged from 5 to 16 years, and as in the first child sample, there were more boys (55 per cent) than girls (45 per cent). Also, PR/CC students (72.1 per cent) outnumbered TR/V students (27.9 per cent). The mean length of residence in Canada – 5. 5 years – was longer than in the first child sample by half a year.

The results from the second child sample, which are presented in the last two columns of Table 6.1, show similar patterns to those of the first child sample. Parents of TR/V second children were more likely than parents of PR/CC second children to indicate their child had difficulties with language and academics, although the majority of both sets of parents did not identify academic difficulties (only 16.3 per cent of TR/V parents and 7.8 per cent of PR/CC parents indicated their child had academic difficulties). However, the majority (61.2 per cent) of TR/V parents identified language difficulties as an issue for their second child, in contrast to 44.8 per cent of PR/CC parents. Again, this can be explained by the fact that the latter group has spent a longer period of time in Canada.

Similar to the first children sample, second children with a temporary status were more likely than their permanent peers to experience an academic decline after moving to Canada (18.2 versus 15.3 per cent, respectively). But, they were also more likely to have improved (29.6 versus 22.2

per cent, respectively). Clearly, the outcomes for TR/V students are not uniform; some do better and some do worse.

There were very few differences between the two status groups in terms of parental interaction with teachers and satisfaction with the parent-teacher relationship for second children. Most of the parents in both status groups had met their child's teacher, though the number was slightly lower for the TR/V group (90 per cent versus 99 per cent of PR/CC parents). We also noticed that slightly more TR/V parents were dissatisfied with the parent-teacher relationship (12.2 versus 9.4 per cent of PR/CC parents) and felt their children had experienced discrimination or were treated unfairly at school (24 versus 20.3 per cent of PR/CC parents).

Finally, in contrast to first children, for whom a temporary status seemed to indicate less involvement in activities, among second children there were no differences in co-/extra-curricular activities between the two status groups. For both status groups, approximately 54 to 55 per cent of children were involved in school activities, and approximately 79 to 80 per cent of children were involved in activities outside of school. It is possible that parents develop a greater awareness of activities by the time their second child is ready to participate, as the average length of residence in Canada in the second children sample was approximately half a year longer than in the first children sample.

Similar to first children, status for second children appeared to be associated with language and academic difficulties at school, and the association was statistically significant ($p < .1$), but it did not appear to affect the parents' access to teachers. However, in contrast to first children, status did not appear to be associated with differential participation in organized activities in or outside of school for second children. As observed with first children, once length of residence in Canada was controlled, the statistical differences in language and academic difficulties between status groups disappeared. These results suggest that some of the issues temporary residents face may be due to the short time spent in Canada. To examine this latter explanation in greater detail, we conducted the analysis again using the newcomer sample of children.

School-Related Experiences, Legal Status, and Newcomer Youth

The number of years of residence in Canada has been shown to affect immigrant children's academic outcomes. A study by Statistics Canada (2004) on immigrant children revealed that, on average, reading scores converged with Canadian-born children after 14 years of residence. The study also noted that while immigrant children started off with a wider language gap, this closed over time and even reversed in many cases (Statistics Canada 2004).

The TKFS survey data contains a sufficient number of newcomer cases to compare status groups (n = 182), however, the sample sizes of the longer-term residents (6 to 12 years) were too small for meaningful statistical analysis, particularly once we disaggregated the sample by legal status. Hence we focused on newcomers. Table 6.2 shows the association between status and school-related experiences by first and second child samples in this restricted newcomer sample (2 to 5 years in Canada).

Comparing the first child subsample of newcomers to the full first child sample (Table 6.1), there was little difference in terms of overall change in academic performance when we examined the association with status. In general, TR/V children were more likely to have both improved (30.6 per cent compared to 22.7 per cent of PR/CC children) and deteriorated (25 versus 20.5 per cent of PR/CC children) in academic performance. Among second children, the pattern shifted slightly: while TR/V children were more likely than PR/CC children to have improved (27 per cent versus 18.6 per cent, respectively), they were less likely to have deteriorated (16.2 versus 23.3 per cent, respectively) in academic performance. This pattern also differed from that of the full sample of second children, as shown in Table 6.1, which revealed that TR/V second children followed a similar split pattern as the first children – that is, they were more likely to have improved and to have worsened in academic performance. Despite all of these patterns, roughly 75 to 80 per cent of all children, regardless of sample, either remained the same or improved after moving to Canada, according to the parents. It is also interesting to note that time in Canada appears to affect PR/CC children more than TR/V children, as the former group reported improving after spending more time in Canada. We draw this cautious conclusion based on the higher percentages of newcomers whose performance deteriorated after moving to Canada relative to the percentages among the full sample (i.e., 20.5 per cent of newcomer PR/CC first children versus 14.6 per cent of full sample PR/CC first children, and 23.3 per cent versus 15.3 per cent of PR/CC second children, respectively) but find it is consistent with past studies (Statistics Canada 2004).

Among newcomers, language was identified as a school-related difficulty for the majority of both first and second children, regardless of status (55 to 68 per cent). However, TR/V newcomer children were more likely to experience language as a school-related difficulty compared to PR/CC newcomer children (67.6 versus 54.6 per cent of first children, respectively, and 62.5 versus 55.2 per cent of second children, respectively). Although academic difficulty was identified by only a small percentage of newcomer families, again we observed some status-related differences. Among PR/CC newcomer first children, 9.1 per cent experienced academic difficulty, while this was the case for 16.2 per cent of TR/V newcomer first children. A similar pattern was observed for newcomer second children as 8.6 per cent of PR/CC children as opposed to 15 per cent of TR/V children reported difficulties with grades.

Regarding interactions with teachers, most, if not all, newcomer parents had met their child's teacher, and this was observed for both first and second children. However, we also observed that, like the full sample, the number was slightly lower for the TR/V newcomer parents than the PR/CC newcomer parents. In spite of these high percentages of newcomer parents having met their children's teachers, not all were satisfied with the parent-teacher relationship. Although the majority of parents in the newcomer and full samples, regardless of birth order and status, were satisfied with the relationship (roughly 57 to 71 per cent), TR/V newcomer parents were more likely to be satisfied compared to PR/CC newcomer parents.

The association between status and perceptions of discrimination in school among newcomers was generally similar to the full sample. TR/V parents were less likely than PR/CC parents to feel their first child had experienced discrimination or had been treated unfairly at school (18.4 versus 22.7 per cent, respectively). On the other hand, TR/V parents of second children were slightly more likely than PR/CC parents to feel their children had been discriminated against or treated unfairly (20 versus 16.7 per cent, respectively).

The association between status and activities was also similar to the full sample (Table 6.1). Among newcomer first children, temporary/visiting status meant a lower likelihood of involvement in school co- or extra-curricular activities relative to PR/CC children (47.4 versus 63.6 per cent, respectively, for co-curricular activities, and 79 to 90.7 per cent, respectively, for extra-curricular activities), although this difference was not statistically significant ($p < .1$). There was little difference in the percentages of student involvement in activities across the two status groups in the second child sample of newcomers, although TR/V students were slightly less likely to participate in school co-curricular activities compared to PR/CC students (50 versus 53.5 per cent, respectively). Finally, it was clear that the majority of students participated in some kind of activity, whether it was at school or elsewhere.

Discussion

The rising numbers of temporary residents in Canada over the past decade, along with restricted avenues for permanent migration, have increased concerns about the living conditions facing non-permanent residents and the consequent impacts on their adjustment and well-being. Given that many non-permanent residents hope to remain on a more permanent basis and many do, it is worthwhile to examine the ways in which their status is linked to particular kinds of experiences.

Our study examined the effects of legal status on school-related experiences among younger students aged five to sixteen years by birth order. Based on responses from parents, we examined post-migration changes in academic performance, academic and language difficulties, relationships with teachers, experiences of discrimination, and co- and extra-curricular involvement. In general, we found some differences among students according to legal status but not uniformly in the expected direction. Differences were observed between permanent residents/Canadian citizens and temporary residents/visitors in the expected direction on academic and language difficulties, interactions with teachers, and co- and extra-curricular involvement for the first-born child (but not for the second-born child).

Temporary residents/visitors were disadvantaged in academic and language ability relative to permanent residents/Canadian citizens as perceived by respondent parents, and this pattern persisted for only/first- and second-born children and for newcomers (those who had lived in Canada from two to five years). Temporary resident/visiting parents may have higher expectations for their children's academic performance and thus have different standards for evaluating their children, or perhaps permanently migrating families are better prepared for schooling in Canada prior to their arrival. Another plausible explanation is institutional: there may be insufficient academic services and supports for temporary residents and visitors and/or a lack of awareness of services that are available. Eligibility requirements for public remedial programs may be inaccessible to those without at least permanent resident status. Moreover, permanent residents are often directed to settlement organizations, whereas temporary residents may be unaware of the range of services available to them in non-profit agencies that do not discriminate by status.

Temporary resident/visiting parents were also less likely to have met their child's teacher. Although the difference by status groups was small, it was noticeable: all but one of the permanent resident/Canadian citizen parents in the sample had met their child's teacher, regardless of the child's birth order, whereas several of the temporary resident/visiting parents group indicated they had not met their child's teacher. Perhaps families living in Canada on a temporary basis feel less compelled to develop a relationship with teachers due to the short-term nature of their stay, or perhaps their jobs or daily activities do not permit them to attend parent-teacher interviews. This latter explanation seems unlikely, as members of temporary resident/visiting families are not likely to be working in Canada; usually one parent works abroad. It seems more likely, given the language difficulties experienced by their children, that temporary resident/visiting parents also face a language barrier when communicating with teachers. This is a common issue for ESL families and it may be alleviated by the presence of bilingual assistants or interpreters (Guo 2010). Nevertheless, despite this potential barrier, these parents tended to be more satisfied with the parent-teacher relationship than their more permanent counterparts.

We also examined participation in co- and extra-curricular activities given the benefits of such activities on social and psychological development and future success (Rees et al. 2008). This was the third area in which temporary resident/visiting children were disadvantaged. However, the association with status was relevant only for first-born/only children. There was no difference in the involvement of second-born children. The birth order pattern in the effect of status may be explained by the lack of knowledge or awareness of temporary resident/visiting families for their first-born/only child. In addition, gender and activity may also play a role. As Rees et al. (2008) show, younger male siblings were more likely to engage in particular extra-curricular activities compared to males who were first-born, while younger female siblings were less likely than first-born females to participate. We did not control for gender in this analysis and we encourage future studies to examine this dimension for extra-curricular participation as well as for other school-related experiences.

Finally, we found minor differences and no clear status patterns when it came to parents' perceptions of discrimination or unfair treatment toward their child in school. Interestingly, a third of families felt either that they had experienced or were uncertain whether they had experienced discrimination, which is an important finding in itself as it shows a number of families may struggle to feel accepted or gain a sense of belonging. Clearly, more needs to be done to address this issue in schools for all immigrant families regardless of status.

This chapter asked whether legal status has any bearing on student and family experiences in schools, and the analysis showed that legal status may be important in a number of areas. However, we take these findings with caution as data limitations and small sample sizes precluded multivariate analysis. Thinking beyond temporary international students from Korea, the findings suggest that temporary students are not substantially different from permanent residents. Although the temporary students may struggle more with academics and language, there is evidence to suggest the differences between them disappear over time. Moreover, the findings suggest that school administrators need not be concerned that parents of temporary students may be less engaged as the results show otherwise. First, parents of temporary students are similarly engaged as parents of permanent students, and second, temporary and permanent students are similarly engaged in activities. Rather, the focus for schools with temporary (and permanent) residents should be on improving language instruction and academic supports.

Our findings encourage future research on the topics of academic performance and language needs, institutional contact, and co- and extra-curricular involvement. How experiences shift and change over time is also an important consideration for future research. Although most of the patterns described above held when we restricted the sample to newcomers who have been in Canada from two to five years, it was not clear whether gaps between status groups increase or decrease over time.

Our findings also point to the importance of addressing systemic disparities among people in different legal categories. Eradicating the disadvantages of temporary legal status will benefit policymakers and society alike. While living in Canada, temporary residents contribute to the social and cultural lives of their communities, as well as to the larger economy. If they transition to permanent residence – which many do (see Lu and Hou in this volume) – a larger gap means they have further to go to catch up with permanent residents and citizens. If they return to their places of origin or move on to a third country, they may help to improve Canada's international relationships (Han and Zweig 2010). As greater numbers of temporary residents arrive and settle in Canada and we gain increased knowledge about the different experiences of residents according to legal status, ensuring equity among status groups will become a priority.

Table 6.1 Legal Status and School-Related Experiences

	First child (n = 128)		Second child (n = 178)	
	PR/CC	TR/V	PR/CC	TR/V
	Per cent		Per cent	
Change in performance				
Improved	28.1	30.8	22.2	29.6
Same	57.3	46.2	62.5	52.3
Worsened	14.6	23.1	15.3	18.2
Language difficulty				
Yes	51.8	70.7	44.8	61.2
No	48.2	29.3	55.2	38.8
Academic difficulty				
Yes	8.2	14.6	7.8	16.3
No	91.8	85.4	92.2	83.7
Met teacher				
Yes	100.0	95.2	99.2	90.0
No	0	4.8	0.8	10.0
Satisfied with parent-teacher relationship				
Satisfied	57.0	66.7	58.6	59.2
Neither	32.6	21.4	32.0	28.6
Dissatisfied	10.5	11.9	9.4	12.2
Experienced discrimination				
Yes	31.4	23.8	20.3	24.0
No	61.6	64.3	66.4	62.0
Uncertain	7.0	11.9	13.3	14.0
School co-curricular involvement				
Yes	59.3	45.2	54.8	54.0
No	40.7	54.8	45.2	46.0
Extra-curricular involvement (outside of school)				
Yes	83.5	76.2	78.7	79.6
No	16.5	23.8	21.3	20.4

Notes: The sample includes children aged 5 to 16 years, living with the responding parent in Canada. PR refers to permanent resident; CC refers to Canadian citizen; TR refers to temporary resident; and V refers to visitor. First child PR/CC n = 86 except for change in performance (82), language difficulty (85), academic difficulty (85), extra-curricular involvement (85). First child TR/V n = 42 except for change in performance (39), language difficulty (41), academic difficulty (41). Second child PR/CC n = 128 except for change in performance (72), language difficulty (116), academic difficulty (116), school co-curricular involvement (126), extra-curricular involvement (127). Second child TR/V n = 50 except for change in performance (44), language difficulty (49), academic difficulty (49), satisfied with parent-teacher relationship (49), extra-curricular involvement (49).

Table 6.2 Legal Status and School-Related Experiences, Newcomers

	First child (n = 82)		Second child (n = 100)	
	PR/CC	TR/V	PR/CC	TR/V
	Per cent		Per cent	
Change in performance				
Improved	22.7	30.6	18.6	27.0
Same	56.8	44.4	58.1	56.8
Worsened	20.5	25.0	23.3	16.2
Language difficulty				
Yes	54.6	67.6	55.2	62.5
No	45.5	32.4	44.8	37.5
Academic difficulty				
Yes	9.1	16.2	8.6	15.0
No	90.9	83.8	91.4	85.0
Met teacher				
Yes	100.0	94.7	100.0	87.5
No	0	5.3	0	12.5
Satisfied with parent-teacher relationship				
Satisfied	56.8	71.1	56.7	61.5
Neither	31.8	18.4	31.7	28.2
Dissatisfied	11.4	10.5	11.7	10.3
Experienced discrimination				
Yes	22.7	18.4	16.7	20.0
No	63.6	68.4	68.3	65.0
Uncertain	13.6	13.2	15.0	15.0
School co-curricular involvement				
Yes	63.6	47.4	53.5	50.0
No	36.4	52.6	46.6	50.0
Extra-curricular involvement (outside of school)				
Yes	90.7	79.0	81.7	82.1
No	9.3	21.1	18.3	18.0

Notes: This sample is the same as in Table 6.1 but restricted to newcomers living in Canada from 2 to 5 years. First child PR/CC n = 44 except for extra-curricular involvement (85). First child TR/V n = 38 except for change in performance (36), language difficulty (37), academic difficulty (37). Second child PR/CC n = 60 except for change in performance (43), language difficulty (58), academic difficulty (58), school co-curricular involvement (58). Second child TR/V n = 40 except for change in performance (37), satisfied with parent-teacher relationship (39), extra-curricular involvement (49).

References

de Haan, Monique. 2010. "Birth Order, Family Size and Educational
   Attainment." *Economics of Education Review* 29 (4): 576–88. https://doi
   .org/10.1016/j.econedurev.2009.10.012.
Fergusson, David M., L. John Horwood, and Joseph M. Boden. 2006.
   "Birth Order and Educational Achievement in Adolescence and Young
   Adulthood." *Australian Journal of Education* 50 (2): 122–39. https://doi
   .org/10.1177/000494410605000203.
Grayson, J. Paul. 2008. "The Experiences and Outcomes of Domestic and
   International Students at Four Canadian Universities." *Higher Education
   Research & Development* 27 (3): 215–30. https://doi.org/10.1080/
   07294360802183788.
Greenman, Emily, and Matthew Hall. 2013. "Legal status and educational
   transitions for Mexican and Central American immigrant youth." *Social
   Forces* 91 (4): 1475–98. https://doi.org/10.1093/sf/sot040. Medline:24511162
Guo, Yan. 2010. "Meetings Without Dialogue: A Study of ESL Parent-Teacher
   Interactions at Secondary School Parents' Nights." *School Community Journal*
   20 (1): 121–40.
Han, Donglin, and David Zweig. 2010. "Images of the World: Studying Abroad
   and Chinese Attitudes Towards International Affairs." *China Quarterly* 202:
   290–306. https://doi.org/10.1017/S030574101000024X.
Kim, Ann H., and Gunjan Sondhi. 2015. "Bridging the Literature on
   Education Migration." *Population Change and Lifecourse Strategic Knowledge
   Cluster Discussion Paper Series/Un Réseau stratégique de connaissances
   Changements de population et parcours de vie Document de travai* 3(1), Article 7.
   http://ir.lib.uwo.ca/pclc/vol3/iss1/7.
Kim, Ann H., Sung Hyun Yun, Wansoo Park, and Samuel Noh. 2013.
   "Explaining the Migration Strategy: Comparing Transnational and Intact
   Migrant Families from South Korea to Canada." In *Koreans in North America:
   Their Twenty-First Century Experiences*, ed. Pyong Gap Min, 103–19. Lanham,
   MD: Lexington Books.
Knight-Grofe, Janine, and Karen Rauh. 2016. *A World of Learning 2016:
   Canada's Performance and Potential in International Education.* Canadian
   Bureau for International Education Report 82.
Rees, Daniel I., Elizabeth Lopez, Susan L. Averett, and Laura M. Argys. 2008.
   "Birth Order and Participation in School Sports and Other Extracurricular
   Activities." *Economics of Education Review* 27 (3): 354–62. https://doi.org/
   10.1016/j.econedurev.2007.04.001.

Resnik, Julie. 2012. "Sociology of International Education: An Emerging Field of Research." *International Studies in Sociology of Education* 22 (4): 291–310. https://doi.org/10.1080/09620214.2012.751203.

Shin, Hyunjung. 2012. "From FOB to Cool: Transnational Migrant Students in Toronto and the Styling of Global Linguistic Capital." *Journal of Sociolinguistics* 16 (2): 184–200. https://doi.org/10.1111/j.1467-9841.2011.00523.x.

Statistics Canada. 2004. "Children of Immigrants: How Well Do They Do in School?" *Education Matters: Insights on Education, Learning and Training in Canada.* October, Number 4. 81–004-XIE. http://www.statcan.gc.ca/pub/81-004-x/200410/7422-eng.htm.

TDSB. n.d. "TDSB Policy P.061 SCH: Students Without Legal Immigration Status." http://ppf.tdsb.on.ca/uploads/files/live/98/1555.pdf (accessed 8 August 2018).

PART III

Local Considerations: Ethnic Communities and Families

7 Adapting to China's Students at the Gateway: Student Stories and the Trajectories of Chinese Community Associations in Vancouver

JEAN MICHEL MONTSION

The metaphor of the gateway has been used by the governments of British Columbia (BC) and Canada to redefine the city of Vancouver's role on the international stage, particularly to privilege its connections to China. "Canada's Gateway to the Asia Pacific," as Vancouver was officially designated by the federal government in 2006, started with investments in transportation infrastructure, which allowed the city to become a key node in the international distribution networks between Asian and North American markets (Evans 2008; Transport Canada 2007, 4–5). Building on this branding exercise, the BC government diversified the meaning of "gateway" to market specific initiatives in education (BC Ministry of Economic Development 2007, 18–20). By shifting the narrative of the gateway from discussions on transport infrastructure, both the federal and provincial governments have developed a hands-off and deregulating approach to gateway developments in the education sector. This approach is based on the belief that the role of governments is to create an environment conducive to individual and private initiatives, which has left community associations in Vancouver on their own to adapt to the consequences of this opening up to Mainland China, especially in post-secondary education (Evans 2010; Mitchell 2001; Mitchell 2004; Montsion 2011).

In this chapter, I am interested in exploring the ways in which Vancouver-based Chinese community associations have been adapting to the BC gateway initiatives in post-secondary education and, more specifically, how these ethnic organizations are relating to international students coming from Mainland China in increasing numbers. By looking at how students from China living in Vancouver do or do not relate to local ethnic-based Chinese associations on and off campus, I present growing social trends relating to Chinese populations and Chinese community politics in Vancouver. More specifically, I stress the increasing importance of community associations in filling the gaps left by a deregulating approach to the recruitment and integration of international students. Notably, I explore the roles played by well-established Chinese organizations, Chinese Christian churches, and newly created Mainlander associations in supporting international students from China, while contributing to the evolving Chinese community politics at the gateway. After framing BC's education gateway initiatives, I will focus on international students' stories and how they perceive and engage with Vancouver-based Chinese community associations. Reflecting broader social trends in Vancouver, I will shed light on the shifting landscape of Chinese community associations and the role of international students in contributing to local community politics.

As a methodological note, it is important to stress that interviews for this research project were conducted in 2008 in Vancouver with university staffers, international students, and representatives from various Chinese community associations, as well as public officials and local experts on recent developments in Chinese community politics in Vancouver. Interviews cited here are taken from a pool of fifty-nine interviews, which helps to make the linkages between state initiatives, the activities of local community associations and universities, and the individual perspectives of international students. Whereas non-student interviewees were selected based on their professional position and involvement in public debates on gateway and Chinese community politics in Vancouver, student participants were recruited through the community association in which they were involved at the time. Although this selection process overemphasizes the voices of students involved with local community associations, it fits well the purpose of this study. The aim is to better understand the evolving community structures supporting Chinese international students in Vancouver, including the students' overall positioning in them and some of their individual perspectives on the matter. As such, these interviews should not be used to make any representative claims on the broader situation of China's international students in Vancouver, but rather to speak to the wide array of reasons for, and profiles of, student involvement in Vancouver-based Chinese community associations, and in a heuristic fashion, to the broader social trends developing in Chinese community politics in Vancouver.

Universities and the Asia-Pacific Gateway

In 2014, the federal government published *Canada's International Education Strategy*, which posits that the main reasons to foster increases in international students are to benefit from the business of international education, to address skilled labour shortages and long-term labour market vitality, to foster innovation and new opportunities for Canadians, and to support a better branding of Canada as a place of learning and educational success (Minister of International Trade 2014, 7–10; see also Trilokekar and El Masri in this volume). Such an approach to international education is familiar to the BC context, which has optimized these strategies since the launch of its education gateway initiative in 2007. With a particular focus on creating synergies and increased innovation through a diversified human capital, the BC government has appropriated the gateway narrative from transportation infrastructure developments to speak of the historical role and competitive advantage of BC in serving as a cultural and educational bridge between Asia and North America.

The BC government's engagement with the education gateway narrative builds on key developments that have occurred since the late 1990s. In line with broader trends in higher education in the Canadian context, the growth of BC's education sector is explained by many factors. One is the new corporatist attitude embraced by educational institutions, and another is the development of publicly sponsored recruitment activities in Asia, from partnerships with local private agents in Asian countries to initiatives such as BC's Offshore School Certification Program, which gives schools in Asia, particularly in China, the ability to offer their students a BC-certified education and the recognition of their credentials when applying to Canadian universities (Waters 2006, 1050–9). Students and their families are also motivated to be active in selecting an institution in BC, because of the province's relative geographical proximity to Asia, the relatively low tuitions in comparison to American schools, and the cultural, ethnic, and family networks already linking BC to various locations in Asia (Kirby 2011, 269). The province's expansion of its education system is also explained by broader considerations of international and national political economy. This includes efforts to shift national attention and initiatives from Central and Eastern Canada to the Pacific Coast and building on its ethnic and family connections to Asia to attract new economic opportunities. International students and skilled migrants are part of that strategy, as the province has committed to use increases in the demand for BC's higher education to train the next generation of workers in line with provincial labour market needs (Bauder 2005, 92; Dennison and Schuetze 2004, 22; Kirby 2011, 268).

The recruitment and retention of international students has become a concrete expression of how the education sector is integrated into the gateway narrative and the related gateway economy. In 2007, BC's minister of economic development stated that the province "has the largest English-as-a-second language market in Canada with approximately 100 organizations operating in Vancouver. British Columbia post-secondary institutions are leaders in international education" (BC Minister of Economic Development 2007, 19). The interest in optimizing the province's support of international students is especially grounded in the business dimension. As a BC official document on Canada's gateway indicates: "many non-commercial activities do, in fact, generate significant economic return to communities. Visits by foreign students to BC educational institutions are a case in point" (Union of BC Municipalities 2007, 9). In this view, the BC government has since 2008 allowed the creation of five new universities out of five former community colleges, as well as a plethora of private vocational training institutes and private degree-granting initiatives, to ensure it can optimize and increase the number of international students to the province, especially those coming from Mainland China (Dennison and Schuetze 2004, 30–1; Levin 2003, 449–51; Montsion 2011, 43).

Besides the revenues gained from its expanding role in the business of international education, the BC government's strategy is also linked to the development of skilled labour at the gateway. As the Greater Vancouver Gateway Council notes:

> Rapid gateway growth is occurring at a time of high economic activity in Western Canada. The situation in the Gateway is compounded by the high cost of housing and an aging workforce. Ways and means must be found to ensure the availability of adequate numbers of skilled employees to meet Gateway needs over the coming decades. (Greater Vancouver Gateway Council 2007, 14)

A priority for governmental strategies is skilled labour, which can be found in graduating cohorts. International students may get incentives from governments, for example, to stay longer in BC, and to work towards fast-tracking their immigration application processes (personal interview with Eric, 21 May 2008). Such a focus on international students as a key immigrant demographic and a potential source of skilled labour echoes trends found elsewhere in Canada, both at the provincial level and nationally (see Trilokekar and El Masri in this volume, 20–1).

Since the explicit marketing of Vancouver as an education gateway in 2007, efforts have been made to increase the number of international students coming from Asia, and especially Mainland China, to BC universities (Illuminate Consulting Group 2014, 6–8). The number of international students in BC during the 2012–13 academic year reached 112,800, with a yearly increase of 6 per cent. Of these students, 25,800 students came from Mainland China, which represents 37.1 per cent of the market for university-level international student enrolments that year. In contrast, students from India made up only 4 per cent of international students coming to the province in 2012–13, although this number does represent an increase of 3,000 students since the 2009–10 academic year. Overall, these increases in the number of international students have helped to generate an estimated $2.3 billion in the provincial economy, creating 25,490 new jobs since 2009–2010 to accommodate the needs and services of the international student population (BCCIE 2014; Illuminate Consulting Group 2014, 7).

As BC's premier, research-intensive university, the University of British Columbia (UBC) has supported Vancouver's gateway education sector by multiplying its presence (i.e., official delegations) and institutional agreements with Mainland China, and by diversifying its research agenda to better represent leadership in bridging Western and Asian societies in knowledge-production mechanisms (UBC 2004; UBC 2008a). Increases in the number of international students are also seen as a way to contribute to more diversity in everyday life on campus and in Vancouver more generally. As the president of UBC stated in 2007:

In Trek 2010, the university established targets for international students. These targets should be understood primarily as attempts to "internally internationalize" the university, thereby enriching the experience of all students, especially those who have stayed at home to study and have not themselves had the opportunity to travel. (UBC 2007)

Between 2000 and 2012, the number of international students enrolled at UBC's Vancouver campus increased from 2,345 to 8,440, making 7 per cent of total enrolment in 2000 and 17 per cent in 2012 (UBC 2012, 5). Of the total number of international students in 2012–13, 29.9 per cent originated from Mainland China or Hong Kong, an increase from

157 in 2000 to 1,222 in 2012–13. Interestingly, the number of Chinese international students has surpassed the number of international students from the United States since 2010, which traditionally has been the largest pool of international students at UBC's Vancouver campus (UBC 2012, 13, 26). In 2015, students from China and Hong Kong made up 39 per cent of UBC's international cohort, while American students represented 10 per cent of it. In contrast, the representation of students from India has increased in a much slower fashion, making up 2 per cent of UBC's international students in 2010 and 4 per cent in 2015 (UBC 2016; for a discussion on the reasons why this number is low relative to Chinese international students, see Illuminate Consulting Group 2014, 7–11).

In line with the provincial emphasis on training international students to meet local labour market needs, UBC had been involved in the sector-based fast-tracking of immigration for many years, namely by facilitating the matching of local employers with international students, especially in the fields of engineering and business (personal interview with Colleen, 18 April 2008). For example, through its Transition Out Program, UBC helps international students get post-graduate work permits in order to work professionally in Vancouver after their studies, which has in turn added many highly skilled workers to the local labour market (UBC 2008b).

China's Students and Their Community Engagement

Such state-driven gateway initiatives do not only impact how a university like UBC adjusts its priorities and programming to cater to increased numbers of international students from China. It also impacts directly the daily lives of international students coming to Vancouver, whether to study before returning to China, or to stay and transition to the local workforce. In this section, I will present three stories that highlight how different students from Mainland China made it to Vancouver to study. Building on these stories, I discuss how these students engage with local Chinese associations in order to examine the role of various community actors that support them during their years of study, whether recognized officially as such or not. I will also explore the role of well-established Chinese community associations such as SUCCESS, the role of Chinese Christian churches, and the role of newly created Mainlander organizations in supporting Chinese international students in Vancouver.

SUCCESS Students: The Stories of John, Katie, and Mindy

John, Katie, and Mindy are three international students from Mainland China that I met while volunteering at a job fair organized by the United Chinese Community Enrichment Services Society (SUCCESS) in April 2008. At that time, all three students were between the ages of eighteen and twenty-one and were studying at various post-secondary institutions in Vancouver. Whereas John wanted to register in a business program at UBC in the fall and find employment in the city to continue living here in the medium-term, Katie and Mindy were more disillusioned with their Vancouver experiences and were looking forward to going back to Fujian, where they are both from. Despite their different views on their years of study at the gateway, they all shared a similar experience of having found SUCCESS and their volunteer work for the organization a main part of their socialization in Vancouver.

John, Katie, and Mindy all shared with me the various reasons they chose Vancouver in the first place, and they described the good and bad aspects of their time in Vancouver. All three students shared with me that they primarily chose Vancouver for their university degree in order to practise their English language skills, and that they viewed the city as a good compromise since they were not able to afford a university in or get a visa to either the United States or England. As a lot of their friends had chosen to immigrate to a different and smaller Canadian province in the Prairies or back East before moving to Vancouver, they denoted how difficult it was for them to survive in the city due to how expensive the tuition fees and the cost of living are in Vancouver. As John indicated, "Its mostly rich Chinese kids here and those who can't find a job soon have to go back" (personal interview with John, 24 April 2008).

The three students' shared socialization experience through their volunteer work at SUCCESS was depicted as a good way of making friends of Chinese origin in Vancouver; this allowed them to speak their language and share important events like Chinese New Year with people for whom it is important, while working towards their permanent residency in Canada. A well-established Chinese community association, SUCCESS is an organization that since the 1970s has relied on the voluntary participation and civic duty of the local Chinese population to give back to their community; hence the organization's emphasis on using volunteering as a recruitment tool, as a socializing practice for newcomers to

Canadian life, and as a basis for grounding its legitimacy in local community politics (Mitchell 2001; Vrasti and Montsion 2014).

Like the other 2,000 registered SUCCESS volunteers, John, Katie, and Mindy were integrated into the SUCCESS family through volunteering, as marketed through various Chinese events, through corporations like Sun Life, or through school counsellors, either in high school or in a post-secondary environment, as laid out in the five to ten memoranda of understanding the organization has with local community colleges and universities, like Langara, Douglas, and UBC (personal interview with Bruce, 9 May 2008). Volunteer work becomes the main socializing parameters to the extent that it helps international students like John, Katie, and Mindy to engage with the local Chinese population of Vancouver, to understand this community's priorities and how best to engage with them. Moreover, it helps some of these students, like John, to utilize and bank this volunteering experience as work experience in service of permanent Canadian residency requirements (personal interview with Bruce, 9 May 2008; personal interview with John, 24 April 2008).

More broadly, integration through volunteering has helped well-established Chinese community associations like SUCCESS adapt to new waves of immigration, notably from Mainland China. Originally a Hong Kongese association, SUCCESS has diversified its recruitment and adjusted its services, notably switching its first line of service to Mandarin, to cater to the 80 per cent of its new clientele (personal interview with Rob, 29 May 2008). As the other well-established Chinese organizations in Vancouver – known collectively as the "Big 5" – have done, SUCCESS relies on this constant renewing of its volunteers to follow and respond to the needs of Chinese newcomers as first respondents, and also to justify its relevance as a legitimate voice of the local Chinese communities in broader municipal, provincial, and federal debates (Vrasti and Montsion 2014). Such a constant renewal of membership also helps the organization justify its social function when applying for government funding, and this is especially notable in the context of the increasing numbers of Chinese community associations trying to compete for the same funding (personal interview with Carl, 3 November 2008).

Struggling to Find the Right Community: The Story of Philip

When I met Philip in 2008, he was two years into a graduate program at UBC, having spent the previous four years in New Brunswick for his undergraduate degree. He was aided in part by financial support received from Project Hope, which allowed him to move to Canada from his hometown in a rural region of south-western China for his studies. Despite finding BC – and more precisely UBC – more populous, beautiful, and Asian than St. Thomas University in New Brunswick, he experienced more isolation and social detachment than he did back East or in China. Philip's story not only depicts the struggle of engaging with the various socializing processes at play on campus and in the city, but also highlights his utilization of a Christian church as a main socializing circle.

Hanging out mostly with international students from the Mainland, with whom he spoke mainly Mandarin, Philip was first shocked at how easy it was to speak Mandarin on campus and in town, and how little incentive there was to integrate to a different community. Engaging somewhat in the events organized by the local Chinese community for Chinese New Year, for instance, Philip had been struggling with pressure to engage in what he considers Western lifestyle choices and activities, as promulgated by various social clubs he encountered on and off campus. Speaking of his own experiences back in China, he stressed the importance of social networks developed in school-related activities and circles as a main socializing force, but he had problems finding one that fit with his needs in Vancouver: "Here, you only go to class together, it is very individual-based. Here, making and maintaining friendships takes time and effort, like going to dance parties. Many Chinese don't get that" (personal interview with Philip, 5 May 2008). He did say that he and his friends chose to participate in some activities organized by Christian churches located very close to campus, which provided space to meet other Chinese international students who did not necessarily buy in to the Western lifestyle.

Chinese Christian churches are especially important for international students from Mainland China. Philip indicated that these churches are a good means to fight off the solitude of studying abroad. By joining these faith-based groups, international students may socialize without participating in Western social practices deemed too different and uncomfortable for many Chinese migrants. More specifically, he described how people in Vancouver speak openly about sexual relations and how most Western social activities are often framed through the appeal of sex; in Philip's view, most Chinese students are uncomfortable with such an approach (personal interview with Philip, 5 May 2008). Whereas Philip found that Christian churches tend to safeguard against these pressures, he also noted that the whole idea of Western and exclusively monotheistic religion is strange to him and his friends, showing the limitations in their engagement with the Christian faith: "Back home ... people deal with loneliness not through one specific religion. It is very flexible, but may bring confusion also, as our ethics is based on Buddhism, Confucianism, Taoism. It's also how we deal with relationships" (personal interview with Philip, 5 May 2008). Chinese Christian churches in Vancouver have become, in his view, a way of socializing, looking at the world, finding friends and other Chinese people, in ways that do not reproduce Western social practices.

This story echoes a broader process at play in Vancouver: the revitalization of many Chinese Christian churches through recruitment practices during new migration patterns from Mainland China. Whereas Caucasian Christian churches have problems finding new members in Vancouver today, Chinese Christian churches are finding new life (Nyíri 2003; Yu 2010). Over the last fifteen years, the increasing number of members from Mainland China has sustained approximately 120 Chinese Christian churches in Greater Vancouver; in terms of individual churches, the numbers of congregants range from 70 members for the smallest churches to more than a thousand members for the larger churches (personal interview with Frida, 6 June 2008). More specifically, Chinese Christian churches are responding to the needs of Chinese newcomers in Vancouver, and especially international students, by directing them to organizations like SUCCESS (Ley 2008, 2064–5). In other words, the intent to join a church is not necessarily based on faith, since Chinese Christian churches offer social services to a specific ethnically defined group whose members seek the familiarity of "speaking the same language" or "being with their own people" (Hiebert and Ley 2003). More concretely, the Bible study groups at these churches are of particular importance, since they not only allow members to share and celebrate their faith but, more importantly, to meet friends from a similar cultural background and combat solitude without falling into a Western lifestyle alien to many from Mainland China (personal interview with Frida, 6 June 2008; personal interview with Philip, 5 May 2008).

Transitioning Out of Being a Student: The Story of Melanie

I met Melanie in May 2008 at a vigil organized by the Chinese Students and Scholars Association (CSSA) at UBC in memory of the victims of the Sichuan earthquakes. Among the seventy people who showed up to the event, Melanie made a point of coming to the vigil even though she had completed her graduate studies in nursing at UBC a couple of years before. Having also worked on campus for a while, she had maintained close ties to the Mainlanders' community on campus. Now, at twenty-four, she was a nurse in Vancouver, a proud Canadian citizen, and a resident of Richmond. As a former international student who had transitioned to being a working professional, Melanie's story speaks to a growing number of Chinese community associations, like the CSSA, that have emerged mostly from and for Mainlanders.

From her experience, most of the new focus on opening up to international students will contribute to the disparity between what is happening on university campuses and the larger community, which favours the children of rich families living in China and Asia in general. Having developed a strong practice of supporting her community of Chinese expats in Canada and at UBC, she pointed to the importance of also supporting other segments of the Canadian population, as well as those international students who may not come from rich families but, like her, have been able to transition into the local workforce. As such, she had a very critical perspective on any government initiatives favouring increases in international students from the Mainland, as most students accepted to Canadian universities do not receive adequate help, especially students from poor families from Canada.

Melanie's story speaks to the role of universities in fostering linkages between current and former international students from China. Attending an event organized by the UBC CSSA, Melanie fits into a specific network created mostly for Chinese students coming from Mainland China. Keeping privileged linkages with the Chinese Embassy in Canada, the CSSA is perceived to be separate and self-isolating from Vancouver's Chinese populations as it organizes based on exclusive language skills, mostly Mandarin. At UBC, the CSSA was formed in the early 1990s and has claimed to be independent from all Chinese governmental directives since the late 1990s. Its membership exploded since it opened to undergraduate students in 2005, and it now possesses between 1,000 and 1,500 members. Its goal is "to serve the students living, starting here" (personal interview with Mike, 19 June 2008). The CSSA wants to make life more convenient and easy for its membership while they are at UBC by providing things like social activities during Chinese New Year and field trips in collaboration with the CSSA at Simon Fraser University. For special occasions, such as the 2008 Sichuan earthquakes, the CSSA has organized specific events like fundraising activities or a vigil to help mobilize resources for disaster relief, and it has offered its members psychological and emotional support (personal interview with Mike, 19 June 2008).

The CSSA's activities have demonstrated self-organization, despite local resources within the Vancouver Chinese communities. For example, for the last three years the association has organized a language school for the children of its members on the UBC campus. Similarly, the CSSA is working towards building networks with corporations in Vancouver, Hong Kong, and Mainland China to find employment opportunities for its members as they approach graduation. The CSSA's main partner, which helps facilitate this process, is the Chinese Embassy in Canada (personal interview with Mike, 19 June 2008).

The CSSA's desire to remain separate from other Chinese community associations in Vancouver, even on campus, stems from its very specific mandate: it caters to Mainlanders. As such, it echoes some other Mainlander organizations created in Vancouver in recent years, including the well-organized Beijing Tong Xiang Kuay (with 1,000 members) and the Canada Wenzhou Friendship Society, as well as trade associations like the Zhong Guo Shuang Kuay. These associations do reflect an everyday life not yet totally anchored in local Chinese social life in Vancouver. They fulfil social functions that are similar to those of SUCCESS and Christian Chinese churches but with specific pretensions of the community and interests they represent: "They want to be one of the leaders, to use China to improve [their members]" (personal interview with Carl, 3 November 2008). With their own connections to the Mainland, they utilize Vancouver as an opening to the Western world, which involves only very limited relations with well-established Chinese community associations in Vancouver.

Community Politics and Shifting Ethnic Claims

With very little help from state and university actors in engaging with local Chinese voluntary associations on and off campus, the search for and integration into a local community at the gateway falls to individuals, including international students. In light of the above-mentioned student stories, Chinese community associations have been actively organizing to fulfil this function, by recruiting and integrating these international students through various mechanisms, such as SUCCESS's memoranda of understanding with post-secondary institutions. Heuristically, this one-on-one student engagement, either based on religion, civic duty, or cultural affinity, helps us to better understand a broader strategic repositioning among Vancouver's Chinese community associations. As student experiences are integrated into broader social trends developing in local community politics, we also gain a better understanding of the shifting meanings of being Chinese and engaging as such at the gateway.

Historically, the Chinese communities of Vancouver are the result of various immigration waves, including the second wave in the 1960s and 1970s from Fujian and Hong Kong, whose members built the Chinatown and lived somewhat separately from the other generations of Chinese newcomers (Mitchell 2004; personal interview with Alex, 14 May 2008). Following the third wave of Chinese immigration to Vancouver (1986–98), during which mostly Hong Kongese and Taiwanese made it to the gateway because of perceived political and economic turmoil at home, a fourth wave, starting in 1999, saw increased numbers of Mainlanders coming to Vancouver for specific reasons and needs; this wave included many international students (Ley 2008; personal interview with Rob, 29 May 2008; Waters 2002).

The positioning of these international students in local Chinese community politics can be understood through broader social trends affecting the city. As newcomers to Vancouver, they encounter already-established structures, mainly created by Hong Kongese, to incorporate and integrate into local social life, including Chinese Christian churches and social services associations such as SUCCESS (Montsion 2012; Olds 1998). Well-established Chinese community associations, whose membership participate in a lot of volunteer work, are the first ones to indicate how inclusive they are to any newcomer in need of support, but they also emphasize how different Chinese newcomers from the Mainland since 2000s are: "People from Hong Kong are used to work for their community but [for Mainlanders coming to us] as newcomers to Canada, they realize a new situation here: they need to work, learn and practice. It's challenging for us" (personal interview with Frank, 22 May 2008).

Despite being mostly run by Hong Kongese, well-established Chinese community associations such as SUCCESS have been playing on a certain ambiguity of what it means to be Chinese in Vancouver in order to adapt to new migration waves, and to integrate newcomers like international students (Vrasti and Montsion 2014). Based on their constant recruitment of newcomers and their economic and political leverage, well-established Chinese community associations often claim to speak for all Chinese in Vancouver (personal interview with Alex, 14 May 2008; personal interview with Carl, 3 November 2008). A Vancouver social city planner indicates that despite these organizations' efforts to open their membership and modify their ways to include newcomers from different Chinese backgrounds, there are strong Chinese ethnic differences and variations: "If people don't accept you ... it's more than language, it's the level of comfort" (personal interview with Vince, 12 June 2008). Besides Katharyne Mitchell's (2001) focus on the ethnicity of Chinese elites, such attitudes can supplement, at least to some extent, our understanding of the creation of these other groups.

A similar experience is witnessed with Chinese Christian churches, which are created, managed, and run mostly by Hong Kongese, and which are adapting to a new membership coming mostly from Mainland China (Nyíri 2003). Speaking of her own struggles as a church manager adjusting to newcomers from the Mainland, Frida has helped create specific services for recent newcomers, including linguistic and social services, and yet she is mostly shocked by the differences in cultural world views. Interestingly, Frida reports one of the main limitations of well-established Chinese community associations and Chinese Christian churches supporting newcomers as follows: "Chinese are helping Chinese. It's not melting people together" (personal interview with Frida, 6 June 2008). As such, she points to the fact that there is little emphasis on integration more broadly across ethnic groups, which not only creates specific challenges for Chinese Christian churches, but also for Christian churches in general, with very little effort being made to bring them together, despite their different ethnic audience (Hiebert and Ley 2003; Yu 2010).

With newly created Chinese community organizations like the CSSA, the Beijing Tong Xiang Kuay, the Canada Wenzhou Friendship Society, and the Zhong Guo Shuang Kuay, membership and community focus are clearer than they are for associations created decades ago. These organizations cater mostly to Mainlanders who generally live in Vancouver for a short time. As such, they have been increasingly vocal since 2005–6 to distinguish their claims from those of well-established Chinese community associations. Notably, in 2008 they organized various events independently from well-established Chinese community associations, integrating international student associations like the CSSA into their circles. After the 2008 snowstorms in China during the Chinese New Year, the 2008 Sichuan earthquakes, and the controversies around the 2008 Beijing Summer Olympics, these Mainlander associations have mobilized newcomers, including international students like Josh, who said that these events "triggered a sense of belonging to the motherland, not in patriotic ways, but as cultural and national pride" (personal interview with Josh, 31 October 2008). Despite the expected mobilization of SUCCESS and other well-established Chinese community associations in response to these events, newly created Mainlander associations have taken an independent approach to the recruitment and mobilization of financial resources (personal interview with Ralph, 18 June 2008). In the view of some community leaders, the 2008 mobilization of Mainlanders in Vancouver has created a change of direction for Chinese community organizations going forward: "This year is remarkable because two events [the earthquakes and the Olympics] through which we see the balance changing" (personal interview with Carl, 3 November 2008).

Despite increased competition among Chinese community associations, some significant steps toward closer linkages between these associations can also be observed. For example, in 2008 the annual SUCCESS fundraising gala featuring Hong Kongese cultural performances and mobilizing both the Hong Kongese networks in Vancouver and China Central Television, included for the first time a cultural gala called "Our Chinese Heart." The event was organized in close collaboration with approximately twenty newly created Mainlander associations, including the CSSA of UBC. Supported by associations such as the Canada Wenzhou Friendship Society and the Beijing Tong Xiang Kuay, this event constituted for many local observers a sign of the growing strength and political importance of these new Mainlander associations in Vancouver's Chinese community. This also highlights a shift in the landscape of Chinese community politics in Vancouver: "Mainland associations have a momentum and more supporters, but economically, they still need to improve. They should find their growing point" (personal interview with Carl, 3 November 2008).

In this view, international students are contributing to the shifting landscapes of Chinese community politics at the gateway. Representing a growing segment of Chinese immigration to Vancouver in terms of ethnic claim, sociological profile, and political allegiance, they are not only recruited to ensure a proper integration into Vancouver's everyday life, but are also integrated into the community politics of the gateway, whether consciously or not. Getting involved in these organizations for such varied reasons as working on a specific visa application, looking for employment, or to give back to the community, international students are also playing a role in legitimating the various Chinese voices in Vancouver and the ways in which these associations are adapting and developing their vision, programming, and future plans at the gateway.

Conclusion

The concept of Canada's Gateway to the Asia Pacific has translated into various governmental initiatives, including in post-secondary education, to facilitate the development of a business-driven, hands-off approach to providing a conducive environment for individuals, universities, and businesses to take the lead in connecting Asian and North American markets. In education, the emphasis has been put on the international education industry and the possibility of using international students to further Vancouver's local economic development. Despite the lack of community engagement in the formulation of the gateway strategies of both the Canadian and the BC governments, the stories and struggles of the international students related here are interesting sites revealing how various community linkages are created and maintained, to cope with the governments' and BC universities' priority to increase the numbers of international students coming from Mainland China.

Moreover, these stories of international students and their everyday engagements with local Chinese community associations at the gateway echo broader social trends emerging in Vancouver, including the use of volunteering to recruit and socialize international students to Vancouver into the set ways of well-established voluntary associations, the growing importance of Chinese Christian churches, and the emergence of new Mainlander associations, defined notably through their exclusive features. Part of a new wave of Chinese immigration to Vancouver, China's international students play a vital role in pluralizing the voices of the local Chinese communities, determining which local community association represents best the Mainlander newcomer perspective in Vancouver, and more broadly, redefining what it means to be and engage as Chinese people at the gateway.

With the increased academic attention in recent years on international education and international students in countries such as Australia, New Zealand, the United Kingdom, and the United States, the conventional focus has been on explaining key developments with reference to differences in policy environments and national contexts (see Kirby 2011; Levin 2003; Waters 2012). This study helps put such a conventional view in perspective, notably by highlighting the unique intersections between the trajectories of some Chinese international students in Vancouver and the various community associations and institutions they encounter. This research not only documents these students' life stories, but also maps their various activities in order to reveal a new dimension of the evolving community politics of Vancouver, where both student migrants and community associations struggle to find the meanings they associate with their encounters with one another, and with the consequences of the government's gateway narrative. By putting the emphasis on these intersections and encounters, this study considers these individual trajectories as an intrinsic part of Vancouver's evolving everyday life, and examines newcomers' contributions and willingness to engage with the city they inhabit while being international students in Canada.

References

Bauder, Harald. 2005. "Habitus, Rules of the Labour Market and Employment Strategies of Immigrants in Vancouver, Canada." *Social & Cultural Geography* 6 (1): 81–97. https://doi.org/10.1080/1464936052000335982.

BC Ministry of Economic Development. 2007. "British Columbia Asia Pacific Initiative." http://www.gov.bc.ca/jtst/down/api_report_2007_small.pdf.

British Columbia Council for International Education (BCCIE). 2014. "Three-year Update on the Economic Impact of International Education in British Columbia." http://www.bccie.bc.ca/sites/bccie_society/files/BCCIE%20 Infographic%20(Web).pdf.

Dennison, John D., and Hans G. Schuetze. 2004. "Extending Access, Choice, and the Reign of the Market: Higher Education Reforms in British Columbia, 1989–2004." *Canadian Journal of Higher Education* 34 (3): 13–38.

Evans, Paul. 2008. "The Asia Pacific Gateway and the Reconfiguration of North America." *Canadian Political Science Review* 2 (4): 93–8.

– 2010. "Gateway Dreams, Gateway Realities: The Governance and Policy Conundrum." Paper presented to the 2nd International Conference on Gateways and Corridors. Vancouver, BC, 17–19 November. http://www.iar .ubc.ca/LinkClick.aspx?fileticket=zfcezM3Vvp0%3D&tabid=380.

Greater Vancouver Gateway Council. 2007. "Vision for the Future of the Greater Vancouver Gateway: Transportation for Liveable Communities in a Global Economy." http://www.gvgc.org/PDF/GVGC%20Vision%202030.pdf.

Hiebert, Daniel, and David Ley. 2003. "Assimilation, Cultural Pluralism, and Social Exclusion Among Ethnocultural Groups in Vancouver." *Urban Geography* 24 (1): 16–44. https://doi.org/10.2747/0272-3638.24.1.16.

Illuminate Consulting Group. 2014. "2014 British Columbia International Education Intelligence Report." http://bccie.bc.ca/sites/bccie_society/ files/2014%20BC%20Intelligence%20Report%20(Web).pdf.

Kirby, Dale. 2011. "Strategies for Widening Access in a Quasi-Market Higher Education Environment: Recent Developments in Canada." *Higher Education* 62 (3): 267–78. https://doi.org/10.1007/s10734-010-9386-7.

Levin, John S. 2003. "Organizational Paradigm Shift and the University Colleges of British Columbia." *Higher Education* 46 (4): 447–67. https://doi.org/10.1023/A:1027375308484.

Ley, David. 2008. "The Immigrant Church as a Urban Service Hub." *Urban Studies (Edinburgh, Scotland)* 45 (10): 2057–74. https://doi.org/10.1177/0042098008094873.

Minister of International Trade. 2014. "Canada's International Education Strategy: Harnessing our Knowledge Advantage to Drive Innovation and Prosperity." http://international.gc.ca/global-markets-marches-mondiaux/assets/pdfs/overview-apercu-eng.pdf.

Mitchell, Katharyne. 2001. "Transnationalism, Neoliberalism and the Rise of the Shadow State." *Economy and Society* 30 (2): 165–89. https://doi.org/10.1080/03085140120042262.

– 2004. *Crossing the Neoliberal Line: Pacific Rim Migration and the Metropolis.* Philadelphia: Temple University Press.

Montsion, Jean Michel. 2011. "Softening Canada's Gateway to the Asia Pacific? Community Perspectives on Vancouver's International Image." *Canadian Journal of Urban Research* 20 (2): 36–55.

– 2012. "A Critique of Everyday International Relations: The Case of Cultural Pluralism in Singapore and Vancouver." *Environment and Planning. D, Society & Space* 30 (5): 930–46. https://doi.org/10.1068/d16310.

Nyíri, Pal. 2003. "Moving Targets: Chinese Christian Proselytising among Transnational Migrants from the People's Republic of China." *European Journal of East Asian Studies* 2 (2): 263–301. https://doi.org/10.1163/157006103771378428.

Olds, Kris. 1998. "Globalization and Urban Change: Tales from Vancouver via Hong Kong." *Urban Geography* 19 (4): 360–85. https://doi.org/10.2747/0272-3638.19.4.360.

Transport Canada. 2007. "Canada's Asia-Pacific Gateway & Corridor: A Strategic Context for Competitive Advantage." http://www.tc.gc.ca/CanadasGateways/APGCI/document/APGC-PCAP_en.pdf.

University of British Columbia (UBC). 2004. "Trek 2010: White Paper." http://www.trek2000.ubc.ca/whitepaper.html.

– 2007. "Where Does UBC Stand? A Letter to the UBC Community from President Stephen J. Toope." http://www.president.ubc.ca/KeyGoals_Community%20Letter%20_2_.pdf.

– 2008a. "Internationalization." http://www.internationalization.ubc.ca.

– 2008b. "International Students Get Involved." http://www.students.ubc.ca/
international/involved.cfm?page=top&view=work.
– 2012. "International Student Enrolment, Vancouver Campus." http://
www.pair.ubc.ca/enrolment%20reports/2012%20International%20
Enrolment%20Report.pdf.
– 2016. "Fact Sheet, Vancouver Campus, Winter 2015." http://pair2016.sites
.olt.ubc.ca/files/2016/04/UBCV-factsheet.pdf.
Union of BC Municipalities. 2007. "BC-Asia Twinning Toolkit: Opening BC
Communities to the World." https://tools.britishcolumbia.ca/Connect/
twinning/Documents/BCAsia_Twinning_Toolkit.pdf.
Vrasti, Wanda, and Jean Michel Montsion. 2014. "No Good Deed Goes
Unrewarded: The Values/Virtues of Transnational Volunteerism in
Neoliberal Capital." *Global Society* 28 (3): 336–55. https://doi.org/10.1080/1
3600826.2014.900738.
Waters, Johanna L. 2002. "Flexible Families? Astronaut Households and the
Experiences of Lone Mothers in Vancouver, British Columbia." *Social &
Cultural Geography* 3 (2): 117–34. https://doi.org/10.1080/146493602201
33907.
– 2006. "Emergent Geographies of International Education and Social
Exclusion." *Antipode* 38 (5): 1046–68. https://doi.org/10.1111/j.1467
-8330.2006.00492.x.
– 2012. "Geographies of International Education: Mobilities and the
Reproduction of Social (Dis)Advantage." *Geography Compass* 6 (3): 123–36.
https://doi.org/10.1111/j.1749-8198.2011.00473.x.
Yu, Li. 2010. "Christianity as a Chinese Belief." In *Asian Religions in British
Columbia*, ed. Larry DeVries, Don Baker, and Dan Overmyer, 233–48.
Vancouver: UBC Press.

Interviews

All names used are pseudonyms.
Alex. Local social services professional, Vancouver, 14 May 2008.
Alfredo. Expert on Chinese Christian movements in the Greater Vancouver,
Vancouver, 18 June 2008.
Bruce. Person involved in SUCCESS's everyday operations, Vancouver, 9 May 2008.
Carl. Local Chinese news director in the Greater Vancouver area, Richmond,
3 November 2008.
Colleen. Administrator, International House, UBC, Vancouver, 18 April 2008.
Eric. Senior Manager, BC Ministry of Economic Development, Vancouver, 21
May 2008.

Frank. Person involved with SUCCESS's everyday operations, Vancouver, 22 May 2008.

Frida. Manager of one of Vancouver's Chinese Christian churches, Vancouver, 6 June 2008.

John. Chinese international student, Vancouver, 24 April 2008.

Josh. Executive member, Chinese Students and Scholars Association of UBC, Vancouver, 31 October 2008.

Katie. Chinese international student, Vancouver, 24 April 2008.

Mindy. Chinese international student, Vancouver, 24 April 2008.

Mike. Former president, Chinese Students and Scholars Association of UBC, Vancouver, 19 June 2008.

Melanie. Canadian nurse of Chinese origin, Vancouver, 30 May 2008.

Philip. Chinese international student, Vancouver, 5 May 2008.

Ralph. Member of one of the newly created Mainlander associations, Vancouver, 18 June 2008.

Rob. Municipal official, City of Vancouver, Vancouver, 29 May 2008.

Vince. Social planner, City of Vancouver, Vancouver, 12 June 2008.

8 "Settlers" Meeting the "Settled": International Students Encountering the South Asian "Diaspora" in Ontario, Canada

GUNJAN SONDHI

Introduction

International students are the fastest-growing stream of new migrants entering Canada. Classed as "temporary migrants" in the Canadian immigration system, international student entries have increased annually at the rate of 4.8 per cent (in comparison, foreign workers have seen a 3.5 per cent annual growth). And of these growing numbers, students from India, make up the second largest group after those from China. As part of the "new" cohort of migrants from India, Indian international students are changing the demographic composition of the Indian community in Canada (Agrawal and Lovell 2010; Sondhi 2013). This "new" cohort, comprised of migrants entering Canada starting in the mid-1990s, is more highly educated and younger than their earlier counterparts.[1] International students, Indian or otherwise, by nature of their status and enrolment in higher education institutions (or HEIs), are more highly educated and younger – some as young as eighteen years of age when they arrive in Canada to pursue undergraduate studies (Sondhi 2013; Sondhi and King 2017).

In recognition of the impact of international students on the economy, labour market, and demographics of Canada (Kim and Sondhi 2015; Lu and Hou in this volume; Walton-Roberts and Hennebry in this volume), there is growing knowledge of the experiences of this group of migrants at the intersection of multiple social locations such as race,

---

1 See Agrawal and Lovell 2010 for a detailed analysis of trends and characteristics of the Indian diaspora in Canada.

class, and gender (Kim and Sondhi 2015; Sondhi 2013; Sondhi and King 2017). This volume is part of that growing body of literature. International students – simultaneously migrants and students – interact with a wide range of people and communities, across myriad social spaces. In the literature, three social spaces have been highlighted that emerge out of interactions with three specific groups[2]: "locals," other international students, and members of the diaspora. Little has been written on this last space of interaction and how those experiences shape international students, and conversely, how new migrants from the "homeland" (re)configure the diasporic community – in this case the Indian community in Toronto.

Within this context, the following discussion draws on gender theory to examine the power geometries of (im)mobilities of not only the subjects but also the associated spaces and practices (Cresswell 2006) between earlier migrant cohorts – the "old" Indian diaspora – and the "new Indians" comprising the current diaspora in Canada. By "new Indians," I mean those with "recent"[3] arrival status in Canada. This chapter explores these two sides of the interaction. First, through an examination of the performance of gender identity, the discussion reveals how the interactions with the "Indian" community in Toronto – a space that already has diverse hegemonic norms and expectations – impact the international student. Second, it looks at the other side of the coin: how international students – the "new" Indians arriving with diverse cultural, political, and social norms – also assert and (re)shape the norms of the community in Toronto. In so doing, this chapter aims to move beyond the traditional modernity framework that is often drawn upon to explain the differences between generations of a diasporic community. Instead, I draw on gender theory – the Butlerian vocabulary of *(un)intelligibility* of gender performances – to highlight the heterogeneity of the Indian diaspora in Toronto, as well as that of the new migrants arriving as international students.

By engaging with these ideas, my focus stretches beyond the mobile subject to include the social relations and emergent spaces within which the mobile

---

2 See Kim and Sondhi 2015 for a detailed review of literature on education migration to Canada.
3 The study specifically focuses on students arriving since 2005, but the "new Indians" focuses on those arriving since 2000, who are more highly educated and younger than their earlier cohorts (Agrawal and Lovell 2010).

subject interacts. The following two sections define the language that is used in this discussion and review the current research in the Canadian context on the experiences of international students. Section four briefly presents the methods of data collection for this research. Section five is divided into three subsections, each one exploring the different gender norms and identities being negotiated between the Indian community in Toronto and international students. Section six provides a concluding discussion.

Gender Theory and Migration

Feminist research has long established the gendered nature of migration (Donato et. al 2014; Kofman and Raghuram 2015; Sondhi and King 2017). Gender here is understood to be a social construction that is reproduced through repeated performances. Drawing upon Butler's interpretation of gender identity (Butler 1999), being a woman or man – possessing masculine or feminine characteristics – is a performance of the hegemonic norms in specific societal contexts. As McDowell (1999) summarizes, "for the majority of the population, [gender identity] is based on that heterosexual regulatory fiction. Through acts, gestures and clothes we construct or fabricate an identity that is manufactured, manifested and sustained through corporeal signs and other discursive beliefs." These performances and their meanings vary across time and space. The bodies that fit the normative gender performances of a space become the *subjects* in those spaces, and those that do not mutually constitute the position of the *abject* in that space. Butler (1999) refers to this as the *matrix of intelligibility*. As bodies traverse spaces they may encounter different meanings and performances of masculinities and femininities. This means that bodies and their performances will be *intelligible* – recognizable and accepted – in some spaces; and that in other spaces, those same bodies and their performances will be *unintelligible* – unrecognizable and unaccepted.

The spatio-temporal fluidity of gender identity is key to understanding migrants' experiences as the identity of a migrant is inherently fluid. As migrants shift from one societal context to another, and from one space to another, they perform their identities in terms of how they seek to present themselves within the specific societal and situational context. Migrants do this through their gestures, clothing, hair, etc. Identity then is (re)shaped continually by location and the societal context (McDowell 1999), and its expression can change from one situation to another, even within the same day. This is also particularly relevant in the case of international students whose identities are continually in motion – moving between and simultaneously possessing multiple identities of student/worker/son/daughter/husband/wife/parent and migrant statuses. They have to continually negotiate different power relations and social and cultural norms as they traverse multiple spaces. Hence, they have to know how to be intelligible in different social spaces.

International Students' Experiences

Migrants' experiences are simultaneously informed by multiple social structures and relations. The hierarchical power relations in each society produce a gendered experience – meaning that how a migrant negotiates everyday life and experiences is shaped according to his/her social location, both in the native and in the host society (Thapan 2005). Both the structural (class, labour market, etc.) and cultural (language, religion, "ways of life," etc.) aspects of both societies are relevant here. These experiences can be divided into three key categories: academic outcomes, social dimensions, and psychosocial well-being and adaptation (see Kim and Sondhi 2015 for a complete review). Results show that there are both positive and negative experiences, and that students often act (or practise avoidance) to achieve the former. The discussion below focuses on the social dimension of the student experience.

Starting with spaces of interactions within the boundaries of the educational institution, a major issue for international students is contact with "Canadians." Although the 2009 survey by the Canadian Bureau for International Education (CBIE) showed more than 70 per cent of international students had some or lots of success with making "Canadian" friends, numerous other quantitative and qualitative studies have shown that international students have struggled to befriend "Canadians," have felt socially excluded, and often wished for a greater degree of interaction (Chira, Barber, and Belkhodja 2013; Li, DiPetta, and Woloshyn 2012; Shin 2014). International students (and their spouses) tend to rely on other international students or co-nationals and co-ethnic communities for friendship and support (Canadian Bureau for International Education 2009; Chira, Barber, and Belkhodja 2013; Ghosh and Wang 2003; Houshmand, Spanierman, and Tafarodi 2014; Moores and Popadiuk 2011).

International students' social lives included other activities at educational institutions and in the outside community. Many of these activities were seen as a positive strategy for social integration and English language acquisition. Studies have shown that international students were actively involved in extra-curricular activities (Brunette et al. 2011; Grayson 2008; Popadiuk 2010). Another activity was part-time paid work, which was highlighted as an integrating and language-learning strategy by some students as well as a strategy to address financial insecurity (Chira, Barber, and Belkhodja 2013). However, it seems less than half of international students have participated in the on- or off-campus labour market (Canadian Bureau for International Education 2009). It is not known to what extent students may participate in the local informal labour market.

International student migration, like international migration generally, is often a family decision and involves spouses/partners and parents who, if they have accompanied students to Canada, face their own integration issues (Martens and Grant 2008; Waters 2002). Although the literature on the parents of international students tends to focus on younger students, studies of university students also recognized the significance of students' relationships with their parents (Waters 2002; Sondhi 2013; Sondhi and King 2017).

In many different types of studies, the experience of social exclusion and discrimination was a common theme (Chirkov et al. 2007, 2008; Houshmand, Spanierman, and Tafarodi 2014; Shin 2013, 2014; Madgett and Bélanger 2008). While the sources of discrimination varied, they included mostly what Houshmand, Spanierman, and Tafarodi (2014) refer to as racial microaggressions, or subtle forms of racism such as exclusion, avoidance, rendering invisible, and taunting accents. Racism in the form of cultural stereotypes (e.g., the cultural inferiority of Asian women) in local media was also found (Park 2010). Such experiences of exclusion have reconfigured international students' identities and objectives by leading to greater cohesiveness with co-nationals and less interaction with English-speaking Canadians, and occasionally, to the reformulation of international students' objectives (Houshmand, Spanierman, and Tafarodi 2014; Shin 2014).

Methods

Data collection included fourteen months of fieldwork in Toronto and New Delhi using mixed methods of data collection. The research was undertaken in both Canada and India to examine "the circulation of cultural meanings, objects, and identities in diffuse time-space"

(Marcus 1995). Ten months of ethnographic research was undertaken in Toronto by the author. In addition, in-depth, semi-structured interviews were conducted with 65 respondents: 22 current students at universities and colleges in Toronto, 23 family members/parents, and 20 students who had returned to New Delhi. Among the 42 students interviewed between Canada and India, 22 were women and 20 were men. Students interviewed in Canada were recruited through a snowballing method. The researcher, for the duration of the Canadian fieldwork, was based at a university in Toronto. This presence facilitated the researcher's access to a large body of students, particularly through Indian student organizations and social media. The recruitment in India started through personal and professional networks and was followed by the utilization of a snowballing method. The parents were also equally divided between those who had daughters studying abroad and those with sons. It also utilized an online survey to facilitate data collection on the socio-economic background and educational profiles of students, past and present, and their families, and to map mobility patterns from various points of origin in India to Canada.

(Re)Configuring Gender Performances to Become (Un)Intelligible

As international students (at both university and college) traversed these multiple spaces, they encountered different discourses concerning the performances of identities, such as that of a student, an Indian, a woman, and a man. Each space that emerged out of social interactions and relations (Massey 1994) with different groups of people (re)produced what were often heteronormative gendered discourses; some of these discourses were intelligible and others unintelligible to the students. The following discussion focuses on how these (un)intelligible performances were negotiated by the students in their interactions with the established Indian community in Toronto. These interactions are presented through a set of case studies. These cases were selected because they highlight the heterogeneity of international students' experiences. One aim is to problematize the often-used archetypes of Indian femininity and remove the exceptionalism through which the experiences of migrants from the Global South are read. Instead, by looking at interaction and negotiation, I want to draw attention away from the cultural exceptionalism of the "migrant" home country by making visible the "cultural" and gendered context of the "host" country as well.

Being Intelligible

Prita, an undergraduate student from an upper-caste Brahmin back-ground, sought out familiar spaces in an unfamiliar environment. Shortly after starting her program in Toronto, she joined the theatre group at her university, as this was something she was involved with in India. While she was familiar with and enjoyed the "theatre" part of the experience, she was uncomfortable with the pressures to perform in a way that was in keeping with hegemonic femininity of that space. The signifiers of the dominant notions of femininity within the theatre group included, but were not limited to, going out clubbing, drinking alcohol, and the norm of having sexual relations outside of marriage. She felt that the people in her theatre group did not understand her choice to defer sex until after marriage. Her choice of not engaging in pre-marital sexual relations was as unfamiliar to them as their choice to have sex before marriage was to her. Young migrants from more sexually conservative countries have expressed a similar dissonance when faced with an environment in which having multiple sexual partners was not just accepted but also encouraged. These youth feel the peer pressure to engage in sexual relations in order to perform the hegemonic gender identities needed to fit in better within a new social space (Hibbins 2005).

Prita's heterosexual femininity was unintelligible among her theatre peers. While she did not explicitly say that she was uncomfortable with people's expectations about sex, she contrasted her experience with the theatre group – whose members were predominantly white/non-Indian – to her experience with the Indian group she had a chance to know over the year.

> I felt that I needed to connect with people, connect with someone. So that's why I joined the [Indian] student club and I made a lot of friends that way. It was not too different for me ... we are from the same background so they understand the limitation

> ... I was more comfortable with this crowd and I was not really comfortable with the other in my first year because I didn't really know what was happening. I didn't know other things so it just made it a bit hard. (Personal interview with Prita, 2010–11)

Prita's gender identity – which included her choice not to have sex–was unintelligible within the social spaces inhabited by the members of the theatre group. However, her gender identity and performances were intelligible within the Indian group made up of her university peers in Toronto. Furthermore, she felt more comfortable in those spaces created through interaction with members of the Indian community than in other spaces. The awareness and acceptance of her gender performance within the "Indian" spaces allowed her to continue asserting her feminine identity.

Prita's case provides a counter-narrative to the sexual liberation experienced by migrants when they move to a "Western" country with more liberal views on sexuality (Ahmadi 2003). Indeed, Prita did not find her experience sexually liberating. She felt a specific heterosexual feminine performance was being forced upon her, one in which she was expected to pursue sexual relations. In response to the pressure to conform to the gender norms and expectations of the "local" space, Prita chose to leave the space for another – one in which her heterosexual femininity was intelligible.

Choosing to Become Intelligible

Prita's story reveals the ease with which she was accepted into the Indian community made up of her university peers. However, many respondents spoke of a different experience – having to reshape and readjust themselves so as to be accepted into the Indian community. As this and the following section show, not all youth feel they fit into the established Indian community in Toronto with the ease that Prita and others experienced. These youth, like Amrita and her friend Anoopa, undertake steps to become more intelligible by reconfiguring their gender performances to match those expected by the older members of the Indian diasporic community, and particularly the Sikh community in Toronto. Amrita and Anoopa, in their mid-twenties at the time of the interview, used to work as nurses in an urban centre in North India. They decided to retrain in Canada with the hope of continuing their professional trajectory here. In the meantime, they went to college in Toronto and survived by working as packers at a manufacturing plant located in Brampton. It was here that they first met members of the Indian community of Toronto – something that they had been actively seeking. They experienced a disjuncture between the gender norms they were familiar with in India and expected to find in Canada, and what they actually encountered in Canada. They were made aware that their behaviour did not fit into the community at their place of work through comments whispered by the older generation of Sikh community members who worked with them:

> The aunties and uncles would keep on staring at us, talking and whispering amongst themselves, making "chee chee" noises.[4] They would ask us what we are doing talking to the boys when we were unmarried. They would keep on telling us that it was not the correct way of doing things. (Personal interview with Amrita, 2010–11)

Amrita and Anoopa's casual association with male friends within the workplace was frowned upon by elder co-workers. They were told that young, single Sikh women should not associate with single men. This was an unfamiliar sentiment among Amrita and Anoopa's social network in India, and the two young women spoke of how frustrating it was to have this pointed out repeatedly.

As many scholars have written, the Sikh community in Canada is often labelled as a traditionalist community that holds on to values, especially with regard to gender roles, from a time when the earlier cohorts settled in Canada (Nayar 2004). Existing work on diaspora and communities abroad has already highlighted the tendency of diasporic communities to adhere to an "older" version of the culture and identity than the one that currently exists in the "home" country (Rayaprol 2005; Thobani 2005). In this body of literature, especially as it relates to South Asian communities, there is a strong sense of a (re)production of an "ideal" nationalistic identity that is tied to patriarchy, wherein women are expected to continue their orthodox gender role of caring and nurturing, and of being the holders of the Indian "cultural" nation; men, by contrast, are expected to preserve their dominant role as head of the household (Radhakrishnan 2009). However, these can also be read as the difference in knowledge of and familiarity with certain practices, and similarly, as an unfamiliarity with other practices. As the discussion in this chapter shows, some practices are unintelligible to others, and therefore the migrants choose to produce those practices with which they are familiar; to choose to leave spaces in which they are continually being constructed as the abject, and inhabit those in which they are the subject. Amrita and Anoopa's experience mirrors these recorded practices of diasporic

---

4 A "chee chee" noise is a way of showing displeasure and indicating that what the person is doing is undesired, shameful, or dirty in some manner.

communities. The disjunctures and conjunctures between the gender expectations and identities of this particular older Indian community in Toronto and the international students – the "new" Indians – is at the heart of the challenges that international students have to negotiate.

As part of this negotiation, Amrita and Anoopa made the choice to appear to "fit" into the norms of the Sikh community with which they associated – namely, by minimizing their interactions with male friends at work. But outside of work, they continued as before. They felt they needed to adapt and fit into the workspace and the wider community since they hoped to stay in Canada upon completing their education. The attempt to "integrate" and be intelligible forced these youth to change their gender performance into one they felt was "conservative" relative to the current gender matrix they inhabited in India.

This disciplining of the behaviour of young Sikh migrants' in homo-social spaces was also imposed upon Anoopa and Amrita's male friends. They, too, spoke about how they felt uncomfortable talking to their female friends in front of the older members of their community at their place of work. Hence, they would discipline their performances to make themselves intelligible at work; then, outside of that space – for example, at college and other social spaces away from the disciplining gaze of older members – they would continue their normal interactions with female friends.

There are more narratives from men about the changes undertaken to become more acceptable within the Indian communities' frame of hegemonic masculinities. In some cases, these changes included cutting one's hair very short or trimming one's beard, thus portraying a "safe" and clean-shaven Indian masculine identity. This "trimmed" look is seen as part of the transnational Indian masculine identity (Gill 2012a, 2012b), an image produced by the "old" Indians abroad, and emulated by "new" Indians "at home."

People reconfigured their performance of gender identity across different class and religious affiliations in similar ways. However, others chose to reject the norms that were imposed upon them by some parts of the South Asian community, withdrawing from many spaces while simultaneously creating new social spaces with other members of the South Asian community who shared an alternate set of communal norms. The section below highlights the experiences of respondents who did not fit into the broad norms of the South Asian community as they negotiated their gender and sexual identities, and who chose to remain unintelligible in those spaces.

Choosing to Remain Unintelligible

Instead of adapting to the expected norms, some students chose to withdraw from the spaces where they were not accepted and took steps to establish and access spaces where their gender and sexual identity were understood.

Two respondents, Nitasha (female) and Mayank (male), were cohabitating at the time I interviewed them. This performance of heterosexuality – the two were living together as an unmarried couple – did not fit within the hegemonic frames of reference of "Indian" spaces in either Toronto or India: their cohabitation produced a subversive queer sexuality. The term "queer" here refers to Manalansan's (2006) broad conceptualization "both as an anti-normative signifier as well as a social category produced through the 'intersectionality' of identities, practices, and institutions" (2006, 225). Even though, individually, Nitasha and Mayank may be intelligible within the spaces of the Indian community, as a pair performing their unmarried heterosexuality they did not fit into the hegemonic masculinities and femininities of most of the South Asian spaces in Toronto. Rather than adapt to the heterosexual marriage norms, they chose to continue living together – thus remaining unintelligible in those spaces. However, they continued to seek out other spaces within and outside the South Asian community where their performances were intelligible, and over the course of several years established a strong social network consisting of members of Indian and non-Indian communities in which their performances were intelligible. In other words, their performances in those spaces were hegemonic rather than subordinate.

Another respondent, Sameer, was a PhD student at the time I interviewed him. He came to Canada in the early 2000s for his undergraduate studies. He first moved from a large Indian city, with a population of over 10 million, to a small city outside of Toronto with fewer than 150,000 people. Sameer had been sexually active with other men by the age of eighteen and before he arrived in Canada. When he arrived in Canada, he felt uncomfortable expressing his sexuality in such a small town, and felt the need to hide his sexuality during his time there. He had the following to say about this experience:

The discourse is that you come here and become more sexually liberated and then do whatever, and then you repress yourself when you go back home.

... I was sexually active before I came here ... Here I repressed myself more than in India. In India I could hook up with someone online and meet up. I would be scared but not so much. But here, in [names city] the Indian community was so small ... much, much smaller ... and the community was very homophobic. I was so scared: what if I got caught? ... I was shit scared that I wouldn't know what to do. *I just didn't know how to be gay here* [my emphasis]. (Personal interview with Sameer, 2010–11)

Limited but growing research on queer sexualities in migration points to greater sexual freedom in "Western" countries than in non-Western countries (Ahmadi 2003; Hibbins 2005; Smith 2012). Smith (2012), in his study of South Asian gay men in Australia, attributes the suppression of young gay men's expressions of sexuality in India to the expectations of marriage, the social stigma of homosexuality, and lastly, the lack of private spaces for sexual exploration. By contrast, living in Australia, far away from their families, these young men feel relatively at ease engaging in sexual exploration due to greater access to private domestic spaces. Sameer's case provides a counter-narrative of the expressions of sexuality in migration. The difference between the Australian and the Canadian experience owes something to the different positionalities of the respondents, which resulted from different age groups and geographical location. The men in Smith's study were either studying or working in Australia, their minimum age was twenty-one, and they were all located in Melbourne, which Smith refers to as a "gay epicentre" (Smith 2012, 95) of the region. By contrast, Sameer, at eighteen, was much younger, and he had moved from the crowded streets of an Indian megacity to a small town in Ontario. Despite Canada's wider public position of being an LGBTQ-inclusive environment, Sameer was left with no access to safe spaces in the small university town. Sameer's relative inexperience when it came to living alone in a new culture, with little support and no access to safe queer spaces, in conjunction with a small population size, left him in a precarious position. His experience reflects the findings that the size and structures of cities and/or urban centres have an impact on migrants' experiences (Di Biase and Bauder 2005).

In the hierarchies of masculinity (Connell 1987), from hegemonic to subordinating to marginal, Sameer was aware of the marginal status of his race, gender, and sexual identity at his academic institution as well as in the wider town (which included a relatively small South Asian community). In order to fit in, he tried to adapt his performances to a less marginal and more intelligible heterosexual masculine performance by dating women. For three years, Sameer internalized the heterosexuality expected in small-town Canada while maintaining that, when he was in India, he "would be gay again." His subjectivities and his performance of sexuality shifted with his physical movement from one country to another. As he said, only in India (in a city with a much higher population density) was he able to fully explore his homosexuality, or he what he called "do[ing] his gay stuff." After several years of this balancing act, Sameer chose to come out the proverbial closet in Canada and make himself unintelligible in the small town to which he had moved, within the South Asian community, the university spaces in which he moved, and the wider town community (which was predominantly white). Sameer's story parallels Prita's experience, and in so doing provides us with a counter-narrative to that of the sexually liberating "West."

The cases presented above, which describe various ways of becoming (un)intelligible across spaces, reveal the complex negotiations that international students undertake within and outside of co-ethnic spaces. These students have to traverse and negotiate several other spaces, build social relationships with others, and then let go of those relationships, simultaneously accepting some gender norms while rejecting others. Prita, Amrita, Anoopa, Nitasha, Mayank, and Sameer – they all experienced multiple versions of being and acting like a man or a woman. And they all at some point or another tried to adapt to the norms of each space – to make themselves a subject of the particular matrix of intelligibility governing their respective spaces. These respondents continually transformed and shifted their gender identities to meet the expectations of the space and to fit in. Their continual transformations of the way they perform gender identity – through the length of their hair, their practise or non-practise of sexuality, and their clothing or make-up – reflect a search for spaces in which they belong. The different gender norms also reflected different class and religious identities, which influenced the participants' decisions as to which spaces to accept or reject, thereby accepting or rejecting specific discursive practices of gender.

Conclusion

This chapter has tried to re-narrate the bodies of international students through the lens of gender. The discussion aims to discredit the often essentialized image of the passive and docile bodies of the subaltern and make visible the agency that international students use to assert, adapt, or transgress the heteronormative matrix that appears to be the dominant discourse within the diverse spaces they inhabit in Toronto.

Overall, the students who had to undertake the least (re)negotiation of gender performances were those whose performances were already intelligible to the Indian community – even within specific cultural groups. Another group of international students finds that if they want to have access to the community, they need to adapt to its norms, even if those are different from the norms observed in India. However, not all choose to adapt to the community. And yet another group, especially those who do not fit into the particular definition of the hegemonic heteronormative matrix of the dominant Indian community, chose to stay away from the majority of the community; instead, they have established their own social spaces among people of Indian background – usually other Indian international students – and others who are also marginalized within the Indian community. This group chose to remain unintelligible, and also to assert their "queer" identity to subvert the dominant heteronormative matrix.

These varying experiences impact international students in different ways. Those who felt the need to, and decided to, adapt to the norms of the diasporic society spoke of feeling dissatisfied with their overall experiences. They often lamented feeling "out of place" and longed for a sense of belonging. Anecdotal evidence has revealed that many of these students have "returned" to India. Students who have taken steps to assert their gender and sexual identities – even if that placed them at the margins of Toronto's Indian community – appear to have established a strong network of people on whom they draw upon. Again, anecdotal evidence, gathered through communications with others in the network, reveals that these students are still in Canada – some having established families and gained permanent resident status.

Hence, this chapter serves three purposes. First, it makes visible the heterogeneity of the student migrants arriving from India, and of the Indian diaspora in Toronto. In doing so, it highlights the intergenerational struggles between migrant cohorts. The current cohort of migrants from India have their own views on gender norms and rights; and they are unashamedly asserting their identities, expectations, and norms in the face of the established South Asian community, while also asserting their identities outside of South Asian spaces – demanding recognition and forcing their bodies and identities to become intelligible (without being exoticized) in the wider Canadian gendered matrix of intelligibility. The nature and composition of the South Asian diaspora in Canada is changing and this "peek" into the interactions between the "new" and "old" Indian migrants shows the complexity of those negotiations.

Second, by discussing the gender matrices of multiple spaces, this chapter has also revealed the "gender matrix" of "Canadian" society, which is often overlooked in the discussion of experiences of migrants in that society. The assumption is often that the Canadian gender matrix is more "progressive" than those from which (non-white) migrants come. But as the cases of Prita and Sameer show, this is not always the case. Western white spaces were shown to be sexually repressive for those who were not willing to become intelligible within that matrix. As a consequence, this chapter provides a counter-narrative, one that challenges the discourse of the "West" as a place of sexual liberation for heterosexual and homosexual gendered identities.

Lastly, the use of gender theory to examine the experiences of this group of highly skilled migrants (and students) allows for a relocation of the body of work on highly skilled mobility. It offers avenues for future research that might not only "bring gender in" migration research, but also reveal new possibilities of analysis and narration.

References

Agrawal, Sandeep. K, and Alex Lovell. 2010. "High-Income Indian Immigrants in Canada." *South Asian Diaspora* 2 (2): 143–63. https://doi.org/10.1080/194 38192.2010.491295.

Ahmadi, Nader. 2003. "Rocking sexualities: Iranian migrants' views on sexuality." *Archives of Sexual Behavior* 32 (4): 317–26. https://doi. org/10.1023/A:1024038931202. Medline:12856893.

Brunette, Michelle K., Michel Lariviere, Robert J. Schinke, Xiaoyan Xing, and Pat Pickard. 2011. "Fit to Belong: Activity and Acculturation of Chinese Students." *Journal of Sport Behavior* 34 (3): 207–27.

Butler, Judith. 1999. *Gender Trouble: Feminism and the Subversion of Identity.* New York: Routledge.

Canadian Bureau for International Education. 2009. *Canada First: The 2009 Survey of International Students.* Ottawa: Canadian Bureau for International Education.

Chira, Sinziana, Pauline Barber, and Chedly Belkhodja. 2013. "Dreaming Big, Coming up Short: The Challenging Realities of International Students and Graduates in Atlantic Canada." *Atlantic Metropolis Centre's Working*

Paper Series 47–2013. http://community.smu.ca/atlantic/documents/ChiraDreamingbigcomingupshort_000.pdf.

Chirkov, Valery I., Saba Safdar, J. de Guzman, and K. Playford. 2008. "Further Examining the Role Motivation to Study Abroad Plays in the Adaptation of International Students in Canada." *International Journal of Intercultural Relations* 32 (5): 427–40. https://doi.org/10.1016/j.ijintrel.2007.12.001.

Chirkov, Valery, Maarten Vansteenkiste, Ran Tao, and Martin Lynch. 2007. "The Role of Self-Determined Motivation and Goals for Study Abroad in the Adaptation of International Students." *International Journal of Intercultural Relations* 31 (2): 199–222. https://doi.org/10.1016/j.ijintrel.2006.03.002.

Connell, R.W. 1987. *Gender and Power: Society, the Person and Sexual Politics.* Stanford: Stanford University Press.

Cresswell, Tim. 2006. *On the Move: Mobility in the Modern Western World.* London: Routledge.

Di Biase, Sonia, and Harald Bauder. 2005. "Immigrant Settlement in Ontario: Location and Local Markets." *Canadian Ethnic Studies* 37 (3): 114–34.

Donato, Katharine M., Bhumika Piya, and Anna Jacobs. 2014. "The Double Disadvantage Reconsidered: Gender, Immigration, Marital Status, and Global Labor Force Participation in the 21st Century." *International Migration Review* (48): 335–76. https://doi.org/10.1111/imre.12142.

Ghosh, Sutama, and Lu Wang. 2003. "Transnationalism and Identity: A Tale of Two Faces and Multiple Lives. "*Canadian Geographer. Geographe Canadien* 47 (3): 269–82. https://doi.org/10.1111/1541-0064.00022.

Gill, Harjant S. 2012a. "Becoming Men in a Modern City: Masculinity, Migration and Globalization in North India." PhD Dissertation, American University. http://aladinrc.wrlc.org/handle/1961/11035.

– 2012b. "Masculinity, Mobility and Transformation in Punjabi Cinema: From *Putt Jattan De (Sons of Jat Farmers)* to *Munde UK De (Boys of UK)*." *South Asian Popular Culture* 10 (2): 109–22. https://doi.org/10.1080/14746689.2012.682858.

Grayson, J. Paul. 2008. "The Experiences and Outcomes of Domestic and International Students at Four Canadian Universities." *Higher Education Research & Development* 27 (3): 215–30. https://doi.org/10.1080/07294360802183788.

Hibbins, Ray. 2005. "Migration and Gender Identity among Chinese Skilled Male Migrants to Australia." *Geoforum* 36 (2): 167–80. https://doi.org/10.1016/j.geoforum.2003.10.003.

Houshmand, Sara, Lisa B. Spanierman, and Romin W. Tafarodi. 2014. "Excluded and avoided: Racial microaggressions targeting Asian international students in Canada." *Cultural Diversity & Ethnic*

Minority Psychology 20 (3): 377–88. https://doi.org/10.1037/a0035404. Medline:25045949

Kim, Ann, and Gunjan Sondhi. 2015. "Bridging the Literature on Education Migration." *Population Change and Lifecourse Strategic Knowledge Cluster Discussion Paper Series/ Un Réseau Stratégique de Connaissances Changements de Population et Parcours de Vie Document de Travail* 3 (1), Article 7. http://ir.lib .uwo.ca/pclc/vol3/iss1/7.

Kofman, Eleonore, and Parvati Raghuram. 2015. *Gendered Migrations and Global Social Reproduction.* Basingstoke, UK: Springer.

Li, Xiaobin, Tony DiPetta, and Vera Woloshyn. 2012. "Why Do Chinese Study for a Master of Education Degree in Canada? What Are Their Experiences?" *Canadian Journal of Education* 35 (3): 149–63.

Madgett, Paul J., and Charles Bélanger. 2008. "International Students: The Canadian Experience." *Tertiary Education and Management* 14 (3): 191–207. https://doi.org/10.1080/13583880802228182.

Manalansan, Martin F. 2006. "Queer Intersections: Sexuality and Gender in Migration Studies." *International Migration Review* 40 (1): 224–49. https:// doi.org/10.1111/j.1747-7379.2006.00009.x.

Marcus, George E. 1995. "Ethnography In/Of the World System: The Emergence of Multi-Sited Ethnography." *Annual Review of Anthropology* 24 (1): 95–117. https://doi.org/10.1146/annurev.an.24.100195.000523.

Martens, Vonda Plett, and Peter R. Grant. 2008. "A Needs Assessment of International Students' Wives." *Journal of Studies in International Education* 12 (1): 56–75. https://doi.org/10.1177/1028315306293547.

Massey, Doreen. 1994. *Space, Place, and Gender.* Minneapolis: University of Minnesota Press.

McDowell, Linda. 1999. *Gender, Identity and Place: Understanding Feminist Geographies.* Minneapolis: University of Minnesota Press.

Moores, Lisa, and Natalee Popadiuk. 2011. "Positive Aspects of International Student Transitions: A Qualitative Inquiry." *Journal of College Student Development* 52 (3): 291–306. https://doi.org/10.1353/csd.2011.0040.

Nayar, Kamala Elizabeth. 2004. *The Sikh Diaspora in Vancouver: Three Generations Amid Tradition, Modernity, and Multiculturalism.* Toronto: University of Toronto Press.

Park, Hijin. 2010. "The Stranger That Is Welcomed: Female Foreign Students from Asia, the English Language Industry, and the Ambivalence of 'Asia Rising' in British Columbia, Canada." *Gender, Place and Culture* 17 (3): 337–55. https://doi.org/10.1080/09663691003737603.

Popadiuk, Natalee. 2010. "Asian International Student Transition to High School in Canada." *Qualitative Report* 15 (6): 1523–48.

Radhakrishnan, Smitha. 2009. "Professional Women, Good Families: Respectable Femininity and the Cultural Politics of a 'New' India." *Qualitative Sociology* 32 (2): 195–212. https://doi.org/10.1007/s11133-009-9125-5.

Rayaprol, Aparna. 2005. "Being American, Learning to Be Indian: Gender and Generation in the Context of Transnational Migration." In *Transnational Migration and the Politics of Identity*, ed. Meenkashi Thapan, 130–49. New Delhi: Sage.

Shin, Hyunjung. 2013. "Ambivalent Calculations in Toronto: Negotiating the Meaning of Success among Early Study Abroad High School Students." *Asian and Pacific Migration Journal* 22 (4): 527–46. https://doi.org/10.1177/011719681302200404.

– 2014. "Social Class, Habitus, and Language Learning: The Case of Korean Early Study-Abroad Students." *Journal of Language, Identity, and Education* 13 (2): 99–103. https://doi.org/10.1080/15348458.2014.901821.

Smith, Geoffrey. 2012. "Sexuality, Space and Migration: South Asian Gay Men in Australia." *New Zealand Geographer* 68 (2): 92–100. https://doi.org/10.1111/j.1745-7939.2012.01229.x.

Sondhi, Gunjan. 2013. "Indian International Students in Toronto: Exploring Young Men Resisting Their Family's Expectations." *South Asian Diaspora* 5 (2): 223–35. https://doi.org/10.1080/19438192.2013.750957.

Sondhi, Gunjan, and Russell King. 2017. "Gendering International Student Migration: An Indian Case-Study." *Journal of Ethnic and Migration Studies* 43 (8): 1308–24. https://doi.org/10.1080/1369183X.2017.1300288.

Thobani, Sunera. 2005. "Cultured Girls: Race, Multiculturalism and the Canadian State." In *Transnational Migration and the Politics of Identity*, ed. Meenkashi Thapan, 252–83. New Delhi: Sage.

Waters, Johanna L. 2002. "Flexible Families? 'Astronaut' Households and the Experiences of Lone Mothers in Vancouver, British Columbia." *Social & Cultural Geography* 3 (2): 117–34. https://doi.org/10.1080/14649360220133907.

9 Global Restructuring, Gender, and Education Migration: Chinese Immigrant Women Professionals in Canada

GUIDA C. MAN AND ELENA CHOU

Introduction

In the last decade or so, there has been a marked increase in the number of students coming from Mainland China to Canada. Data on international students reveal the extent to which students from Mainland China are impacting the Canadian educational system. Between 2006 and 2014, for example, the number of Chinese students present in Canada increased from 49,579 to 128,750 (CIC 2015, 34). During that same period, the number of international students arriving in Canada from China annually more than doubled, from 24,070 in 2006 to 62,262 in 2014 (CIC 2015, 36), comprising, respectively, 19 per cent and 29 per cent of the total number of international students arriving in Canada for those years. To put this into perspective, the number of permanent residents from Mainland China numbered 33,518 in 2006 (13 per cent of the total number of permanent residency permits granted, and the second-most populous source country after India) and 24,640 in 2014 (10 per cent and the third-most populous source country after the Philippines and India, respectively) (CIC 2014). The majority of Chinese in Canada reside in the census metropolitan areas of Vancouver and Toronto; in 2001, 72 per cent of all Chinese lived in these two cities (Statistics Canada 2007), and by 2011 it still remained high, at 71 per cent (Statistics Canada 2013).

There is ample data, as well as sufficient literature, examining how Chinese students fare in the Canadian post-secondary system (see, for example, Wong 1979 and Minichiello 2001) and looking at their motivations for choosing Canada for their university education (see, for example, Waters 2006; Chen 2007; Lu, Zong, and Schissel 2009). However, there has been relatively little research on those who take the immigration pathway to Canada from China for education purposes. In particular, little research has focused on the gendered experiences of these immigrants. In this chapter, we focus on the experiences of highly educated Chinese women who immigrate to Canada for the purpose of enabling their children to obtain a Canadian education.

Focusing on education migration as a gendered process and a strategy for social reproduction, this chapter investigates how Chinese immigrant women and their families adopt transnational migration practices as a strategy to provide what they perceive as better educational opportunities for their children and for themselves. Our research starts with Chinese immigrant women's individual articulations of their own migration trajectories. We also explore how their education migration strategies are embedded in the context of changing social, economic, political, and cultural processes in both China and Canada, and how these have made Canada a desirable destination for education migration. We will present our data analysis by first exploring these women's motivations for immigration. We will then explain education (im)migration and the experiences of Chinese immigrant women professionals, as well as their transnational strategies for social reproduction. Finally, we will end the chapter with some concluding observations.

Framework and Methodology

The conceptual framework and methodology of this study is informed by feminist theory and institutional ethnography (Smith 1987, 2005), and we seek to address the intersections of gender, race, and class (see, for example, hooks 1984; Ng 1993). The study puts Chinese immigrant women professionals at the centre of this inquiry, and links their accounts of their experiences to the larger processes in which their experiences are embedded. The goal is to investigate how individual immigrant women as subjects account for their situations, and to demonstrate how their subjective experiences are articulated within larger social, economic, political, and cultural processes.

Research Design

In-depth interviews were employed as the primary data collection method for this research. A life history approach (Cole and Knowles 2001) was used to interview the participants. Each interview lasted at least two hours. The research subjects analyzed for this chapter were immigrant women professionals from Mainland China, one of the largest immigrant groups in Canada. With the exception of three interviews, which were conducted by a research assistant alone, all the interviews were conducted in pairs by the principal investigator assisted by a research assistant. The research assistant's job was to take detailed impression notes, focusing on the interviewee's emotions. The study was restricted to within Ontario and largely within the Greater Toronto Area (GTA), where the majority of immigrants reside (CIC 2014). This chapter derived its analysis from sixteen immigrant women from Mainland China who immigrated to Toronto between 1998 and 2008, when immigrants from Mainland China became the largest immigrant group in Canada. We adopted a multi-pronged approach in our sampling by contacting various sources: the community and professional networks we have established from previous projects and outreach, the ethnic media (newspapers and websites), and posting in community centres and grocery stores. We used a snowball sampling method to generate additional participants from our original list of participants. The women were interviewed in the language of their choice, either in Mandarin (their native language) or in English. We included those women who have a university degree/college diploma; who have worked as a professional (e.g., as an accountant, teacher, engineer, medical doctor, etc.) before immigrating to Canada; and who were married/divorced at the time of the interview, have at least one child, and have immediate or extended family members in their home country.

Data Analysis

The data for this chapter is derived from an analysis of sixteen in-depth interviews with Mainland Chinese immigrant women from a larger Social Sciences and Humanities Research Council–funded research project entitled "Transnational Migration Trajectories of Immigrant Women Professionals in Canada: Strategies of Work and Family" (henceforth TTWF).[1] The project focused on two groups of immigrant women professionals: those from Mainland China, and those from India.

---

1 The TTWF project was supported by Social Sciences and Humanities Research Council of Canada Research Grant no. 410-2009-2453 to Guida Man as principal investigator, and T. Das Gupta, K. Mirchandani, and R. Ng (deceased) as co-investigators.

The data analysis of this chapter focuses on Chinese immigrant women who worked as professionals in their home country. Of the sixteen women interviewed, ten identified their children's education as one of the reasons, if not the sole reason, for their decision to immigrate to Canada. All sixteen of the women were highly educated and worked as skilled professionals in Mainland China. At the time of immigration, all had at least one university degree. Their degrees were in various fields such as medicine, education, engineering, physics, sociology, biochemistry, IT, business administration, accounting, and English literature. Eight of the women had master's degrees, including one woman who had two master's degrees. One woman had a PhD. The women ranged in age from thirty-five to sixty-four at the time of the interviews. Fifteen were married, and one was separated from her common law spouse. All of the women had at least one child, and three had two children. Prior to coming to Canada, three had worked as physicians; six as high school, college, or university teachers in various fields; two in accounting; two in sales; one as an operations manager in the IT field; one in telecommunications engineering; and one as a social worker for the government. In terms of the immigration process to Canada, seven of the women were the principal applicants through the Federal Skilled Worker stream, primarily because they had more points in their immigration application compared to their spouse. Two of the women immigrated alone to Canada, one against the wishes of her spouse, who remained in China with their son.

Motivation for Immigration: Social Reproduction and Children's Education

Most Mainland Chinese families immigrate to Canada as a family unit. However, due to unemployment and underemployment, some husbands opt to return to China to continue their work or business, while the wives typically stay in Canada to care for children and to ensure that the children could ease into the Canadian educational system. Confucian ideals, which in recent years have been revived in China as part of the economic restructuring project, thrust individual families, particularly mothers, into positions of responsibility for their children's education and well-being. This is reminiscent of the ideology of intensive mothering in Western cultures, which induced women to be the sole carer of their children. At the same time, gendered processes of social reproduction further require mothers to be primarily responsible for the work of mothering.

Social reproduction refers to the myriad activities that sustain and reproduce the labour force, as well as the institutions and ideologies that help support and/or maintain those activities (Bakker 2007). These include activities required for daily sustenance; institutions and activities related to generational reproduction, such as education, employment, and care work; and institutions and activities related to the biological reproduction of the population (Bezanson and Luxton 2006; Bakker 2007; Steans and Tepe 2010).

Furthermore, "particular patterns of social reproduction are shaped by and also shape socio-economic and political orders" (Bakker and Silvey 2008, 3). Thus, we need to examine social reproduction in relation to globalization and the interrelations between economies in the Global North and the Global South, the public and private spheres, and the local and the global (Bakker and Silvey 2008). Education migration highlights the transnational dimension of social reproduction and also outlines how education migration as a strategy of social reproduction is dialectically contingent upon particular social, political, and economic contexts (see Kim 2015).

A recurring theme in the interviews for the women who decided to immigrate primarily for their children's education was their perception, whether real or imagined, that the Chinese educational system was too rigid, too demanding, or too academically competitive for their children. They voiced their preference to have their children educated in a more relaxed and less difficult educational environment, similar to the kind found, or perceived to be found, in Canada. Xui,[2] for example, stated:

> [The] reason I wanted to immigrate was for my child. My child faced so much pressure when trying to get into a better school in China. It is very competitive in China. (TTWF, CH10)[3]

---

2 All names are pseudonyms, as interviewees are assured of confidentiality and anonymity.

3 "CH10" refers to Mainland Chinese immigrant interviewee number 10. Since the research involves immigrant women from Mainland China and from India, "CH" is used to indicate Mainland Chinese immigrant women, while "IN" is used to indicate Indian immigrant women. For the purpose of this chapter, only the analysis of Mainland Chinese immigrant women professionals is used.

Similarly, another woman, Ping, was also concerned about the demanding school system in China, which she did not want her son to experience:

> [Students have] much heavier workloads [in China] compared to the students [in Canada]. Here they learn in school by playing, [and there are] a lot of opportunities to explore the world. But in China, [there are] very high academic demands. So for them, it's a heavy burden ... I don't want that to happen to my son, because I was a victim of that educational system. (TTWF, CH04)

The women's negative perception of the education system in China, along with their preference for Western education and their complaints about the high cost of living in China, can be linked to the larger context of economic restructuring in China. In the post-Mao era, Chinese reformers began to dismantle the rigid structure of the planned economy. As part of this new economic strategy, the Chinese state began integrating into the global capitalist economy by selling off state-owned enterprises while encouraging foreign direct investment (Boyd 2006).

Furthermore, China's rapid economic transformation over the last three decades has been accompanied by the emergence of a new middle class. According to a 2001 study undertaken by the Chinese Academy of Social Sciences, the middle class – consisting of managers, private entrepreneurs, professional and technical workers, and clerical workers – accounted for 15 per cent of the Chinese workforce in 1999 and was expected to grow to 19 per cent by 2003 and 25 per cent, or about 170 million people, by 2010 (Flew 2006, 422).

In the post-reform era, middle-class managers and professionals, along with private entrepreneurs, have now become the central players in the rising rural and urban market economies in China (Bian 2002). Zhang (2005) points out that prior to these reforms, only a few high-ranking Chinese Communist Party (CCP) cadres were able to enjoy an affluent lifestyle based on their elite political status rather than their personal wealth. Increasingly, however, status and wealth are no longer acquired solely through party membership, although CCP members and their families continue to maintain lives of privilege.

An emerging aspect of the rapidly growing middle class in China is its aspirational character. Wealthy middle-class Chinese are able to use their financial power to pursue lifestyles that are not affordable to the majority of the population (Zhang 2005; Deng 2006; Woronov 2011). Hence, although the middle classes encompass varied occupations, incomes, and social levels, their cultural and consumption practices, which are based on the values and lifestyle of "a small group of well-educated urban consumers ... ideologically dominate the concept of urban citizenship today" and therefore serve as the aspirational model for modern Chinese values and behaviour (Woronov 2011, 80). Activities such as eating foreign food and consuming foreign goods, for example, have become one of the primary ways for members of the Chinese middle class to define themselves as distinct individuals and as professionals (Zhang 2005).

The aspirations of this growing middle class are exemplified by an increasing sense of cosmopolitanism. These cosmopolitan aspirations have been facilitated in large part by the emergence of the English language, through histories of colonization and imperialism, as the dominant language of globalized capitalism, and in a globalized context in which Western cultural and social norms are promoted and privileged (Matthews and Sidhu 2005; Waters 2005; Igarashi and Saito 2014; Kim 2015). This cosmopolitanism not only refers to developing international tastes in consumption, but also in a greater awareness of the differences between Chinese and Western social norms, values, and lifestyles. Such awareness may extend to criticisms of Chinese institutions, such as the country's education system. As such, English-language education in a Western setting becomes not only a market commodity for the Chinese middle class, but also a marker of class distinction linked with values of worldliness, modernity, and progress (Matthews and Sidhu 2005; Waters 2005; Tsang 2013).

Lei, for example, recounted how she felt that her son was being treated unfairly by some of his teachers in China, and she expressed hope for a less difficult experience for him in Canada:

> My son was very naughty. He had good marks and he is a very smart boy. But they didn't like him, and ... remember the national sports games and they had the opening? Their school chose to have a performance there, and my son practiced, and one day the teachers said, "...we worry about you naughty kids; you may make trouble." So they removed him from the performance. They treated kids not fairly. They told some kids they were stupid or they had lower marks or they were something ... you know what they say? They are very discriminatory things. I don't feel good [about it].

Many middle-class Chinese women believe the Western education system provides a better environment for their children's social development. As Lei explained, she wanted a Western education for her son:

> My son of course is considered smart, but naughty. So he is ... considered... not advanced or not brain advanced [according to the Chinese educational system] ... So my son was not very positive in learning. So that's why I want a chance for him to get Western education. (TTWF, CH06)

Another woman, Ping, voiced her perception of the competitiveness in Chinese education vis-à-vis what she perceived to be a healthier lifestyle in Canada:

> Because, I believe the education ... the kids can do more [in Canada], really, to learn everything ... how to socialize with people, everything, like the spiritual part. So, I would like to have my son live a very healthy lifestyle; not everything is only work, money. That was my concern. High competition sometimes has a very negative impact on young kids. (TTWF, CH04)

Some parents who cannot afford or do not want to pay the high cost of an international education for their children choose to immigrate to a Western country so that their children will obtain a Western education. The countries that are typically favoured in this regard include Canada, Australia, and to a lesser extent, the United States. Many Chinese immigrants are aware of the prospect of possible downward mobility in the new country. They were willing to make the sacrifice for the sake of their children's education. For some families, their children's education is only one factor, albeit a major one, in their decision to emigrate. Other factors – such as the fear of increasing economic insecurity, a lack of trust in the Chinese government, or the escalation in human rights violations – cumulate to erode confidence in their country. As the expansion of the free market system results in growing occupational and economic instability, guaranteed or lifelong employment can no longer be taken for granted. Ping, for example, notes that the cost of living in China is rising, particularly when it comes to medical expenses and the cost of education, and highlights the difficulties in finding a "decent job" in China. These combined reasons provide the motivation for middle-class Chinese to immigrate to Canada.

While these women's narratives highlight their belief in the assumed superiority of Western education over that found in China, a body of literature has emerged to challenge this taken-for-granted perception. Song (2016a, 2016b), for example, is particularly critical of the Western emphasis on "critical thinking," a skill students from Asian countries are perceived as especially lacking due to what is presumed to be their more rigid and conservative styles of pedagogy, which emphasize rote learning and memorization. She argues that "critical thinking" is an ethnocentric and culturally specific concept that characterizes Chinese students as "deficient" in comparison to their Western counterparts. Nevertheless, the women's views emphasize how these binary descriptions of Western and Chinese education systems have become "part of the 'social imaginary' in the globalisation of higher education" (Song 2016b, 143).

The aspirations of the growing middle class in China and the globalization of education have facilitated the popularity of Western education as a form of cultural capital integrally linked to social reproduction. The globalization of education involves the marketization of education focused on the intense recruitment of international students, primarily from Asian countries to English-speaking ones (Matthews and Sidhu 2005). As Igarashi and Saito (2014) note, the "globalization of education helps institutionalize Western academic qualifications as proxies of cosmopolitanism as globally-circulable cultural capital" (233). Cultural capital broadly refers to the institutionalized forms of knowledge, such as qualifications and educational certificates, which can be used or converted by its bearer to gain greater prestige, honour, social status (symbolic capital), or economic benefits (economic capital) (Bourdieu 1986, 243–5). Thus, for some women obtaining a Canadian education for their children can be seen as an investment, one that will enhance their children's future assets, particularly in a context where their a priori middle-class status in China will no longer guarantee a prosperous or stable future. The erosion or elimination of entitlement programs and benefits for Chinese state employees, such as for housing, child care, and pensions (Hung and Chiu 2003), in addition to the ongoing economic changes in China, have intensified the precariousness of middle-class life there. As such, an English-language, Western-based education is perceived as a way for middle-class Chinese to preserve and perhaps even improve their class status as well as their chances for intergenerational mobility (Huang and Yeoh 2005; Waters 2005; Tsang 2013).

Thus, framed within an increasingly precarious social and economic context and a highly competitive educational environment in China, the cultural capital accrued through a Canadian education can be viewed as a safety net within which middle-class professional women can ensure a more stable career and economic future for their children. Although these women may currently be experiencing precarious employment, downward career mobility, or transnational family situations, education migration to Canada is viewed as a strategy by which they can maintain and reproduce their middle-class status through their children.

Other women decide to invest not only in their children's education, but in their own as well. Lynn's decision to immigrate to Canada was driven by a desire to advance her own career as well as her son's education. She had completed a master's degree in the Netherlands before applying to pursue a doctoral degree at the University of Toronto. Here is what she told us:

> In his school, some of [my son's] classmates went to study in European countries like the UK, or Australia, so he said he would like to study abroad. Then I said it's hard there.

> Here it's easy. Why not I go first and then he came [afterwards] … In China, it's also challenging to find a position in a university nowadays. It's quite challenging for new grads. (TTWF, CH16)

Education (Im)migration and the Experience of Chinese Immigrant Women Professionals

Some Chinese immigrant women note that Canada is considered "easy" to apply to for immigration, and Canadian universities are also perceived as "relatively easy" to get into compared to Chinese universities. For example, here is what Jing said:

> Canada is easy to apply … You know in China, there is a big competition for kids to go to university. I think here it's relatively easy for kids to go to university. (TTWF, CH03)

The relative ease with which these highly educated and skilled women professionals are able to immigrate to Canada can be explained as a product of the ascent of neo-liberal economics in Canada. During the post–Second World War era, from 1945 to 1975, Canada joined other Western liberal democracies in its focus on developing a Keynesian welfare state with the goals of full employment and broad social security coverage (McBride 2005; Workman 2009). Since the 1970s, and continuing into the 1980s and 1990s, a neo-liberal economic policy began to take hold throughout the West, exemplified by the policies of the right-wing conservative governments of Margaret Thatcher in Britain and Ronald Reagan in the United States. The election of Brian Mulroney's Progressive Conservative Party in 1984 heralded the emergence of neo-liberal ideology and economic practice in Canada.

This trend has continued through changes in governments. The Liberal government of Jean Chrétien, elected in 1993, did not reverse this path, but rather continued the dismantling of the Keynesian welfare state in Canada. The Liberal Party focused on neo-liberal fiscal policies, such as balanced budgets and privatization. Massive cuts in federal funding were made to education, health care, and housing, and funding to provinces for social welfare programs was severely reduced. Funding in these areas have not been restored by subsequent federal governments. A more insidious ideological effect of the expansion and normalization of neo-liberal economic policy in Canada is the way in which individuals, rather than the state, are now responsible for their own well-being.

Neo-liberal economic and social policies have also permeated various Canadian institutions, including Canadian immigration policy. Although Canada eliminated its race-based immigration policy in 1967 in favour of a points-based system, Canadian immigration policy has shifted to reflect neo-liberal ideology. There is an increasing emphasis on human capital, which manifests in a preference for immigrants who will benefit the Canadian economy, increase Canada's economic competitiveness abroad, and bolster international trade (Abu-Laban and Gabriel 2002; Man 2002, 2004). Canadian immigration policy currently favours highly skilled and well-educated immigrants who are self-sufficient and therefore not dependent, and are unlikely to become a "burden" on, the state (Abu-Laban and Gabriel 2002; Man 2002). Social scientists have highlighted the numerous ways in which gender bias operates in Canadian immigration policy (see, for example, Arat-Koç 1999; Mojab 1999; Man 2004; Boucher 2016). This includes the division between principal and secondary applicants rooted in a male breadwinner/female dependent model, which has negative implications for women who generally tend to be the secondary applicants while being equally skilled or qualified, as well as immigrant selection criteria that does not take into account the different life courses of men and women, the latter of whom are more likely to be engaged in non-continuous employment due to care work.

Concurrently, policies pursued at various governmental levels and by educational institutions have aimed to position Canada as an attractive destination for economic immigrants, particularly those who immigrate for the sake of education. While international students are not immigrants, and they are not the focus of this chapter, it should be mentioned here that they are also being increasingly targeted by Canadian educational institutions as a source of revenue, as well as to diversify or enhance the existing Canadian student body (see Kwak 2013).

However, despite Canada's reputation as an immigrant-friendly nation with a generous welfare state, its neo-liberal economic climate and the continual cutbacks to its social welfare system have resulted in many highly skilled immigrants finding themselves underemployed and without the resources and support needed to maximize their potential in Canada. Although such immigrants have been recruited specifically for their high value as human capital, they are prevented from working in their professions in Canada by various institutional and structural barriers. Numerous studies have outlined the particular struggles that highly educated immigrants face in Canada (see, for example, Mojab 1999; Reitz 2001; Anisef, Sweet, and Frempong 2003; Man 2004, 2015; Li 2008; Sakamoto, Chin, and Young 2010; Goldmann, Sweetman, and Warman 2011; Sweetman 2014). These include, among others, the lack of recognition of international education and work experience by Canadian employers, racism and sexism in Canadian society, transnational portability of human capital (education, skills, etc.), quality of education from the source country, the requirement by some employers for "Canadian experience," lack of fluency in English or French, and lack of familiarity with Canadian work culture (i.e., "soft skills").

As would be expected, the ten women in this study who immigrated to Canada for their children's education are all currently experiencing de-skilling, downward career mobility, and precarious employment. One reason for this is that their training in China was in different education and technological systems, with distinct rules, regulations, and norms compared to those in Canada. Jing and Xui, for example, were both medical doctors in China but neither are currently employed as doctors, as their medical degrees are not recognized in Canada. Jing works as a technical assistant in a doctor's office while enrolled in a registered practical nurse program at Seneca College, while Xui works as a technician in a sleep clinic. Mei and Ai both worked as accountants in China; Mei is currently taking English classes while Ai is completing an undergraduate degree in accounting at a university in Toronto. Both Min and Lynn were employed as university teachers in China – Min at the associate professor level. However, they both came to Canada as PhD students, and neither have found steady employment in the university sector (higher education) in Canada.

Transnational Strategies for Education Migration

Among the Chinese women who immigrated to Canada for their children's education, six are currently living in transnational familial arrangements. Such family arrangements, in which family members reside separately in different countries or territories, are used to accommodate families' social reproductive goals (Man 2012). In all of these families, the husbands have returned to China while the wives have stayed in Canada with their children. Periodically, the husband visits his wife and children; the wife and children also visit the husband when time and money permit. This particular transnational familial arrangement, also known as the "astronaut family" arrangement (Man 1995; Bula 2016), is deemed necessary when the husband is not able to find employment in Canada commensurate with his employment in China, or when he is not willing to give up his current position in China for a potentially lower status or lower-paying position in Canada. However, it is the wife in Canada who experiences de-skilling and downward career mobility. Hence, education migration to Canada can come at an enormous personal cost in terms of family separation and emotional strain, and with negative career implications for the wife in particular, at least at the initial stage of their migration.

Ai and her husband, for example, would both like their children to remain in Canada, at least until they graduate from high school. However, because her husband is unwilling to move to Canada due to his inability to find acceptable employment, this transnational familial arrangement is something that Ai and her husband are willing to endure for the sake of their children's education. Here is what Ai said:

> He [My husband] wants the child to stay in Canada at least until high school graduation. But now I have doubt myself. Considering my mom's health and his situation, I may return earlier [to China] than I expected. My husband will not move here because he can't find a job over here and he is satisfied with his job in China. Maybe he will immigrate after his retirement. (TTWF, CH12)

Similarly, Tina and her husband are currently in a transnational familial situation, as they both prefer their daughter to be educated in Canada.

They run an import-export business together, with Tina handling affairs in Canada and her husband in China. However, the separation is placing a heavy strain on their relationship. Although Tina's husband feels that "China's environment is not good for [their] daughter's healthy growing [*sic*]," he is not willing to consider moving to Canada permanently. When asked to elaborate on their future plans, Tina replied:

> She [My daughter is] is 13 years old and in grade eight. I cannot leave while my daughter is here. So there is not a perfect solution. He's pessimistic in these two years. Sometimes he thinks maybe we have to break up. (TTWF, CH14)

On the other hand, unlike Ai and Tina, Mei's child remains in China with her husband, who has a stable job there. Rather than risking being unemployed or underemployed, Mei's husband has decided to stay in China with their daughter, while Mei stays in Canada to obtain her citizenship. Mei prefers that her daughter receive her elementary education in China, and the plan is for her daughter to join Mei in Canada for her secondary education. In the meantime, Mei is willing to endure living on her own in Canada. When asked about her decisions, she reflected and had this to say:

> [My husband and I] had planned to study here [in Canada]. We're young. We can do whatever we want after finishing school. But now we have a child, stability is more important. We are not sure, but we prefer to have our child educated here, so I myself [will] stay here and give it a try. (TTWF, CH09)

As the interview data from Ai, Tina, and Mei suggest, education migration can be seen as a strategy for reproducing the class and social status of middle-class families. As well, by securing a desirable Western education, these middle-class parents are hopeful that their children will be rewarded with good jobs and economic security, which will in turn ensure their own old age security. These parents' current struggles and sacrifices are expected to pay off in the future for their children. These sacrifices, however, are gendered. For those families living in transnational familial arrangements, it is invariably the women who stay in Canada alone to care for the children, and who deal with de-skilling and downward career mobility. These women must also bear the dual burden of paid employment and unpaid housework and childcare in Canada, without support or assistance from their husbands, other family members, or hired help. Hence, while education migration is used as a strategy for social reproduction, and in the reproduction of class and social status, the gendered construction of social reproduction is also duplicated and accentuated in transnational families.

Conclusion

This chapter illustrates that education migration functions as a strategy for social reproduction for highly educated Chinese immigrant women in the context of an increasingly globalized economy. In China, the expansion of the free market over the past thirty years has resulted in increasing economic and occupational instability alongside a rapidly growing middle class. The social and economic mobility of this middle class has boosted the popularity of Western education as a desirable form of cultural capital for the social reproduction of the next generation, and the reproduction of middle-class status. In Canada, policies pursued at various governmental levels and by educational institutions have positioned the country as an attractive destination not only for economic migrants, but also for education migrants. The decision of the women in this study to immigrate for their children's education cannot be separated from the social, economic, and political processes taking place in China and in Canada in the context of global economic restructuring. Hence, education migration is as much an undertaking by Chinese immigrant women using their individual agency as it is an enterprise rooted in larger social institutions and organizations.

As a final point, we can see how education migration as a strategy for social reproduction also functions as a source of hope for these highly educated women who are struggling in Canada with de-skilling, downward career mobility, and unstable or precarious employment, as well as prolonged family separation. The promise that a Canadian education holds for their children's future provides them with a basis for viewing their sacrifices and current struggles as worthwhile. Min, for example, believes that despite the sacrifices she has made in her personal life to ensure her daughter can receive a Canadian education, the hardships she has endured and will continue to endure will ultimately benefit her daughter:

Sometimes I feel regretful [about coming to Canada]. But considering my daughter's education, I don't regret. I think Canada is more suitable for my daughter's development in a long run. From the viewpoint of the family life, I feel a little regretful. The quality of my life decreased greatly. Although I don't want to put any pressure on myself, some pressure from the outside is tangible. It exists, and you cannot ignore it, even though you want to ignore it. For example, the living conditions. I live in such a small apartment, and I don't have a car, although it's not because I cannot afford it, but I dare not drive. And I'm far away from my parents and always worried about them. My husband is not around and I'm also worried about his health, safety, etc. So I have some regrets, but this is life. It depends on how you view it. If we cannot live here permanently together as a whole family, maybe it's a better option to let my daughter study alone abroad in the future when she grows up, considering education in Canada is an advantage for my daughter. (TTFW, CH15)

References

Abu-Laban, Yasmeen, and Christina Gabriel. 2002. *Selling Diversity: Immigration, Multiculturalism, Employment Equity, and Globalization.* Toronto: University of Toronto Press.

Anisef, Paul, Robert Sweet, and George Frempong. 2003. "Labour Market Outcomes of Immigrant and Racial Minority University Graduates in Canada." *Journal of International Migration and Integration* 4 (4): 499–522. https://doi.org/10.1007/s12134-003-1012-4.

Arat-Koç, Sedef. 1999. "NAC's Response to the Immigration Legislative Review Report: Not Just Numbers: A Canadian Framework for Future Immigration." *Canadian Woman Studies/les cahier de la femme* 19 (3): 18–23.

Bakker, Isabella. 2007. "Social Reproduction and the Constitution of a Gendered Political Economy." *New Political Economy* 12 (4): 541–56. https://doi.org/10.1080/13563460701661561.

Bakker, Isabella, and Rachel Silvey, eds. 2008. *Beyond States and Markets: The Challenges of Social Reproduction.* New York: Routledge.

Bezanson, Kate, and Meg Luxton, eds. 2006. *Social Reproduction: Feminist Political Economy Challenges Neo-Liberalism.* Montreal: McGill-Queen's University Press.

Bian, Yanjie. 2002. "Chinese Social Stratification and Social Mobility." *Annual Review of Sociology* 28 (1): 91–116. https://doi.org/10.1146/annurev.soc.28.110601.140823.

Boucher, Anna. 2016. *Gender, Migration and the Global Race for Talent.* Manchester: Manchester University Press. https://doi.org/10.7228/manchester/9780719099458.001.0001.

Bourdieu, Pierre. 1986. "The Forms of Capital." In *Handbook of Theory and Research for the Sociology of Education*, ed. J.G. Richardson, 241–58. New York: Greenwood Press.

Boyd, Rosalind. 2006. "Labour's Response to the Informalization of Work in the Current Restructuring of Global Capitalism: China, South Korea, and South Africa." *Canadian Journal of Development Studies* 27 (4): 487–502.

Bula, Frances. 2016. "Astronaut Wives: Chinese Spouses Looking for Belonging in Vancouver." *Vancouver Magazine*, 8 November. http://vanmag. com/city/astronaut-wives-chinese-spouses-looking-belonging-vancouver/.

Citizenship and Immigration Canada (CIC). 2014. *Facts and Figures 2014— Immigration Overview: Permanent Residents*. http://www.cic.gc.ca/english/ pdf/2014-Facts-Permanent.pdf.

– 2015. *Canada Facts and Figures: Immigrant Overview Temporary Residents 2014*. Ottawa: Research and Evaluation Branch. http://www.cic.gc.ca/english/ pdf/2014-Facts-Figures-Temporary.pdf.

Chen, Liang-Hsuan. 2007. "Choosing Canadian Graduate Schools from Afar: East Asian Students' Perspectives." *Higher Education* 54 (5): 759–80. https:// doi.org/10.1007/s10734-006-9022-8.

Cole, Arda L., and J. Gary Knowles, eds. 2001. *Lives in Context: The Art of Life History Research*. Walnut Creek, CA: AltaMira Press.

Deng, Peng. 2006. "From Outcasts to Honored Guests: The Changing Fortune of Private Entrepreneurs in China and the Struggle for CCP Legitimacy." *Journal of Third World Studies* 23 (1): 23–49.

Flew, Terry. 2006. "The New Middle Class Meets the Creative Class: The Masters of Business Administration (MBA) and Creative Innovation in 21st-Century China." *International Journal of Cultural Studies* 9 (3): 419–29. https://doi.org/10.1177/1367877906066887.

Goldmann, Gustave, Arthur Sweetman, and Casey Warman. 2011. *The Portability of New Immigrants' Human Capital: Language, Education and Occupational Matching. IZA Discussion Paper No. 5851*. Bonn: Institute for the Study of Labour. http://citeseerx.ist.psu.edu/viewdoc/download?doi=10.1.1. 477.7021&rep=rep1&type=pdf.

hooks, bell. 1984. *Feminist Theory: From Margin to Center*. Cambridge, MA: South End Press.

Huang, Shirlena, and Brenda S.A. Yeoh. 2005. "Transnational Families and Their Children's Education: China's 'Study Mothers' in Singapore." *Global Networks* 5 (4): 379–400. https://doi.org/10.1111/j.1471-0374 .2005.00125.x.

Hung, Eva P.W., and Stephen W.K. Chiu. 2003. "The Lost Generation: Life Course Dynamics and Xiagang in China." *Modern China* 29 (2): 204–36. https://doi.org/10.1177/0097700402250740.

Igarashi, Hiroki, and Hiro Saito. 2014. "Cosmopolitanism as Cultural Capital: Exploring the Intersection of Globalization, Education and Stratification." *Cultural Sociology* 8 (3): 222–39. https://doi.org/10.1177/1749975514523935.

Kim, Ann H. 2015. "Structuring Transnationalism: Mothering and the Educational Project." In *Engendering Transnational Voices: Studies in Family, Work, and Identity*, ed. Guida Man and Rina Cohen, 235–45. Waterloo: Wilfrid Laurier University Press.

Kwak, Min-Jung. 2013. "Rethinking the Neoliberal Nexus of Migration, Education, and Institutions." *Environment & Planning A* 45 (8): 1858–72. https://doi.org/10.1068/a43493.

Li, Peter S. 2008. "The Role of Foreign Credentials and Ethnic Ties in Immigrants' Economic Performance." *Canadian Journal of Sociology* 33 (2): 291–310.

Lu, Yixi, Li Zong, and Bernard Schissel. 2009. "To Stay or Return: Migration Intentions of Students from People's Republic of China in Saskatchewan, Canada." *Journal of International Migration and Integration* 10 (3): 283–310. https://doi.org/10.1007/s12134-009-0103-2.

Man, Guida. 1995. "The Experience of Women in Chinese Immigrant Families: An Inquiry into Institutional and Organizational Processes." *Asian and Pacific Migration Journal* 4 (2–3): 303–26. https://doi.org/10.1177/011719 689500400207.

– 2002. "Globalization and the Erosion of the Welfare State: Effects on Chinese Immigrant Women." *Canadian Woman Studies/les cahiers de la femme* 21/22 (4/1): 26–32.

– 2004. "Gender, Work and Migration: Deskilling Chinese Immigrant Women in Canada." *Women's Studies International Forum* 27 (2): 135–48. https://doi.org/10.1016/j.wsif.2004.06.004.

– 2012. "Working and Caring: Examining the Transnational Familial Practices of Work and Family of Recent Chinese Immigrant Women in Canada." *International Journal of Interdisciplinary Social Sciences: Annual Review* 6 (3): 199–212.

– 2015. "Maintaining Family Through Transnational Strategies: The Experience of Mainland Chinese Immigrant Women in Canada." In *Engendering Transnational Voices: Studies in Family, Work, and Identity*, ed. Guida Man and Rina Cohen, 33–51. Waterloo, ON: Wilfrid Laurier University Press.

Matthews, Julie, and Ravinder Sidhu. 2005. "Desperately Seeking the Global Subject: International Education, Citizenship and Cosmopolitanism." *Globalisation, Societies and Education* 3 (1): 49–66. https://doi.org/10.1080/14767720500046179.

McBride, Stephen. 2005. *Paradigm Shift: Globalization and the Canadian State*. Halifax: Fernwood Publishing.

Minichiello, Diane. 2001. "Chinese Voices in a Canadian Secondary School Landscape." *Canadian Journal of Education* 26 (1): 77–96. https://doi.org/10.2307/1602146.

Mojab, Shahrzad. 1999. "Deskilling Immigrant Women." *Canadian Woman Studies/les cahier de la femme* 19 (3): 110–14.

Ng, Roxana. 1993. "Racism, Sexism, and Nation Building in Canada." In *Race, Identity and Representation in Education*, ed. Cameron McCarthy and Warren Crichlow, 50–9. New York: Routledge.

Reitz, Jeffrey G. 2001. "Immigrant Skill Utilization in the Canadian Labour Market: Implications of Human Capital Research." *Journal of International Migration and Integration* 2 (3): 347–78. https://doi.org/10.1007/s12134-001-1004-1.

Sakamoto, Izumi, Matthew Chin, and Melina Young. 2010. "'Canadian Experience,' Employment Challenges, and Skilled Immigrants: A Close Look Through 'Tacit Knowledge.'" *Canadian Social Work Journal* 10 (1): 145–51.

Smith, Dorothy. 1987. *The Everyday World as Problematic: A Feminist Sociology.* Toronto: University of Toronto Press.

– 2005. *Institutional Ethnography: A Sociology for People.* Toronto: Altamira Press.

Song, Xianlin. 2016a. "'Critical Thinking' and Pedagogical Implications for Higher Education." *East Asia (Piscataway, NJ)* 33 (1): 25–40. https://doi.org/10.1007/s12140-015-9250-6.

– 2016b. "Changing Social Relations in Higher Education: The First-Year International Student and the 'Chinese Learner' in Australia." In *Universities in Transition: Foregrounding Social Contexts of Knowledge in the First Year Experience*, ed. Heather Brook, Deane Fergie, Michael Maeorg, and Dee Michell, 127–56. Adelaide: University of Adelaide Press.

Statistics Canada. 2007. *The Chinese Community in Canada.* https://www150.statcan.gc.ca/n1/pub/89-621-x/89-621-x2006001-eng.htm.

– 2013. *Immigration and Ethnocultural Diversity in Canada.* Ottawa: Minister of Industry. http://www12.statcan.gc.ca/nhs-enm/2011/as-sa/99-010-x/99-010-x2011001-eng.pdf.

Steans, Jill, and Daniela Tepe. 2010. "Introduction—Social Reproduction in International Political Economy: Theoretical Insights and International, Transnational and Local Sitings." *Review of International Political Economy* 17 (5): 807–15. https://doi.org/10.1080/09692290.2010.481928.

Sweetman, Arthur. 2014. "The International Portability of Migrant Human Capital." In *Matching Economic Migration with Labour Market Needs*, OECD/EU, 229–48. Paris: OECD Publishing. https://doi.org/10.1787/9789264216501-10-en.

Tsang, Eileen Yuk-Ha. 2013. "The Quest for Higher Education by the Chinese Middle Class: Retrenching Social Mobility?" *Higher Education* 66 (6): 653–68. https://doi.org/10.1007/s10734-013-9627-7.

Waters, Johanna L. 2005. "Transnational Family Strategies and Education in the Contemporary Chinese Diaspora." *Global Networks* 5 (4): 359–77. https://doi.org/10.1111/j.1471-0374.2005.00124.x.

– 2006. "Geographies of Cultural Capital: Education, International Migration and Family Strategies Between Hong Kong and Canada." *Transactions of the Institute of British Geographers* 31 (2): 179–92. https://doi.org/10.1111/j.1475-5661.2006.00202.x.

Wong, Angelina T. 1979. "The Contest to Become Top Banana: Chinese Students at Canadian Universities." *Canadian Ethnic Studies* 11 (2): 63–9.

Workman, Thom. 2009. *If You're in My Way, I'm Walking: The Assault on Working People Since 1970.* Halifax: Fernwood Publishing.

Woronov, T.E. 2011. "Learning to Serve: Urban Youth, Vocational Schools and New Class Formations in China." *China Journal (Canberra, ACT)* 66: 77–99. https://doi.org/10.1086/tcj.66.41262808.

Zhang, Qing. 2005. "A Chinese Yuppie in Beijing: Phonological Variation and the Construction of a New Professional Identity." *Language in Society* 34 (3): 431–66. https://doi.org/10.1017/S0047404505050153.

10 "A Typical *Girogi* Family Experience?" The Transnational Migration and Heterogeneous Identity Formation of *Girogi* Families in Toronto, Canada

MIN-JUNG KWAK, WANSOO PARK, EUNJUNG LEE,
SANGYOO LEE, AND JEONG-EUI LEE

Introduction

Over the past four decades, Canada has become a major destination for international education migration. In 2001, Canada started admitting over 130,000 international visa students annually, and by 2013, that number had grown to 200,000 (CIC 2014). Between 2004 and 2013, almost 1.5 million international students received permits to study in Canada and 15 per cent (approximately 225,000) of those students were from South Korea (ibid.). The previous literature, however, testifies that this number does not accurately reflect the actual number of education migrants from South Korea because Korean education migration is practised through many different types and categories of migration. These include permanent migration, visitors, working holiday visa holders, temporary work permit holders, and parents/guardians accompanying young international students (Kwak 2012). In this chapter, we pay particular attention to one specific type of education migrant: those who maintain a transnational family arrangement between South Korea and Canada.

Transnational families, whose members are separated across borders, are not a novel phenomenon in the history of human migration. For a long time, labour migrants have moved around the world, leaving behind their families in search of better economic opportunities. However, the phenomenon of families *choosing* to live transnationally for the purpose of their children's education is fairly new and it has drawn much scholarly attention within migration studies. It is known to be an East Asian trend, and terms such as "astronaut families," "study mothers," and "parachute kids" have become popular in Canada and elsewhere (Waters 2002; Yeoh, Huang, and Lam 2005). These transnationally split households are often portrayed as usually middle- to upper-class families in which the mother moves abroad with her young child(ren) while the father remains in the home country working to financially support the two households. The mothers and children often move to English-speaking countries or places where affordable and competent international education is available. For Korean families, Canada has been a popular destination mainly due to active recruitment strategies and policies set out by the Canadian government and educational institutes to generate revenue for severely reduced public education funding in the host society (Johnstone and Lee 2014).

Girogi families are the Korean version of the transnational East Asian astronaut family and they have characteristics and migration goals similar to other East Asian astronaut families. The name *girogi* (wild geese) is believed to have originated as a reference to these families' seasonal migration. Traditionally in Korea, a pair of wooden crafted *girogi* also symbolizes a long-lasting and affectionate bond characterized by a conjugal relationship and is often displayed in wedding ceremonies as a blessing.

Due to some negative media attention on family separation and the discontents of early education migration syndrome, the neutral or even positive meanings of the original *girogi* couple/families have been somewhat tainted over time.[1] However, this does not mean that everyone has the same negative perception of *girogi* families and their experiences. While a growing number of studies has investigated the experiences of *girogi* families in the United States and Canada, many have focused on a limited number of *girogi* family experiences, and they report similar positive and negative outcomes. Our analysis adds to the existing literature but explores more *complex aspects* of these experiences. Drawing upon interview data of ten *girogi* mothers and ten *girogi* children in Toronto, we argue that there is no single, typical *girogi* family experience; rather, there are myriad complexities of motivation, identity formation, and acceptance and resistance of stereotypes of the "typical *girogi* family."

---

1 Although the term "*girogi* mother" is received negatively by some lone mothers, the authors decided to use the term consistently along with "*girogi* families" and "*girogi* fathers" as they are widely used in the literature on Korean transnational families. Rather than studying the contested nature and meaning of term use, we pay more attention to different reception of the term among Korean mothers.

Methodology

The data for this chapter are drawn from the Toronto Korean Family Study of Children (TKFSC project), which was built upon the survey project Toronto Korean Family Study (TKFS: PI – Ann Kim). According to preliminary findings from the earlier survey, children's education was an important objective of migration for many participants. Whereas the survey investigated the migration strategies and settlement experiences of Korean immigrant families in Toronto in general, the TKFSC underlined the experiences and perspectives of the children and their families and attempted to capture their nuances using qualitative research approaches.

The TKFSC research team conducted a total of 62 semi-structured interviews with Korean (im)migrant parents and their children. Among them, 20 interviews were with the mothers and children of 10 *girogi* families (10 mothers and 10 children). In terms of family structure, our research participants are distinctive, maintaining transnational households between Korea and Canada. The child participants ranged between 11 and 17 years of age at the time of the interviews. For families with more than one child between the ages of 6 and 17, we interviewed the child who was most willing to speak to us. Usually, the mothers recommended one. These research participants are by no means a representative sample of Korean immigrant families in Toronto. We were more interested in exploring the particular experiences of transnational families within the Korean-Canadian community.

The interviews were conducted by bilingual interviewers in either Korean or English, depending on the participant's preference, in a familiar setting. Participants were asked about their experiences of coming to Toronto as well as living and learning in the city. They were also asked how this experience had influenced their views of self, their future plans, their relationship with family, and their relationships with peers at school. Each interview, which lasted between sixty and ninety minutes, was recorded and then transcribed verbatim in either Korean or English. The transcripts were coded through MAXQDA software by bilingual research assistants.

In this chapter, we pay particular attention to migration objectives and processes and to changes in family relations in order to explore differences and similarities among the ten *girogi* families. While as mentioned, the data are by no means based on a representative sample of Korean *girogi* families, they do provide qualitative details that allow us to focus on various heterogeneities and idiosyncrasies among the ten families in their pre- and post-migration processes.

A Frame of Analysis

Our analysis has been guided by several areas of scholarship, including globalization, Korean migration, international education, global citizenship, and identity studies.

Globalization, International Students, and Girogi Families

A myriad of factors have contributed to the emergence of the internationally split household arrangement known as the *girogi* family. These factors include the hegemony of English as the language of the global economy; active recruitment by the host countries; the Korean government's globalization policy of the mid-1990s and the subsequent increase in access to overseas educational opportunities for younger children; and Koreans' dissatisfaction with their public education system. The central goal of the *girogi* arrangement is to obtain the best opportunities for the children's education (Finch and Kim 2012; Johnstone and Lee 2014). Even though most Korean international students are still at the college and postgraduate level, the number of early study abroad (ESA) students (elementary school through to high school) has shown an increasing trend (Finch and Kim 2012; Shin 2014).

Girogi families' split household arrangements range from short-term, lasting a couple of years, to long-term, lasting a decade or more, and require considerable flexibility to adapt to changing circumstances (Finch and Kim 2012). Regardless of the length of the *girogi* project, Korean *girogi* families are viewed as deeply traditional in that they seek to maintain or improve family status through education and they assume a traditional Korean family structure with an indissoluble marriage and strongest bonds between the mother and children. At the same time, they take advantage of the latest technology to maintain communication among the dispersed family members.

The *girogi* family phenomenon captures a moment in the ideological and practical reworking of fundamental values such as education, family, and citizenship in a global and transnational context (Finch and Kim 2012). *Girogi* families choose early study abroad as the best strategy to acquire high-status Western educational and linguistic capital, even while facing marginalization as an ethno-racial minority within another social hierarchy after migration (Shin 2014). For example, in her Toronto-based ethnographic study of Korean international students, Shin (2014) reported that a twelfth grader faced racial slurs such as "yellow monkey" and had difficulty making friends when both white Canadian students and other Korean immigrant students were unwelcoming towards her. Nancy Abelmann's (2009) work on the post-secondary experiences of fifty Korean-American students at the University of Illinois also highlights the existence of implicit racism and the need to reconsider the meaning of "comfort zones" for these students. Abelmann (2009) argues that what some popular American journalists labelled "co-ethnic segregation by choice" should not be taken at face value. Rather, there are structural pressures that encourage these students to stay in their comfort zone during their college years. The aspirations and expectations as regards their education, social mobility, and identity formation are all situated within an entangled web of South Korean society, American or Canadian multicultural society, and family and intergenerational tension, which are exacerbated by an intergenerational linguistic and cultural gap that goes beyond the typical intergenerational tension family would experience during children's adolescence period.

The question of whether the intergenerational cultural gap results in intergenerational conflicts has also not yet been conclusively answered. For example, some studies (Choi, He, and Harachi 2008; Tardif and Geva 2006) report that the intergenerational cultural gap has a positive influence on intergenerational conflicts, while others report either no relationship between the two dimensions (Lim et al. 2008) or positive acceptance of the cultural gap as an asset for the family (Barcallao and Smokowski 2007). In our small sample of *girogi* families, the findings on intergenerational relations and conflicts were rather mixed as well.

Identity Issues: Global Citizen, Korean, and Canadian/American?

Rey Chow's approach to ethnicity and identity formation provides useful conceptual insights for our data analysis (Bowman 2013). Chow problematizes the existence of origin as a unitary formation and further probes *ethnicity* as a singular cultural identity. She further touches upon the complexity and lack of unity in an entangled identity formation of gender, sexuality, race, and ethnicity through the lens of visual cultural studies. According to Chow (1991), the well-known discourse around the representation and reproduction of racialized others through popular visual media analysis is too simplified. In her own words, she notes that

> the most difficult question surrounding the demarcation of boundaries implied by "seeing" have to do not with positivistic taxonomic juxtapositions of self-contained identities and traditions in the manner of "this is you" and "that is us," but rather, who is "seeing" whom, and how? What are the power relationships between the "subject" and "object" of the culturally overdetermined "eye"? (Chow 1991, 3)

Directing our gaze toward a certain social group represents a clear or simple demarcation between "you" and "us," and we need to consider who we are, whom we are studying, and how we are viewing them (i.e., in what context). The production and reproduction of essentialized identity formation have not only been a racist or patriarchal project carried out by hegemonic power. In many cases and places, the labelling and characterization of a social/cultural group is often led by the marginalized. In Chow's understanding, it is far more complex to define a social/cultural group as one or typical.

Echoing Chow's insights, the identity issues of *girogi* families reflect complex negotiations and reconfigurations within and across nation-state boundaries (Finch and Kim 2012). Korean *girogi* mothers believe that English will make their children members of a cosmopolitan set (Song 2010). Social class intersects with other social identity categories such as race, ethnicity, citizenship, and immigration status within the host country to shape the identities of *girogi* mothers and their children. Korean *girogi* children often experience linguistic and racial stigmatization and downward social mobility (Shin 2014). Shin found that Korean international high school students in Toronto invested in a class-based consumption of Korean language and culture to contest the racial and linguistic stigmatization they experienced in the local context and to index their cosmopolitanism (Shin 2014). Song (2010) notes that among *girogi* families the Korean language is perceived as part of the national identity, yet at the same time, there is a strong desire for English as an economic commodity and a means of becoming cosmopolitan. Korean "glocalization" drives *girogi* families to transnational migration as an educational strategy, but their identities are strongly rooted in Korea.

The Korean identities of short-term migrants expecting to return to Korea within a few years remain strongly intact. One of the mothers interviewed in Song's (2010) study stated that, "the benefits of English do not compensate for the cost of losing Korean for her children's lives" (35). However, long-term migrants who live in the host country for five years or longer were more likely to consider immigration options due to the financial strain caused by higher tuition fees for international students. In addition, the longer they stay in the foreign country, the more acculturated the children become compared to their mothers. This acculturation gap, or intergenerational cultural dissonance between parents and children over cultural values, is considered a normative experience among immigrant families (Choi, He, and Harachi 2008).

Some *girogi* children may try to distinguish themselves from immigrants by identifying as transnational, cosmopolitan, and wealthy modern citizens (Shin 2014). One *girogi* child, Jenny, from Finch and Kim's (2012) study, was born in the host country but raised in Korea. She interacted with both Korean immigrants and Korean international students but still struggled with the racist attitudes of white Americans. In addition, tensions with her mother emerged around her nationality and citizenship during her high school years. Jenny complained that "it was really unfair to not be able to be full American, just because my dad was in Korea."

Girogi mothers' identities are strongly traditional with regards to gender, especially since they are seen as managers of their children's education, a function through which they demonstrate their whole-hearted commitment to motherhood (Finch and Kim 2012). At the same time, *girogi* mothers reshape their maternal selves and renegotiate gendered roles in response to the experience of living in a foreign country, physically separated from their husbands and in-laws (Jeong, You, and Kwon 2014), even though the gender roles are not drastically changed by having a split household (Finch and Kim 2012). For middle-class *girogi* mothers, the husband's social status in Korea is a very important part of their identity, even if the mothers need to take a lower-status job to supplement family income (Finch and Kim 2012). In addition, a number of *girogi* mothers flexibly reconfigured their social identities in order to secure legal residency in the host country by acquiring business visas or becoming full-time students, even though they had given up full-time jobs and careers in Korea (Jeong, You, and Kwon 2014). *Girogi* fathers' self-image assumed a critical role in the father's adaptation to the long-term separation from family members (Kim 2006). Fathers who perceived themselves as being the centre and provider of the family and as serving rather than sacrificing for the family had better family relationships.

Prejudice, Stigma, and Criticism

Prejudice, stigma, and criticism against *girogi* families exist in South Korea, and such negative attitudes are often exacerbated by the mass media. Filtered through the lens of the mass media, the visual and textual representation of *girogi* mothers, children, and families has been highly provocative and has caused social controversy. Some cartoon images of *girogi* mothers having an affair with local men, along with low-resolution images of middle-aged Korean women playing golf and young teenagers hanging out in the entertainment district, were aired in the news media. What was more problematic was that the media's depiction was accepted as a representative and impartial view of the *girogi* family experience. Rey Chow (1993) effectively warned us about the dangers of media representation:

> The obsession with visuality means also the obsession with a certain understanding of visuality, namely, that visuality exposes the truth ... All sensations merged into the sensation of seeing and the epistemological and moral imperative of watching. It was believed that by watching – that is, by concentrating all media into that of sight – we would be able to prevent disasters from happening ... Alternatively, visuality was believed to be scientific. The other culture [here, *girogi* families] was "observed" through our electronic windows as a biological "culture" would be observed under a scientist's microscope. Whether theological or scientific, moreover, the media believed themselves to be transparent, impartial – nonexistent. (166)

In Finch and Kim's (2012) study, *girogi* mothers expressed anger about the portrayal offered in mass media and academic articles, which they believed misrepresented their situation. Earlier studies reported that the long-term split-household arrangements of *girogi* families caused deteriorating family relationships and psychological and financial problems (Choi, He, and Harachi 2008; Kim 2006), but more recent studies report that *girogi* couples maintain or even strengthen their relationships (Chiang 2008; Finch and Kim 2012; Jeong, You, and Kwon 2014). Jeong, You, and Kwon (2014) also pointed out the importance of considering these families' relationships prior to living apart, because their lives and relationships, although changed, continue on even though the family is living in two different countries. Both Korean mothers (Jeong, You, and Kwon 2014) and Taiwanese mothers (Chiang 2008) revealed that freedom from their responsibilities as wives and daughters-in-law was a motivating factor in their decision to migrate.

In addition, Kim (2010), who conducted qualitative interviews with sixteen *girogi* mothers in the United States, contends that these mothers can be categorized into three distinctive types based on their adaptation outcomes: integration, self-actualization, and separation. Integration-type mothers carefully plan for their family's transnational separation. They secure jobs in the United States and actively interact with Americans in the hope of integrating into American society. They do not limit their identity to motherhood but work very hard to earn American credentials and to get jobs. Self-actualization-type mothers consider the short time in the United States as an opportunity to build career skills or experiences they can capitalize on when they return to Korea. Separation-type mothers tend to avoid interactions with Americans, mainly fulfilling their emotional needs through the local Korean community.

Motivation and Pre-migration Context

For many Korean families, the children's education is known to be a major motivating factor for emigration and it is even more so for *girogi* families. In the previous literature, East Asian transnational families were often described as having three main characteristics: a split household, a mother and children staying in the host country pursuing a Western education, and a father staying in the home country providing financial support (Waters 2002; Yeoh, Huang, and Lam 2005; Jeong and Bélanger 2012). While pursuit of an overseas education for children is one of the main defining attributes of *girogi* families, several participants in our study told us otherwise. Six *girogi* mothers told us that their own desire to experience life abroad, existing family networks, and even marital discord were the main reasons for moving to Canada and maintaining a separated family. Seeking a better place for their children's education was a secondary motivating factor rather than the main one.

INYOUNG[2]: In my mind ... Actually between my husband and me, we had this firm agreement.
INTERVIEWER: Ah?

---

2 Pseudonyms are used throughout to protect the identity of research participants.

INYOUNG: That is … if any opportunities were given, I can go [abroad]. We have been married for twenty years. We were happily married and known to be a model couple. But, we had this consensus that both my husband and I can do whatever we wish to do after our forties. So the decision was totally based on my free will and desire to move to Canada. (Personal interview with Inyoung, 20 June 2012)

This may reflect the fact that our sample included *girogi* families who initially came to Canada as permanent immigrants. However, even some mothers who accompanied children with international student visas cited their own objectives or motivations as important factors. For example, Ayoung, who was an active career woman in Korea, told us that her decision to bring her son to Canada was motivated by her wish to take a break from work and spend time with her own family in Toronto. Examining pre- and post-migration trajectories seems crucial to fully understanding the experiences of transnational families (Jeong and Bélanger 2012). Beyond the simple link between education migration and transnational family formation, our participants reveal that much more complex dynamics underlie their decision-making. Several mothers and children told us that living apart or having little time with their spouse/father was not a new experience. For Jungeun, the mother of a grade 11 international student, migration to Canada was a way to escape marital discord and the financial burden caused by her husband. In cases like hers, the adjustment and adaptation of mothers and their children seemed to be rather easier. The gaps left by absent fathers were often filled by the mothers' family network or friends.

Analysing the motivating factors for migration among our ten *girogi* mothers, we found that children's education was a major factor but not the most important one. Also, it was not a defining attribute of *girogi* families. As reflected in other chapters in this volume, education migrants include a wide range of people with different objectives. Education migration, then, should be regarded as another form of migration, one that goes beyond the experience of studying and living abroad as international students.

Identity Issues and Family Relationships

Critiquing Aiwa Ong's analysis of Hong Kong transnational families in the United States, Waters (2002) noted that living as a transnationally separated family may not be a good model of a successful migration family. Waters's case study of lone mothers in Vancouver revealed that such forms of family separation may be interpreted as an example of middle-class privilege in the pursuit of flexible citizenship, but they also resulted in negative consequences. A major challenge typically faced by these *girogi* families was the worsening relationships between family members, especially between the father and children, due to prolonged separation. In our sample, Chaeyoun, who lived apart from her husband for three years, said that while her relationship with him remained unchanged, her children were starting to feel some distance from their father. On the other hand, other mothers and children in our sample claimed they maintained good family relations through frequent phone calls and virtual meetings. For example, Bona, who came to Canada three years ago, said the physical separation had brought her family emotionally closer together than before. Her two children knew that their father was making sacrifices for them and she herself felt greater empathy towards him as they grew older.

Such efforts to stay close and affectionate also disguise family problems. Eunyoung shares her family's experience as follows:

EUNYOUNG: Yes, of course I tell my husband whenever there are issues with the kids. Then, he talks to the kids on the phone. He doesn't even get mad because he doesn't see the problems with his own eyes. He talks to the kids nicely and it looks like the problems are solved. But, they are not. The problems are still there. Nothing is solved.

INTERVIEWER: Aha.

EUNYOUNG: According to other girogi mothers who live overseas, girogi fathers should not scold their children when they visit them in Canada or the US. It usually escalates the already deepening gap between fathers and children. Fathers are told they should only say nice things to the children in order to maintain a good relationship. But, once they arrive in Canada, they start to witness the messy situation going on with their children.

INTERVIEWER: Once fathers get to see with their own eyes ...

EUNYOUNG: That's right. I always talk to my husband ahead of time [whenever he visits us]. Don't ever say "don't do this and that" or "you can't do this and that" to Eric [her son]. I advise him that he should try to be nice to him, pretending he doesn't know what's really going on. I told him just to be a nice and gentle daddy while I play a role of evil mom. But then, once he is here, he sees the behaviour problems of the kids. Once, my husband talked to the kids about not spending too much time on the computer. Of course, they said they wouldn't but then, they play on the computer every day. It is no use. I totally regret bringing my kids to Canada. (Personal interview with Eunyoung, 11 June 2012)

As discussed in earlier studies of transnational family relations (Waters 2002, Jeong and Bélanger 2012), some *girogi* mothers in our study felt liberated from their duties and responsibilities as daughters-in-law and wives in Korea. For example, Inyoung, who came to Canada four years ago, explained that "some *girogi* mothers complain about separation from their husbands, but for me, it is just so much fun. I can't say this is totally a good thing but that is the truth."

Aside from these few exceptional cases, many mothers complained about the increased pressure they felt from being solely responsible for the children's care and education. For *girogi* mothers the difficulties of parenting are escalated, not only by the absence of the father, but also when they start to notice a generational gap in integration. As time passes, children often gain fluency in English and Canadian culture much faster than their mothers. Some mothers and children experience communication problems. Eunyoung complained that these problems often resulted in arguments with her daughter. She noted that, "when my daughter says something in English, I don't understand. Then we start arguing because she complains that I don't even understand what she is trying to say." When children realize that their *girogi* mother is not fluent in English, they look for other ways of solving issues that occur outside the home. For example, Cloe, who is in grade 6, was unwilling to talk to her mother about some of the problems she faces at school. She would rather talk to her school teacher, counsellor, or principal:

INTERVIEWER: If you, uhm. If you ... would have been in that kind of situation, what do you think you could do?

CLOE: I'd tell my ... um, my, the teacher? But I would, but I don't think I'd tell my mom cause, because it'd be kind of private and she'd get all worried and stuff. And I just don't wanna upset her.

INTERVIEWER: You don't want your mother worried about you?

CLOE: Yea. Because it's like school and stuff, and I think teacher and if it's very serious, I think I'd tell my, I'd tell the principal or the teacher.

INTERVIEWER: Ok. So, are you uh, do you feel comfortable telling your teachers about those kinds of concerns and issues?

CLOE: Yea, I'd be com ... confident, because it's like, bullying. (Personal interview with Cloe, 24 July 2012)

A similar observation was reported in Cho's (2011) study, which was conducted in Canada. One high school student spoke of the important role played by a Korean counsellor: "I am very thankful for Miss Kim because she seems like my mother. She goes to the hospital with me, goes out with me during the weekend, invites me to her house, and checks with me about my medication each morning" (Cho 2011, 101). In our study, Bona also shared a similar experience, noting that her children do not want her to participate in curriculum nights or any other school events because they are ashamed of her lack of fluency in English. Her younger child, who is in grade 8, often lectures Bona about Canadian culture and manners. As Bona notes, "she [my daughter] always says, Mom, you can't do this and that. That is considered rude here in Canada." Bona's report on what her younger daughter told her is indicative of the intergenerational cultural gap between the mother and more acculturated children. The acculturation process for parents and children is often different, and research on immigrant families has reported that parents tend to stick to their heritage culture, while children accepts the norms and values of dominant culture of the hosting country, which creates an acculturation gap (Lim et al. 2008).

Children who come to Canada at an earlier age or who spend some time overseas before arriving in Canada tend to integrate into the Canadian school system and culture more easily than those who arrive in later years. Benjamin and David in our child-participant sample, for example, said they did not have much trouble adjusting to the new school system in Canada and were able to excel academically as both had attended an English/international school before. There were individual variations among children as well. Not all children who arrived in Canada at an earlier age experienced a smooth transition; however, early exposure to an English educational environment did help many students.

Such discussions of the integration and settlement experiences of *girogi* children often led to questions about identity that explored how *girogi* children identified themselves and foresaw their future between Korea and Canada. Interestingly, our research participants showed that length of stay in Canada was important but not the sole determinant of successful integration in the host society. Rather, the sense of belonging in Canadian society was more significantly related to how they maintained close connections with Korea and the Korean community in Canada. Howard and Gary are good examples from our study. They are both grade 10 students and have been in Canada about six to seven years. Both came to Canada with their families under a permanent migration program but currently live apart from their fathers, who live and work in Korea. When we asked them how they identified themselves, they responded in different ways. Howard had this to say:

The way I think, and the way I view stuff, is a lot more different from how, Korean ... people do. I guess, you can say that I'm white washed now because I'm used to Canadian culture more. So ... I'm just better off with Canadian people. (Personal interview with Howard, 17 August 2012)

By contrast, Gary stated the following:

Ah ... for sure, when I introduce myself, I think I tend to show the more Korean side of me. I am a Canadian ... but I was Korean. And, at home, if I only speak English and do not interact with Korean people at all, I think I would have become only Canadian. But then, the environment I am living in is just so Korean. So, even if I am a Canadian, I speak Korean and don't feel anything holding me back at all ... (Personal interview with Gary, 17 August 2012)

Awareness of self-identity as a minority, or more specifically, being Korean in the host country, influences how these children behave in their daily interactions with classmates and teachers at school. Their skin colour, race, ethnicity, and citizenship become topics of discussion, writing, and education in their school environment or everyday activities. They become more aware of their skin colour, nationality, and citizenship, factors they were not conscious of in the ethnically homogeneous Korean educational environment. In Finch and Kim's study (2012), as children adjusted to an unfamiliar school environment, which represents multiple challenges including language, they became used to being part of a racial and ethnic minority. Earlier studies of Korean *girogi* children found that some became subjects of discrimination as well. Shin (2014) noted that one of her interviewees was mocked for her Korean accent in Canada and bullied with racial slurs by white classmates in New Zealand. The *girogi* children in our study managed such sensitive issues in their own ways with the resources available to them. As noted above, some chose not to rely on their own mothers, unlike most children. Also some children started to experience problems communicating with their mothers. When the children do not feel the need to maintain cultural and social linkages with home (i.e., the Korean community in Canada or family, friends, and relatives in Korea), they tend to identify themselves more as Canadian than Korean. Howard is a good example as he has not talked to his own father in Korea for several years, and he began to identify himself as being better off with Canadian people.

Reactive Views on Prejudice, Stigma, and Criticism

Compared to Korean immigrants who often give up their middle- or upper-middle-class identities after arriving in the new country, *girogi* families tend to maintain a strong middle- and upper-middle-class identity. The cosmopolitan, wealthy, modern, and consumerist behaviours and attitudes reported by Shin (2014), based on her ethnographic observations of four high school students, may not just represent *girogi* children. It is quite possible that the mothers of these children have promoted such lifestyles and attitudes, which may be perceived negatively within Korean immigrant communities. At the same time, they are also perceived as affluent/powerful consumers within the Korean immigrant community market as well as in the Canadian education market. At first, the influx of international students and *girogi* mothers was viewed as an important economic opportunity for the Canadian education industry in general and for Korean immigrant entrepreneurs specifically (Kwak 2013). At the same time, however, there has been some prejudice and stigma attached to lone mothers with young children. Some mothers openly discussed their discomfort or distaste for these views of fellow Koreans in Toronto.

Dohee, a *girogi* mother who came to Canada with her two children, had no plans to stay in the country permanently. She talked about the distance she felt when she started interacting with different groups of people within the Korean immigrant community:

DOHEE: But then ... I think I feel that I am closer to and share common ground with other *girogi* mothers here in Toronto or my friends in Korea. But, I think I am quite different from Korean immigrants who have lived here for long.

INTERVIEWER: Really? How do you feel different?

DOHEE: What I found is that the ways of thinking of those old immigrants are quite different from mine. So, I became very conscious about sharing my thoughts with them, especially with views on children's education. For example, those old immigrants [Korean immigrants who lived in Canada for long periods] don't usually seek tutoring services for their children. They think that we [*girogi* families] are rich and thus can afford tutoring. That is not true though. We are just the same middle-class families who live on monthly wages. I just care about my children's education and that's why I have been spending extra money for tutoring ... Since I got to

learn that people were talking about me and my family behind our backs,
I started to keep everything related to my children's education a secret.
(Personal interview with Dohee, 29 August 2012)

The feeling of distance was not just shared by *girogi* mothers; several
girogi children also told us that Korean immigrant kids were usually the
ones who made fun of them during their adjustment period at school.
The gap between the different lifestyles and world views starts at a very
early stage and often deepens over time. Heejin, who came to Canada
six years ago with her two children, told us that she and her children
were hiding the fact that they were in Canada on student visas. Korean
mass media has played a critical role in producing stereotypes of *girogi*
families as a deviant form of family. Some of the earlier media reports on
girogi mothers were even harsher. The mothers were often described as
irresponsible and unfaithful women who enjoyed living lavishly on their
husbands' sacrifices. Almost all *girogi* mothers who participated in our
study complained about this prejudice and stigma tied to their status.
The mass media's representation of *girogi* mothers, children, and families has been highly controversial and even hostile as it is viewed as a nor-
malized and accurate image of who they are (Chow 1993). Addressing
the rumours of *girogi* mothers being unfaithful, Hwajeong responded
very sarcastically, emphasizing her upper-middle-class background:

People say that many *girogi* mothers have affairs with the guys [Korean
immigrant men] here in Canada, neglecting their husbands back home.
I think ... it is in fact quite contrary ... You see, considering the job
background of those *girogi* mothers' husbands ... They are all professionals
like doctors, professors, and highly paid managers in some big companies.
Why would we become interested in those Korean guys here? At best, they
are merely real estate agents. [laughs] ... That is just nonsense and a simple
prejudice from those old immigrants. (Personal interview with Hwajeong,
17 August 2012)

While most *girogi* mothers and children tend to take a defensive stance
against such prejudice and stigma, we also found that some mothers and
girogi children did not mind being labelled as a "*girogi* mother" or "international student." For example, Chaeyoun, who came to Canada three
years ago as a permanent migrant and now lives apart from her husband, said she totally accepted being called a *girogi* mother. She rather
wished that she and her husband could become an "eagle father" and
"eagle mother" who were able to travel more frequently between Korea

and Canada with better economic status. Also, some international students who arrive with good English skills from previous exposure to an English education environment reported an easier adjustment to school in Canada. They often got along well with Canadian students immediately upon arrival and became the subject of jealousy from those who experienced language barriers and social limitations. Not all *girogi* mothers and families were victimized by prejudice and stigma, rather some actively fought against these negative views by arming themselves with a higher-class identity.

Conclusion

In this chapter, we examined the heterogeneous nature of this transnational migration group and its identity formation, with the focus on young (K–12) Korean students and their mothers in Toronto, Canada. Although international education is known to be a growing form of transnational migration, the experiences of young students and their families have been under-studied and subsequently portrayed as homogenous. Drawing upon semi-structured interview data collected in Toronto, Canada, we explored the ways in which the students and their mothers, as active agents and actors in transnational migration, flexibly negotiate and reconstruct their identities beyond the pervasive, so-called typical preconceptions of such separated families.

While analysing the interview transcripts of ten *girogi* mothers and ten *girogi* children in Toronto, we soon realized it was difficult to generalize about their experiences. Except for the commonality of being a family separated between Korea and Canada, their experiences were varied in terms of migration objectives, perspectives on ethnic and class identity, and trajectories of changing family relations. Globalization has had the effect of displacing pre-existing identities of spaces. Cultural differences, travelling bodies, displaced identities, and diasporic solidarity and connections are each prevalent in the global era. However, it is critical to remember that even in the pulverized space of postmodernity and rapid globalization, spatial identity and hegemonic power relations have not become irrelevant. Rather, they have been reshaped into more complex and pluralistic forms involving more than one place and various individual characteristics. Echoing Chow (1991), the many differences observed among the ten *girogi* families testify to the impossibility of defining their group identity by a few main characteristics. Such family arrangements, despite being the subject of prejudice and media backlash, represent some positive changes in conjugal and family relations. It was also interesting to find that *girogi* families face constant power struggles and negotiations with other members of the Korean-Canadian community. Some *girogi* mothers engaged their class status to resist the harsh prejudice against them. Our analysis begs further comparative research on the experiences of Korean *girogi* families in different places such as the United States, Australia, and other Asian countries.

References

Abelmann, Nancy. 2009. *The Intimate University: Korean American Students and the Problems of Segregation*. Durham, NC: Duke University Press.

Bacallao, Martica.L, and Paul R Smokowski. 2007. "The Costs of Getting Ahead: Mexican Family System Changes After Immigration." *Family Relations* 56 (1): 52–66. https://doi.org/10.1111/j.1741-3729.2007.00439.x.

Bowman, Paul. 2013. *Reading Rey Chow: Visuality, Postcoloniality, Ethnicity, Sexuality*. New York: Peter Lang. https://doi.org/10.3726/978-1-4539-1089-4.

Chiang, Lan-Hung Nora. 2008. "'Astronaut Families': Transnational Lives of Middle-Class Taiwanese Married Women in Canada." *Social & Cultural Geography* 9 (5): 505–18.

Cho, E.S. 2011. "Challenges and Support Plan for the Unaccompanied Early Study Students from Korea: A Case Study of Canada" (in Korean). *Studies on Korean Youth* 22 (1): 87–114.

Choi, Yoonsun, Michael He, and Tracy W Harachi. 2008. "Intergenerational Cultural Dissonance, Parent-Child Conflict and Bonding, and Youth Problem Behaviors among Vietnamese and Cambodian Immigrant Families." *Journal of Youth and Adolescence* 37 (1): 85–96. https://doi.org/10.1007/s10964-007-9217-z. Medline:18645631

Chow, Rey. 1991. *Woman and Chinese Modernity: The Politics of Reading Between West and East*. Minneapolis: University of Minnesota Press.

– 1993. *Writing Diaspora: Tactics of Intervention in Contemporary Cultural Studies*. Bloomington: Indiana University Press.

Citizenship and Immigration Canada (CIC). 2014. *Facts and Figures 2013: Immigration Overview – Permanent and Temporary Residents*.

Finch, John, and Seung-Keung Kim. 2012. "Kirogi Families in the US: Transnational Migration and Education." *Journal of Ethnic and Migration Studies* 38 (3): 485–506. https://doi.org/10.1080/1369183X.2012.658548.

Jeong, Junmin, and Danièle Bélanger. 2012. "Perspectives and Experiences of Kirogi Mothers." In *Korean Immigrants in Canada*, ed. Ann Kim and Samuel Noh, 259–84. Toronto: University of Toronto Press.

Jeong, Yu-Jin, Hyun-Kyung You, and Young In Kwon. 2014. "One Family in Two Countries: Mothers in Korean Transnational Families." *Ethnic and Racial Studies* 37 (9): 1546–64. https://doi.org/10.1080/01419870.2012.758861.

Johnstone, Marjorie, and Eunjung Lee. 2014. "Branded: International Education and 21st-Century Canadian Immigration, Education Policy, and the Welfare State." *International Social Work* 57 (3): 209–21. https://doi.org/10.1177/0020872813508572.

Kim, K.H. 2010. "Adaptation Process of the Korean 'Geese Mother' in the U.S.A.: A Grounded Theory Approach" (in Korean). *Journal of Korean Family Relations* 14: 211–39.

Kim, S.S. 2006. "The 'Kirogi' Fathers' Change of Lives and Adaptation Problems." *Journal of Korean Home Management Association* 24 (1): 141–58.

Kwak, Min-Jung. 2012. "Consuming Canadian Education: International Student Experiences of Migration, Education and Living between Seoul and Vancouver." In *Korean Immigrants in Canada*, ed. Ann Kim and Samuel Noh, 88–114. Toronto: University of Toronto Press.

– 2013. "Rethinking the Neoliberal Nexus of Education, Migration, and Institutions." *Environment & Planning A* 45 (8): 1858–72. https://doi.org/10.1068/a43493.

Lim, Soh-Leong, May Yeh, June Liang, Anna S. Lau, and Kristin McCabe. 2008. "Acculturation Gap, Intergenerational Conflict, Parenting Style, and Youth Distress in Immigrant Chinese American families." *Marriage & Family Review* 45 (1): 84–106. https://doi.org/10.1080/01494920802537530.

Shin, Hyunjung. 2014. "Social Class, Habitus, and Language Learning: The Case of Korean Early Study-Abroad Students." *Journal of Language, Identity, and Education* 13 (2): 99–103. https://doi.org/10.1080/15348458.2014.901821.

Song, Juyoung. 2010. "Language Ideology and Identity in Transnational Space: Globalization, Migration, and Bilingualism Among Korean Families in the USA." *International Journal of Bilingual Education and Bilingualism* 13 (1): 23–42. https://doi.org/10.1080/13670050902748778.

Tardif, Christine, and Esther Geva. 2006. "The Link Between Acculturation Disparity and Conflict Among Chinese Canadian Immigrant Mother-Adolescent Dyads." *Journal of Cross-Cultural Psychology* 37 (2): 191–211. https://doi.org/10.1177/0022022105284496.

Waters, Johanna L. 2002. "Flexible Families?: 'Astronaut' Households and the Experiences of Lone Mothers in Vancouver, British Columbia." *Social & Cultural Geography* 3 (2): 117–34. https://doi.org/10.1080/14649360220133907.

Yeoh, Brenda S. A., Shirlena Huang, and Theodora Lam. 2005. "Transnationalizing the 'Asian' Family: Imaginaries, Intimacies and Strategic Intents." *Global Networks* 5 (4): 307–15. https://doi.org/10.1111/j.1471-0374.2005.00121.x.

PART IV

The Post-student Experience

11 Student Transitions: Earnings of Former International Students in Canada's Labour Market

YUQIAN LU AND FENG HOU

Introduction

Every year, tens of thousands of international students from over a hundred countries are attracted to Canada's classrooms to pursue high-quality education. Since the 1990s Canada has experienced rapid growth in the number of international students. At present the country ranks seventh worldwide in annual number of international students. According to a strategic plan released in early 2014, the Canadian government hopes to attract 450,000 international students by 2022, which will double the number of international students currently studying in the country (FTD 2014).

This rapid inflow has infused a large amount of financial resources into Canadian educational institutions and created job opportunities for Canadians (FTD 2014). It has also provided Canada with a large pool of candidates from which to select well-educated immigrants. Among the temporary foreign residents who received student permits from 1990 to mid-2014, more than 270,000, or 19 per cent, have become permanent residents. This is a major source of young, diverse, and vibrant workers for the Canadian labour force. To attract highly educated international students and to facilitate their transition to immigrant status, Citizenship and Immigration Canada (CIC) implemented important changes in the late 2000s to allow international students to seek work opportunities and apply for permanent resident status after finishing their university education.

Landed immigrants who first arrive in Canada as international students have some advantages over other immigrants: they come to Canada at a relatively young age; their Canadian educational qualifications, unlike foreign credentials, are easily assessed by prospective employers; they tend to have some proficiency in one of the country's official languages; and they have gained knowledge about the Canadian labour market and have had opportunities to establish social networks that could facilitate their job search. Accordingly, they should be expected to face fewer barriers to their socio-economic integration.

The empirical evidence, however, seems to suggest that the Canadian study experience does not necessarily guarantee an immigrant's economic success in the Canadian labour market. A government evaluation report shows that previous Canadian study experiences are not positively associated with immigrants' earnings (CIC 2010). Similarly, Hou and Bonikowska (2015) found that immigrants with only pre-landing Canadian study experience but no prior work experience in Canada had only a small earnings advantage at the time of landing over immigrants without any pre-landing Canadian experience, and this small advantage was entirely attributable to their longer stay in Canada.

Although these results are counterintuitive, they are consistent with empirical findings in two other traditional immigrant countries – the United States and Australia. Lowell and Avato (2014) found that former student visa holders in the United States started with lower earnings and had flatter earnings growth than former temporary work visa holders. Lowell and Avato suggest this may be because student visa applicants undergo a less-selective screening process compared to temporary work visa applicants, who have to demonstrate they possess the job-ready skills and abilities sought by US employers.

Hawthorne and To (2014) show that in Australia, former international students who lack advanced English ability and who are not in high-demand fields fare poorly in terms of employment and earnings compared with skilled immigrants. They argue that many foreign students face barriers, including poor English ability, inadequate quality control of the private-training sector, and cultural and linguistic enclosure.

These empirical studies point to the great heterogeneity that seems to exist among international students. Host-country education in and of itself does not necessarily generate a clear advantage for immigrants in the host country's labour market unless it is combined with other characteristics that facilitate socio-economic integration.

This chapter examines factors associated with successful labour market performance among landed immigrants in Canada who are former international students. The analysis focuses on how immigrants' earnings are affected by the following factors: levels of education pursued and attained in Canada, work experience in Canada during or after studies, language, age at landing, and source region.

The analysis starts with a brief introduction of the data sources and data linkage. The next section presents the rates of transition from international students to permanent residents by various characteristics. Then, the characteristics of landed immigrants who are former international students are briefly described. For simplicity, these immigrants are referred to as IS (i.e., international student) immigrants in this chapter. Finally, the factors affecting earnings among IS immigrants are examined, followed by some concluding remarks.

Data Sources

The overarching data source for this study is the Canadian Employer-Employee Dynamics Database (CEEDD). The CEEDD is an employer-employee matched data bank created and maintained by Statistics Canada. It links various administrative data sets and contains information on Canadian business enterprises and the workers they employ.

For the purpose of this study, three input data sets in CEEDD are used to construct the analytical file. The first is the Temporary Residents (TR) file. The TR file is created by CIC and contains socio-demographic and administrative information on all non-permanent residents in Canada. Foreign students were identified among non-permanent residents as anyone who ever held a student permit issued by CIC.

The second data source is the Immigrant Landing File (ILF), which contains the socio-demographic characteristics at landing of immigrants who have arrived in Canada since 1980. This study uses the following characteristics at landing: highest level of completed education, class of immigration, mother tongue, and self-reported official-language abilities.

The third data set is the T1 personal tax file, which includes annual information on demographic characteristics, income, and taxes for tax filers. This study draws earnings, current age, marital status, and province of residence from the T1 file.

The three source files are linked together with the Linkage Control File (LCF) created by Statistics Canada. The LCF contains individuals' social insurance numbers (SIN) as well as other basic demographic characteristics. Former temporary residents were probabilistically matched to the LCF based on their first and last name, date of birth, gender, postal code, claim date, and family indicator from the TR file. The SINs of linked temporary residents were then obtained from the LCF, yielding a linkage key containing both the CIC client identification number and the SIN. Next, a deterministic linkage based on the SIN was established between these temporary residents and their filing records in the T1 file and ILF.

International Students in Canada

As shown in chapter 1 of this volume, the number of temporary foreign residents who hold student permits has been rising continuously since 1990. In the early 1990s, Canada received a yearly average of 31,000 international students, and the annual level doubled by the end of the 2000s before further expanding to 96,000 in the early 2010s (Table 11.1).

Table 11.1 Demographic Characteristics of International Students at Their First Student Permits, Canada

	First student permit in				
	1990–4	1995–9	2000–4	2005–9	2010–13
Gender	Per cent				
Male	51	50	51	54	55
Female	49	50	49	46	45
Age at first student permit					
< 18	33	25	22	25	21
18–24	41	49	55	55	58
25+	26	26	23	21	20
Level of study at first student permit					
Primary and secondary	43	28	24	25	22
Trade	10	15	15	12	6
Post-secondary, other	21	24	27	25	34
Bachelor's	10	13	16	19	18
Above bachelor's	8	8	8	10	11
Other	8	12	10	8	8
Source country/region					
Northern and Western Europe	17	17	13	13	10

	First student permit in				
	1990–4	1995–9	2000–4	2005–9	2010–13
Southern and Eastern Europe	5	4	3	4	4
Africa	8	6	6	7	7
China	5	5	15	16	24
India	1	1	3	5	13
Japan	11	13	9	6	4
South Korea	3	15	20	19	9
Other Asian countries	26	16	13	14	14
United States	10	9	7	6	4
Other	13	15	13	11	11
Destination of first student permit					
Atlantic	5	4	5	6	5
Montreal	13	13	12	11	11
Quebec, other	7	6	4	4	4
Toronto	11	12	16	16	22
Ontario, other	27	21	18	18	21
Prairies	14	14	12	11	10
Vancouver	11	20	20	20	16
British Columbia, other	13	12	13	13	12
Territories	0	0	0	0	0
Number of observations	158,443	218,740	329,639	339,778	384,807

Data Source: Citizenship and Immigration Canada, Temporary Residents File.

Table 11.1 summarizes the age, level of study, source region, and destination distribution of international students at the time of their first student permits. In any given year, the majority of international students arrived at age 24 or younger. Over the past two and a half decades, the age structure has become more concentrated towards the 18–24 range – the main age range for post-secondary education. The trend in the age structure corresponds to changes in the level of study. In the early 1990s, 43 per cent of international students came to attend primary and secondary schools and 18 per cent pursued university education. The pattern was reversed by the early 2010s, when more international students attended universities (29 per cent) than primary and secondary schools (22 per cent).

Similar to the trends in other English-speaking developed countries (see Shu and Hawthorne 1995), the composition of source country/region has changed considerably since the 1990s. In terms of broad source regions, increasingly, international students have come from Asia, while the number of students from the United States and Europe has declined over the past two and a half decades. The share of international students from Africa has fluctuated narrowly between 6 per cent and 8 per cent. In the early 1990s, Japan and the United States were the two top source countries of international students to Canada. They were replaced by South Korea and China by the early 2000s. In the early 2010s, China and India together accounted for 37 per cent of all international students. China and India were also the two top source countries of international students in the United States and Australia in the early 2010s. China alone accounted for about 30 per cent of all international students in each of those two countries.

The geographic distribution of international students within Canada generally follows the patterns observed among new immigrants. The majority of international students were located in Ontario, British Columbia, and Quebec, particularly in the metropolitan areas of Toronto, Vancouver, and Montreal.

Transition to Permanent Residents

International students come to Canada for different reasons. Some of them appreciate the quality of education in Canada and intend to return to their home countries with qualifications obtained from their Canadian education. Other students may want to stay after graduation to gain work experience in an advanced economy and build an international network. Furthermore, a substantial share of international students hope to become immigrants so they can work and reside in Canada permanently (van Huystee 2011; Arthur and Flynn 2013).

The longitudinal feature of the CEEDD allows the calculation of the cumulative rate of transition from international students to permanent residents starting from the year first study permits are obtained. Figure 11.1 presents cumulative transition rates among international students who obtained their first student permits in the 1990–4, 1995–9, 2000–4, and 2005–9 periods.

Figure 11.1 Cumulative Rates of Transition to Permanent Residence among International Students

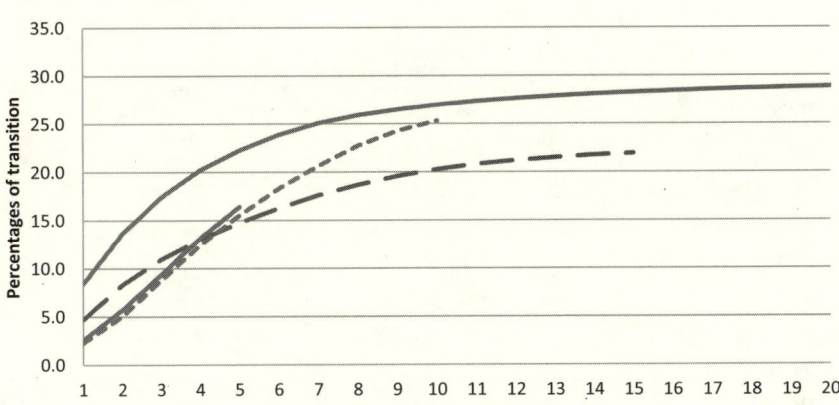

Among students in these four arrival cohorts, those in the early 1990s cohort were more likely to become permanent residents in Canada. By the end of their tenth year, the transition rate for this group reached 27 per cent. Those who arrived in the 2000s had lower transition rates in the initial years after obtaining their first study permits than the 1990s arrivals. However, after their fifth year, those who arrived in the 2000s surpassed the late 1990s cohort in the transition rate. By the end of their tenth year, about one-quarter of the early 2000s cohort had become landed immigrants in Canada.

The existing data indicated that most of the transitions to permanent residence occurred within the first ten years after the first study permit. Therefore, ten-year transition rates were calculated by international students' characteristics for those who arrived before 2005 (Table 11.2).

Male international students tended to have higher transition rates than females by two percentage points. This gender difference has been stable since the early 1990s. The transition rates were more evenly distributed across age groups in the early 2000s than in the 1990s. In the 1990s, those who first obtained their student permits between the ages of eighteen and twenty-four were the least likely to become permanent residents. By the early 2000s, the transition rate for this age group increased considerably.

Table 11.2 Cumulative Transition Rates by the End of the Tenth Year since the First Student Permit

	Obtained the first student permit in		
	1990–4	1995–9	2000–4
Gender	Per cent		
Male	28	21	26
Female	26	19	24
Age at first student permit			
< 18	33	26	24
18–24	20	16	25
25+	30	24	28
Level of study at first student permit			
Primary and secondary	31	25	25
Trade	25	10	13
Post-secondary, other	23	17	26
Bachelor's	22	21	32
Above bachelor's	33	42	49
Other	21	14	15
Source country/region			
Northern and Western Europe	14	13	16
Southern and Eastern Europe	38	35	36
Africa	38	46	55
China	61	57	47
India	47	53	55
Japan	7	6	6
South Korea	23	12	14
Other Asian countries	36	24	32
United States	20	16	16
Other	24	17	17

Data Source: Citizenship and Immigration Canada, Temporary Residents File.

In the early 2000s, international students who came to Canada to study for bachelor's or graduate degrees had the highest transition rates across all levels of study. In particular, close to one-half (49 per cent) of international students who arrived between 2000 and 2004 and pursued graduate degrees obtained permanent residence in Canada in the following ten years, compared with the corresponding rate of 33 per cent for the 1990–4 arrivals and 42 per cent for the 1995–9 arrivals. Similarly, the transition rate among international students who came to Canada to study for bachelor's degrees also increased. These increases likely reflect various modifications to the points system of immigrant selection over the 1990s and 2000s. These modifications enhanced the requirements on educational attainment and language ability in evaluating economic immigrants, and thus would benefit international students who came to Canada for university education.

The transition rates also differed by source country/region. International students from Northern/Western Europe, the United States, Japan, and South Korea had much lower transition rates than those from Southern/Eastern Europe, other parts of Asia, and Africa. In particular, the transition rates among international students from India, Africa, and China were about three times higher than among those from Northern/Western Europe and the United States.

The large variation in the transition rates by source country/region may be related to the differences between Canada and various source countries in terms of economic development, job opportunities, and social and political environments. It is possible that international students from countries with lower levels of economic development and less favourable social and political environments are more motivated to seek permanent residence in Canada. Figure 11.2 demonstrates the relationship between gross domestic product (GDP) per capita (in 2005 constant US dollars) of international students' source countries and their transition rates by the end of the tenth year after their first student permits. In the chart, each bubble represents a source country. The location of the bubble indicates a source country's position in the log of GDP per capita and the transition rate of their international students in Canada. The size of the bubble is weighted by the number of students. The chart reveals a strong negative association between a source country's GDP per capita and its international students' rate of transition to permanent residence in Canada.

A linear-probability regression model, applied in analyses where the dependent variable has only two possible outcomes, was estimated to predict becoming a landed immigrant (versus remaining a temporary resident) using source-country GDP per capita – whether English or French is an official language in the source country – and level of civil

Figure 11.2 Transition Rates and Source Country's Log GDP Per Capita

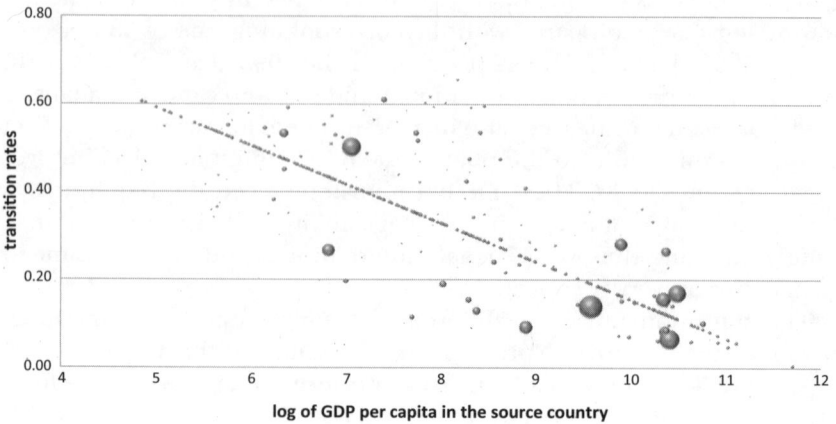

liberty as predictors. The model results show that a one-point increase in the log of source-country GDP per capita was associated with a decrease in the transition rate of eight percentage points. Meanwhile, the transition rate increased by nine percentage points if international students came from source countries with English as an official language, and by eight percentage points if French is an official language in the source country, compared with source countries where neither English nor French is an official language. International students from source countries with English or French as an official language likely benefitted from their high proficiency in English or French when they applied for permanent residence in Canada. Furthermore, the regression results show that a higher level of civil liberty in the source country was associated with lower transition rates. This implies that Canada's social and political environment is an important reason for many international students to seek permanent residence here.

It is also revealing that the transition rates among international students from different source countries/regions have moved in different directions since the early 1990s. Among the early 1990s arrivals, 61 per cent of Chinese students became landed immigrants within ten years of receiving their first student permit, but the transition rate declined to 47 per cent among the early 2000s cohort (Table 11.2). This decline may be a result of the rapidly expanding economy in China, which has become increasingly attractive to Chinese students abroad. Likely for the same reason, there was a large decline in the transition rates in the 1990s among international students from South Korea. In comparison, the transition rates have increased continuously among international students from India and Africa.

Characteristics of Immigrants Who Are Former International Students

Table 11.3 presents sex composition, age, level of study, and source region – all characteristics measured when international students obtained their first study permits – among immigrants who are former international students (IS immigrants). These characteristics were determined by the distribution of former international students and transition rates by these characteristics.

Although there were similar numbers of male and female international students in the 1990s and early 2000s, male international students had higher transition rates, resulting in more male IS immigrants than female IS immigrants. From the early 1990s to the early 2000s, the share of IS immigrants who held their first student permits before they turned 18 declined, while the share of those aged 18 to 24 at the time of first student permit increased considerably, from 33 to 55 per cent. These changes were the combined result of the rising share of international students who arrived between the ages of 18 and 24 and their increased transition rates.

Related to the change in age structure, the distribution of IS immigrants by the level of study at the first student permit changed markedly from the early 1990s to the early 2000s. While in the early 1990s about 45 per cent of IS immigrants came to Canada initially to study at primary and secondary school, this share decreased to 19 per cent in the early 2000s. In comparison, only 20 per cent of IS immigrants in the early 1990s came to study for bachelor's or graduate degrees, but this share increased to 38 per cent in the early 2000s. International students who initially studied at primary or secondary school arrived predominantly as minors and their transition to permanent residency was almost entirely as dependents in the economic class or as family class members. Conversely, the transition pathways were more diverse for international students who came to study for bachelor's or graduate degrees. Most of them applied as principal applicants in the economic class, and recent policy changes have made this pathway increasingly prevalent.

Driven by the changes in the source country/region composition and transition rates among international students, most IS immigrants

Table 11.3 Demographic Characteristics at First Arrival among Immigrants Who Were Former International Students

	Obtained the first student permit in		
	1990–4	1995–9	2000–4
Gender	Per cent		
Male	52	53	53
Female	48	47	47
Age at first student permit			
< 18	37	29	17
18–24	33	40	55
25+	30	31	28
Level of study at first student permit			
Primary and secondary	45	32	19
Trade	9	8	8
Other	6	9	7
Post-secondary, other	19	20	29
Bachelor's	9	14	20
Above bachelor's	11	17	18
Source country/region			
Northern and Western Europe	8	10	7
Southern and Eastern Europe	7	7	5
Africa	12	14	13
China	12	15	28
India	3	3	6
Japan	3	4	2
South Korea	3	10	10
Other Asian countries	34	19	16
United States	6	6	4
Other	12	13	9

Data Source: Citizenship and Immigration Canada, Temporary Residents File and Immigrant Landing File.

originated from Asia. In particular, the share of IS immigrants from China increased monotonically from the early 1990s to the early 2000s. Note that the source country/region composition of IS immigrants will continue to change significantly as China and India became the top two source countries of international students to Canada by the early 2010s, and students from those two countries tend to have relatively high transition rates, even though the transition rate among international students from China has fallen.

Table 11.4 summarizes the years of study and work experience in Canada that IS immigrants acquired before becoming landed immigrants, as well as characteristics that were collected at the time of landing. From the early 1990s to the early 2000s, there was a large shift in the years of study completed in Canada among IS immigrants, with a steady increase in the share of those completing at least three years of study. Among immigrants who first arrived as international students in the early 2000s, 53 per cent studied three to four years and another 27 per cent studied five or more years in Canada. There was also a decrease of ten percentage points in the share of IS immigrants who did not have some work experience in Canada before landing compared to the 1990s cohorts. Among the early 2000s arrivals, about 49 per cent of IS immigrants did not have any work experience in Canada at landing (in contrast to 59 per cent in the early 1990s cohort), while 22 per cent had worked in Canada in high-skilled jobs (versus 20 per cent in the early 1990s cohort).

The average age of IS immigrants at landing also increased. About 71 per cent were aged twenty-five years and over among the early 2000s arrivals, compared with 52 per cent among the 1990s arrivals (Table 11.4). Similarly, with the rising share of international students who came to study for university degrees and their rising transition rates, the achieved educational attainment of IS immigrants at landing increased significantly. The share of IS immigrants with bachelor's or graduate degrees surged from 36 per cent among the early 1990s arrivals to 56 per cent among the early 2000s arrivals.

Not surprisingly, the majority of IS immigrants spoke one of Canada's official languages. Only about 7 per cent of IS immigrants among the early 2000s arrivals spoke neither English nor French, compared with 25 to 37 per cent of all immigrants aged fifteen or over who arrived in Canada during the late 2000s and early 2010s (CIC 2014). Over the 1990s, the share of IS immigrants who did not speak English or French decreased, as did the share of IS immigrants whose mother tongue was English.

Table 11.4 Characteristics at Landing among Immigrants Who Were Former
International Students

	Obtained the first student permit in		
	1990–4	1995–9	2000–4
Years of study in Canada before landing	Per cent		
2 years or less	43	34	21
3–4 years	41	43	53
5 years or more	17	23	27
Had work permit in Canada before landing			
with high skill	20	18	22
with low skill	4	3	4
skill level unknown	17	17	25
no work permit	59	63	49
Age at immigration			
< 18	25	19	10
18–24	24	19	20
25 and above	52	62	71
Education qualifications at landing			
Primary and secondary	43	31	22
Trade	5	3	2
Post-secondary, other	15	17	20
Bachelor's	17	26	35
Above bachelor's	19	23	21
Canadian official Language ability at landing			
English mother tongue	18	16	10
French mother tongue	7	8	7
Other mother tongue, speaking English	55	55	63
Other mother tongue, speaking French	4	3	2
Other mother tongues, bilingual	5	8	11
Not speak English or French	12	10	7
Class of immigration			
Economic, principal applicant	30	39	48
Economic, spouse or dependent	32	26	22
Family	30	28	23
Refugee	5	7	8
Other	3	1	0
Number of observations	41,196	43,671	71,004

Data Source: Citizenship and Immigration Canada, Temporary Residents File and
Immigrant Landing File.

An important change was the large increase in the share of IS immigrants who were principal applicants in the economic class, from 30 per cent among the early 1990s arrivals to 48 per cent among the early 2000s arrivals. This trend was likely a response to government policy changes that made it easier for international students to work and apply for immigration. This trend signalled a major shift in the transition pathways to permanent residence for international students. Increasingly, IS immigrants initiated the application themselves, while in the past more of them were dependents in the economic class or sponsored in the family class.

The change in admission classes through which international students transition to immigrant status is also an underlying reason for many changes in the characteristics of IS immigrants observed earlier. Under the points system Canada uses to select immigrants, principal applicants in the economic class receive high points for being of prime working age, proficient in the official languages, and having work experience in Canada and university degrees. The share of immigrants with these characteristics would certainly increase as more IS immigrants obtained their permanent residence as economic principal applicants rather than as dependents. For instance, among IS immigrants with only primary or secondary education at landing, only 4 per cent were principal applicants, and this share did not change across the arrival cohorts. In comparison, among IS immigrants with a bachelor's degree, 67 per cent were economic principal applicants among the early 2000s arrivals, a large increase from 52 per cent among the early 1990s arrivals.

What Factors Are Associated with Integration in the Labour Market?

The descriptive statistics outlined above reveal vast heterogeneity in educational attainment, work experience in Canada, language ability, age at landing, and source countries among IS immigrants. Because Canadian employers and the structure of the economy value these characteristics differently, the heterogeneity naturally leads to individual variations in performance in the Canadian labour market. This section examines how common predictors of labour market outcomes, including human capital factors such as education and work experience, and immigrant-specific factors such as age at landing, language, source region, and immigration class, affect the earnings of IS immigrants. In particular, the analysis evaluates these predictors, examining how their relative importance changes with more years after immigration.

Knowledge of the relative importance of various predictors of immigrant labour market outcomes is pertinent to immigrant selection. Canada's points system for selecting economic immigrants allocates different points to various human capital factors, including age, education, language ability, and work experience. The newly implemented Express Entry system also uses these factors to screen individuals who are interested in immigrating to Canada as skilled workers before they are formally invited to apply. Since the points system was first established in 1967, the factors and points assigned to each factor have been altered many times at least partly as a way to improve immigrants' integration into the Canadian labour market. For instance, changes in the selection system in the early 1990s and again in the early 2000s enhanced the roles of education and language under the assumption that these are the most critical factors for immigrants to perform well in a knowledge-based economy and to adapt to changes in economic conditions (Picot, Hou, and Qiu 2014). Beach, Green, and Worswick (2011) demonstrated that altering the characteristics (e.g., education and language) of immigrants via the points system could indeed affect entry earnings. Among a number of recommendations, they argued that the average age of economic immigrants should be reduced given that younger immigrant workers achieve greater labour market success than older immigrants, and that the emphasis on foreign work experience should be discounted since there were no economic returns from foreign work experience according to empirical studies. A more recent empirical analysis by Bonikowska, Hou, and Picot (2015) shows that among factors used in the points system, language ability and work experience in Canada prior to landing are the best predictors of entry earnings (first two years after landing) for economic immigrants. However, education and age at landing are the best predictors of earnings about ten years after immigration. To what extent these empirical findings for immigrants in general are applicable to immigrants who are former international students in Canada is addressed below.

The analysis approach is based on ordinary least square (OLS) regression models. Annual earnings, including paid employment and self-employment earnings, are used as the outcome. The study sample includes immigrants who obtained their first study permits in or after 1990, became landed immigrants between 1990 and 2002, were aged 20–44 at landing, and reported positive annual earnings. The restriction on the landing period ensures that all immigrants in the sample have been landed for at least 10 years. Annual earnings in a given year are expressed in 2010 constant Canadian dollars and the natural logarithm of annual earnings is used in the regression models. The predictors include age at landing, years of study in Canada prior to landing, level of study at the first study permit, work experience in Canada before landing, educational attainment at landing, language ability at landing, class of immigration, and source region. Control variables include months of being a full-time student in the year when earnings data were collected, province of residence, and arrival cohort based on the year of obtaining the first study permit (1990–4, 1995–9, and 2000–4). The categories of the predictors can be found in Table 11.5. To examine whether the relative importance of these predictors changes as immigrants stay longer in Canada, models are estimated respectively for immigrants in their first 2 years after landing, 5 to 6 years after landing, and 9 to 10 years after landing. Analyses are conducted for men and women separately.

Table 11.5 presents the unstandardized coefficients of the regression models. Since the dependent variable is the natural logarithm of annual earnings, the coefficient of an independent variable in the model can be interpreted approximately as percentage differences (the coefficient times 100) in earnings associated with a one-unit change in a continuous predictor or between a given category and the reference category in a categorical predictor. For instance, in the model for IS immigrant men in the first 2 years after landing, 1 extra year of study in Canada prior to landing was associated with 1 per cent higher annual earnings, but this effect was not statistically significant. This coefficient increased to 0.02 (or 2 per cent) in the model for men 5 to 6 years after landing, and by 9 to 10 years the coefficient remained positive and statistically significant. These results suggest that more years of study in Canada prior to landing, net of educational levels achieved, had a positive effect on earnings in the long run. Similar effects for years studying in Canada were observed for immigrant women, and the long-term positive effect was stronger among women than among men.

The initial level of study at first study permit in Canada also mattered for earnings after immigration, even when we controlled for completed education. IS immigrants who came initially to pursue university degrees earned 15 to 41 per cent more than those who first came to attend elementary or high school. The effects of first study level remained strong nine to ten years after immigration and were similar for women and men. Since international students who started at elementary or high

Table 11.5 Regression Coefficients of Log Annual Earnings among Immigrants Who Were Former International Students

Men	Years after landing		
	1–2	5–6	9–10
Level of first study (ref: high school or less)			
Trade	0.13*	0.22***	0.10
Some post-secondary	0.05	0.22***	0.09*
Bachelor's degree	0.15**	0.39***	0.32***
Graduate degrees	0.26***	0.40***	0.41***
Other	0.05	0.07	−0.02
Years of study in Canada	0.01	0.02**	0.01*
Canadian work experience before landing (ref: no exp.)			
High-skilled experience	0.5***	0.41***	0.35***
Low-skilled experience	0.47***	0.27***	0.27***
Skills not identified	0.36***	0.26***	0.17***
Age at landing (ref: 20–4)			
25–9	0.26***	0.03	−0.07
30–4	0.14***	−0.08	−0.21***
35–9	0.07	−0.25***	−0.30***
40–4	0	−0.34***	−0.59***
Educational attainment at landing (ref: high school or less)			
Trade	0.51***	0.33***	0.18**
Some post-secondary	0.47***	0.42***	0.32***
Bachelor's degree	0.79***	0.7***	0.60***
Graduate degree	0.83***	0.8***	0.76***
Language ability (ref: English mother tongue)			
French mother tongue	−0.15*	−0.07	−0.03
Other mother tongue, speaking English	−0.14**	−0.11*	−0.12*
Other mother tongue, speaking French	−0.28***	−0.17*	−0.20**
Other mother tongues, bilingual	−0.27***	−0.17**	−0.17**
Not speak English or French	−0.72***	−0.71***	−0.49***
Class of immigration (ref: Family class)			
Economic, principal applicant	0.34***	0.2***	0.16***
Economic, spouse or dependent	−0.44***	−0.2***	−0.02
Refugee	−0.09	−0.11	−0.04
Other	−0.14	0.22	0.11

| | Years after landing | | |
Men	1–2	5–6	9–10
Source country /region (ref: the United States)			
Northern and Western Europe	0.10	0.13	0.16
Southern and Eastern Europe	0.04	0	−0.01
Africa	−0.22**	−0.19*	−0.17*
China	−0.36***	−0.28**	−0.31***
India	0.02	0.10	0.04
Japan	−0.09	0.10	0.09
South Korea	−1.18***	−0.91***	−0.78***
Asia, other	−0.42***	−0.48***	−0.38***
Other	0.06	0.10	0.02
Intercept	9.05***	9.67***	10.12***
R squared	0.162	0.137	0.103
Observations	35,101	31,300	27,797

| | Years after landing | | |
Women	1–2	5–6	9–10
Level of first study (ref: high school or less)			
Trade	0.24***	0.05	0.13*
Some post-secondary	0.03	0.07	0.11*
Bachelor's degree	0.39***	0.37***	0.38***
Graduate degrees	0.36***	0.31***	0.38***
Other	0.06	0.00	−0.01
Years of study in Canada	0.01	0.05***	0.04***
Canadian work experience before landing (ref: no experience)			
High-skilled experience	0.67****	0.56***	0.39***
Low-skilled experience	0.75***	0.53***	0.46***
Skills not identified	0.64***	0.5***	0.26***
Age at landing (ref: 20–4)			
25–9	0.07	−0.12**	−0.12**
30–4	−0.15**	−0.17***	−0.13**
35–9	−0.23***	−0.08	−0.20**
40–4	−0.14	−0.11	−0.29***

Table 11.5 (continued)

Women	Years after landing		
	1–2	5–6	9–10
Educational attainment at landing (ref: high school or less)			
Trade	0.28***	0.26***	0.08
Some post-secondary	0.41***	0.30***	0.28***
Bachelor's degree	0.69***	0.55***	0.49***
Graduate degrees	0.72***	0.63***	0.72***
Language ability (ref: English mother tongue)			
French mother tongue	−0.27**	−0.16	−0.04
Other mother tongue, speaking English	−0.23***	−0.39***	−0.32***
Other mother tongue, speaking French	−0.60***	−0.66***	−0.28**
Other mother tongues, bilingual	−0.31***	−0.26**	−0.29***
Not speak English or French	−0.84***	−0.72***	−0.79***
Class of immigration (ref: Family class)			
Economic, principal applicant	0.76***	0.65***	0.45***
Economic, spouse or dependent	−0.12**	0.08	0.11*
Refugee	−0.16	0.18	0.08
Other	0.33*	0.69***	0.14
Source country /region (ref: the United States)			
Northern and Western Europe	0.28**	0.58***	0.42***
Southern and Eastern Europe	0.22*	0.72***	0.68***
Africa	−0.06	0.43***	0.36***
China	−0.01	0.69***	0.61***
India	−0.07	0.48***	0.58***
Japan	−0.21*	0.39***	0.29**
South Korea	−1.27***	−0.38**	−0.20
Asia, other	−0.28**	0.24*	0.34***
Other	0.04	0.54***	0.46***
Intercept	8.46***	8.49***	8.89***
R squared	0.134	0.094	0.088
Observations	29,625	27,373	25,069

Data Source: Citizenship and Immigration Canada–Temporary Residents File and Immigrant Landing File; and Statistics Canada–T1 tax data.
Note: all models also include months of full-time study in a given year after immigration, arrival cohorts, and provinces of residence. The sample includes immigrants who arrived initially as international students since 1990 and became landed immigrants between 1990 and 2002. *Significant at 5%; **Significant at 1%; ***Significant at 0.1%.

school mostly arrived with their families, they may not be as independent and motivated as those who came at an older age to pursue post-secondary education.

Work experience in Canada before landing, particularly skilled work experience, had a strong positive effect on post-immigration earnings. The effect of pre-landing work experience tended to decrease with increased years after immigration, but remained large nine to ten years after immigration. A previous study found that the earnings advantage of immigrants with pre-landing work experience in Canada stemmed mostly from a better match between skills and Canadian labour market demands (Hou and Bonikowska 2015). The same may also apply to IS immigrants. It is possible that IS immigrants who found jobs before landing either studied in fields that were in high demand or had better skills and stronger motivations than other IS immigrants.

The effect of age at landing varied noticeably with years since landing and by sex. Among IS immigrant men, those aged 25–34 years had higher initial earnings than their younger or older peers, likely because they were more fully engaged in the labour market than their younger peers and preferred by employers over older immigrants. However, as the years after immigration increased, particularly to 9 to 10 years, a steep negative association between age at landing and annual earnings appeared. This is consistent with the findings of earlier empirical studies that younger immigrants tend to have better integration outcomes in the long run. Compared with men, the penalty of older age was less severe among IS immigrant women.

Educational attainment at landing was strongly and positively associated with earnings among both IS immigrant men and women. Interestingly, the effect of Canadian university education at landing among IS immigrants remained consistent in the short and long run. This differs from recent findings for immigrants in general, for whom the benefits of university education increase substantially with years after immigration (Picot, Hou, and Qiu 2014). The differences in the effect of university education between IS immigrants and regular immigrants likely reflect the impact of the location where the education is acquired. Educational credentials acquired in Canada can be easily evaluated by Canadian employers, thus the earnings returns on Canadian university education were high upon entry to the labour market and remained high over time. In comparison, many foreign-educated immigrants cannot find jobs commensurate with their qualifications when they first arrive, thus the earnings returns on foreign education are low initially, but can increase over time as highly educated immigrants are generally more flexible in adjusting to changes in labour market demands and they can gradually demonstrate their skills and abilities on the job.

Ability in one of Canada's official languages was a strong predictor of earnings among IS immigrants. Those who did not speak English or French at landing had a large earnings disadvantage, even though this disadvantage was somewhat mitigated as these IS immigrants stayed more years in Canada and likely learned some English or French. Compared with IS immigrants whose mother tongue was English or French, those who had another mother tongue, but were able to speak either or both official languages, also had significant earnings disadvantages in the short and long terms.

The earnings of IS immigrants varied by immigration class. Immigrants in different entry classes (e.g., family class versus economic principal applicants) differ not only in the observed characteristics – education, official language, pre-landing work experience in Canada, age at landing – but also in unobserved abilities, motivations, and preparedness for the Canadian labour market. For both men and women, economic principal applicants had higher earnings compared to all other classes, but the advantage was more than twice as large among women as among men. In contrast, the disadvantage of being a spouse or dependent in the economic class was much larger among men than among women. Since most economic principal applicants are men, those men who gain permanent residence as a spouse or dependent may have lower human capital relative to the female principal applicant in the family and also to average immigrant men. Conversely, immigrant women who were principal applicants may have acquired more skills and abilities relative to their male partners and also to average immigrant women.

Finally, there were large earnings gaps among IS immigrants from various source countries/regions. Compared with those from the United States, IS immigrant men from South Korea, China, "other" Asian countries, and Africa earned significantly less both in the short and long terms. Among IS immigrant women, the disadvantages were limited to those from South Korea, Japan, and "other" Asian countries in the first two years after landing. By nine to ten years, immigrant women from Southern/Eastern Europe, China, and India earned higher incomes compared to other major source country/region groups.

The above discussions of regression coefficients reveal how strongly the variation in a particular predictor is associated with earnings, but they do not show the relative importance among predictors. The relative importance of predictors of immigrant earnings can be evaluated by the extent to which a predictor "explains" or "accounts for" the variation in earnings. A predictor that accounts for a larger share of the variation in earnings is considered to be more important, as indicated by the contribution of each predictor to the total R squared in a regression model. The total R squared in a regression model ranges between 0 and 1. A higher R squared implies that the included predictors account for a larger portion of variance in the outcome variable; in other words, together they explain more of the variation in positive earnings. A predictor's contribution to the total R squared contains a unique component and a common component. The unique component is determined by first running the full model, and then dropping the variable of interest from the regression. The resulting reduction in the R squared is regarded as the unique contribution of the predictor in explaining the variance of immigrant earnings. However, a predictor may partially operate in combination with another predictor, so the joint presence of two or more predictors would have an additional contribution to the model R squared. This additional, or "common," contribution can be identified through the "commonality analysis" (Nathans, Oswald, and Nimon 2012). As the number of predictors increases, the number of possible combinations of these predictors for commonality analysis becomes large quickly. To maintain a manageable analysis, only the two-way combinations of four key human capital factors are included in the calculation of common contribution. Table 11.6 presents the unique and common contributions of major predictors included in the regression models by years after landing and sex.

Among IS immigrant men, the most important predictors in explaining variations in earnings in the first two years after landing were source region, immigrant class, pre-landing work experience in Canada, and educational attainment. Over time, the relative importance of immigration class diminished and the role of pre-landing work experience in Canada also declined. By nine to ten years after immigration, educational attainment and source region remained the most important predictors of earnings, while the level of the first student permit, pre-landing work experience in Canada, and age at landing were also relatively important. The common contribution of various two-way combinations of predictors did not play a large role. Similarly, among IS immigrant women, immigration class, pre-landing work experience in Canada, source region, and educational attainment were the predominant predictors of earnings in the initial years after immigration. But the explanatory

Table 11.6 The Relative Importance of Predictors of Immigrant Earnings by Years after Immigration

	Men			Women		
	Years after landing			Years after landing		
	1–2	5–6	9–10	1–2	5–6	9–10
R squared of the full model	0.16	0.14	0.10	0.13	0.09	0.09
Unique contribution						
Age at landing	0.002	0.002	0.004	0.002	0.000	0.001
Canadian work experience	0.008	0.006	0.004	0.014	0.009	0.005
Level of first student permit	0.001	0.003	0.005	0.003	0.002	0.003
Language	0.003	0.004	0.002	0.003	0.003	0.003
Education qualifications at landing	0.007	0.007	0.008	0.006	0.004	0.006
Source country/region	0.012	0.011	0.009	0.013	0.010	0.007
immigration class	0.009	0.003	0.001	0.017	0.010	0.005
Common contribution						
Age at landing, Canadian work experience	0.000	0.000	0.000	0.000	0.000	0.000
Age at landing, education qualifications	0.002	0.000	−0.001	0.000	0.000	0.000
Canadian work experience, education qualifications	0.002	0.002	0.002	0.002	0.001	0.001
Language, Canadian work experience	0.001	0.001	0.001	0.001	0.001	0.001
Language, education qualifications	0.001	0.001	0.001	0.000	0.000	0.000

Data Source: Citizenship and Immigration Canada–Temporary Residents File and Immigrant Landing File; and Statistics Canada–T1 tax data.

power of these predictors weakened over time, and by nine to ten years, source region, education, pre-landing work experience in Canada, and immigration class each played similarly reduced roles.

While previous studies found language ability to be one of the most important predictors of immigrant earnings both in the short and long terms, this was not the case here for two reasons. First, study experience at Canadian educational institutions might have reduced the variation in English or French proficiency among IS immigrants. Second, source regions were controlled in the regression models, thereby eliminating some of the effects of language abilities. It is possible that the crude categories of self-reported language abilities in the data do not fully capture individual variations in English/French proficiency, and this limitation may be somewhat mitigated by the inclusion of source regions. If source regions were excluded from the models, language became similarly important as educational attainment, but remained not as important as immigrant class and pre-landing work experience in Canada in determining initial earnings. In predicting earnings nine to ten years after immigration, language ability was similarly important as pre-landing work experience in Canada, level of the first student permit, and educational attainment at landing when source regions were excluded from the models.

Conclusions

This chapter first described the transition rates from international students to permanent residents, and the characteristics of immigrants who are former international students (IS immigrants). It further examined the factors associated with the earnings of this group of immigrants in the Canadian labour market.

As the number of international students has increased continuously since the 1990s, more of them arrived at age eighteen years and over and came to pursue university degrees. The composition of source regions has also changed. While Japan and the United States were the two top source countries in the early 1990s, they were replaced by South Korea and China by the early 2000s, and China and India took the top two spots in the early 2010s. In terms of transitions to permanent residence, about 20 to 27 per cent of international students switched their status by the tenth year after their first student permits, depending on arrival cohorts.

The period from the early 1990s to the early 2000s witnessed a major shift in the transition pathways to permanent residence for international students. IS immigrants increasingly initiated the application as principal applicants rather than being admitted as spouses or dependents in the economic class or family class. Accordingly, more IS immigrants were of prime working age, proficient in one or both official languages, and had university degrees and work experience in Canada. The rates of transition to permanent residence differed greatly by source country. International students from countries that were less developed and had less-favourable social and political environments were more likely to become landed immigrants in Canada.

The heterogeneity in the characteristics of IS immigrants leads to large variations in their labour market outcomes. Regression analysis suggests that IS immigrants enjoyed clear advantages in annual earnings if they first came to Canada to pursue university education, obtained bachelor's or graduate degrees, had high proficiency in English or French, landed at a younger age, and were economic principal applicants. Among IS immigrant men, those from the United States and Europe had much higher earnings than those from developing countries. In terms of the relative importance of the observed predictors, source region, immigrant class, pre-landing work experience in Canada, and educational attainment played the predominant roles in determining earnings in the first two years after landing among IS immigrant men and women. Educational attainment and source region remained the most important predictors of earnings nine to ten years after immigration. The effect of source region to a large extent likely captures the role of proficiency in Canada's official languages in determining immigrants' earnings.

International students who pursue university education and acquire work experience in Canada during or immediately after their study will benefit from the recent policy changes in immigration selection. The Express Entry system, introduced at the beginning of 2015, emphasizes young age, university education, English or French proficiency, and work experience in Canada in determining whom will be invited to apply as skilled-worker immigrants. International students have advantages in all these aspects over individuals who have never worked or studied in Canada. Furthermore, the current implementation of the new system gives overriding propriety to applicants who have a job offer from Canadian employers or who are nominated by provincial governments. To secure the transition to permanent residents, international students need opportunities and the ability to find jobs in Canada. It would certainly help for them to study in high-demand fields, improve their English or French proficiency, and establish some social networks.

References

Arthur, Nancy, and Sarah Flynn. 2013. "International Students' Views of Transition to Employment and Immigration." *Canadian Journal of Career Development* 12 (1): 28–37.

Beach, Charles, Alan Green, and Christopher Worswick. 2011. *Toward Improving Canada's Skilled Immigration Policy: An Evaluation Approach.* Toronto: C.D. Howe Institute Policy Studies.

Bonikowska, Aneta, Feng Hou, and Garnett Picot. 2015. "Which Human Capital Characteristics Best Predict the Earnings of Economic Immigrants?" Working Paper. Ottawa: Statistics Canada.

Citizenship and Immigration Canada (CIC). 2010. *Evaluation of the Federal Skilled Worker Program. No. Ci4–54/2010E-PDF.* Ottawa: Evaluation Division.

– 2014. *Facts and Figures 2013.* Ottawa.

Foreign Affairs, Trade and Development Canada (FTD). 2014. *Canada's International Education Strategy: Harnessing Our Knowledge Advantage to Drive Innovation and Prosperity.* Ottawa: Cat. No.: FR5–86/2014, ISBN: 978–1-100–23110–5.

Hawthorne, Lesleyanne, and Anna To. 2014. "Australian Employer Response to the Study-Migration Pathway: The Quantitative Evidence 2007-2011." *International Migration (Geneva, Switzerland)* 52 (3): 99–115. https://doi.org/10.1111/imig.12154.

Hou, Feng, and Aneta Bonikowska. 2015. *Earnings Advantages of Immigrants Who Were Skilled Temporary Foreign Workers.* Analytical Branch Research Paper. Ottawa: Statistics Canada.

Lowell, Lindsay, and Johanna Avato. 2014. "The Wages of Skilled Temporary Migrants: Effects of Visa Pathways and Job Portability." *International Migration (Geneva, Switzerland)* 52 (3): 85–98. https://doi.org/10.1111/imig.12133.

Nathans, Laura L., Frederick L. Oswald, and Kim Nimon. 2012. "Interpreting Multiple Linear Regression: A Guidebook of Variable Importance." *Practical Assessment, Research & Evaluation* 17 (9): 1–19.

Picot, Garnett, Feng Hou, and Theresa Qiu. 2014. *The Human Capital Model of Selection and the Long-Run Economic Outcomes of Immigrants.* Analytical Studies Research Branch Research Paper Series 361. Ottawa: Statistics Canada.

Shu, J., and Lesleyanne Hawthorne. Nov 1995. "Asian female students in Australia: Temporary movements and student migration." *Journal of the Australian Population Association* 12 (2): 113–30. https://doi.org/10.1007/BF03029313. Medline:12321978

van Huystee, Monica. 2011. *A Profile of Foreign Students Who Transition to Permanent Resident Status in Atlantic Canada.* Ottawa: Citizenship and Immigration Canada, Research and Evaluation.

12 Bumpy Roads: Tracing Pathways into Practice for International Students in Nursing

MARGARET WALTON-ROBERTS AND JENNA HENNEBRY

Introduction

This chapter considers the transition process from education to employment for internationally educated nurses (IENs) who enter Canada
through educational pathways. Navigating through a myriad of professional regulatory requirements, educational requirements, and immigration regulations slows and sometimes halts the process by which
these nurses attempt to stay and work in Canada. Current policy developments allow for postgraduate college programs to act as an entry into
a "two-step" migration process for IENs to obtain permanent residency
and employment in Canada. Given the Canadian Nurses Association's
(CNA) prediction that Canada will face a shortfall of 60,000 nurses by
2022, and the growing number of, and government interest in, international student migrants, this chapter provides an analysis of IEN postgraduate trajectories to determine if international student pathways are
an effective and ethical way to fill labour market gaps. While scholars
have examined the growing tendency of international students to enter
Canada for the purpose of migration (Ortiz and Choudaha 2014), few
studies track IEN pathways through the licensure process or evaluate
their employment outcomes (Shaffer and Dutka 2013). In this chapter
we highlight the intricacies of the student-to-labour-market pathway in
Ontario by examining the intersections between changing immigration
policy and professional nursing regulatory change, highlighting some of

This research has benefitted from funding from CERIS Ontario Metropolis and the
Social Science and Humanities Research Council of Canada. We thank Jennifer Guo, Kira
Williams, Amy Arbuckle, and Gabriel Williams for assistance with this research.

the challenges international students in nursing face on the bumpy road to professional practice.

Nursing as a Globally Mobile Profession

The international migration of health professionals is not a new phenomenon; however, owing to the global nursing shortage in many of the countries in the Global North today, the stock of nurses living and working overseas has significantly increased over the past two decades and nursing is increasingly characterized as a mobile profession (Kingma 2006). Yet, this does not necessarily translate into enhanced mobility for nurses themselves, and what mobility exists is certainly not without costs and consequences for migrants and their families. For nurse-migrants, the direction and scope of migratory flows are reliably determined by the interaction of a set of "push" and "pull" motivators (Connell 2010). Political, social, and economic insecurities, substandard working conditions, and undesirable quality of living are commonly cited factors that drive nurses to emigrate. On the other hand, IENs choose their overseas destination based on a set of factors related to a country's attractiveness, which includes opportunities to gain higher income, standard of living, and prospects for career advancement (Home 2011).

In much of the Global North, particularly in the United States, the United Kingdom, Canada, Australia, Ireland, and New Zealand, the hiring of IENs is regarded as a "quick fix" to curtail the effects of nursing shortages and to increase labour market flexibility (Valiani 2012). Keeping in mind that in Canada it takes, at minimum, a four-year baccalaureate or equivalent to become a registered nurse (RN), and up to seven years of training to become a nurse practitioner (NP), recruiting IENs allows countries to sidestep the time investment to train nurses domestically (Yeates 2010, 424–5). The Global North, in competing for IENs, has rolled out a series of strategies, including active international nurse recruitment campaigns, bilateral state agreements (including mutual trade agreements), changes to immigration regulations (including opportunities to apply for permanent residence, citizenship, and family reunification), and new foreign credential recognition and licensing policies, all aimed at successfully integrating overseas nurses into the local nursing workforce (Yeates 2010, 427). Correspondingly, in several countries of the Global South, especially the Philippines, India, China, and the newly independent states of the former Soviet Union (NIS), there is a deliberate effort to overproduce nurses for overseas employment (Brush and Sochalski 2007). It is, however, often the private education sector that provides this export-directed training, resulting in lower-quality training and poor regulatory oversight (Reynolds et al. 2013).

Global (Nurse) Care Chains, Perverse Subsidies, and Ethical Recruitment

The convergence of these "push" and "pull" motivators, on both an individual and institutional level, together with the shifting political economy of feminized, care-oriented migration, gives shape to a "global nursing care chain" (Yeates 2010, 426), wherein poorer countries situated at the lower end of the chain export valuable nursing human resources upwards along the chain to supply richer countries (Yeates 2010, 426). This phenomenon is broadly mirrored in the distinctive migratory patterns of nurses from the Philippines, India, China, and countries in Sub-Saharan Africa moving to developed countries in the Global North (OECD 2007, 173). For instance, IENs represented 10.7 per cent of the combined nursing workforce of OECD member countries, equal to a total of 711,877 nurses (OECD 2007, 165). In 2001, 85 per cent of all working Filipino nurses (or 150,000 in absolute numbers) were documented as working overseas (Aiken et al. 2004, 75). In 2010, the top source countries for internationally educated RNs in Canada included the Philippines (32.4 per cent); the United Kingdom (16.3 per cent); India (6.5 per cent); and the United States (6.3 per cent). The top source countries for internationally educated registered practical nurses (RPNs) included the Philippines (35.2 per cent); the United Kingdom (16.2 per cent); the United States (10 per cent); and India (7.3 per cent) (CIHI 2011,70). In addition, migration trajectories are not always straightforward, with many IENs working in one or more countries prior to coming to Canada, often after prolonged separation from their families, who remain in their countries of origin (George 2005). Table 12.1 illustrates the country of training for nurses who applied to the College of Nurses of Ontario in 2014, revealing the dominance of less-developed countries. Table 12.2, on the other hand, indicates the country of last permanent residence for IENs who come to Canada, which includes the United Arab Emirates, Saudi Arabia, and Hong Kong – key markets for nurses engaging in multiple migrations.

Due to the uneven geographical distribution of nurse migration between destination and source countries, the deliberate sourcing of nurses from countries with health systems most severely crippled by long-term nursing shortages is seen as unethical recruitment. For instance,

Table 12.1 Top Ten Countries of Last Residence for IENs Entering Canada, 2011

Rank	Country	2011 Total	2002–11 Growth
1	Philippines	8,439	52.6%
2	Hong Kong	1,025	3200.0%
3	India	832	320.0%
4	United Kingdom	514	54.8%
5	China	408	167.0%
6	Taiwan	351	356.0%
7	France	331	27.8%
8	Saudi Arabia	160	83.9%
9	Singapore	152	2000.0%
10	UAE	143	169.0%
-	Rest of the World	2,650	33.8%
-	Total	15,005	66.7%

Source: CIC, 2013a

Table 12.2 Country Where Applicants to the College of Nurses of Ontario were Originally Trained, 2014

Country of training (Canada excluded)	Number of applicants in the reporting year
India	1,871
Philippines	1,034
United States	122
Iran	106
Jamaica	69
Nigeria	64
Pakistan	54
United Kingdom	51
Nepal	28
China	26

Source: CNO annual report to the Office of the Fairness Commission, p. 29. Available at http://www.cno.org/globalassets/1-whatiscno/newsreleasesandnotices/notices/nursingfairregistrationpracticesreport2014.pdf.

countries in Sub-Saharan Africa are projected to reach an estimated nursing shortfall of 600,000 nurses while they continue to be exporters of nurses (ICN 2004, 5). A series of global voluntary codes of conduct, the Commonwealth Code of Practice for the International Recruitment of Health Workers (adopted in 2003), and the WHO Global Code of Practice on the International Recruitment of Health Personnel (adopted in May 2010), aim to both discourage dependency on nurse migration as a "quick fix" solution, and to discourage the recruitment of nurses from countries that would be most severely impacted. In 2005 the CNA officially recognized "the right of individual nurses to migration and confirm[ed] the potential beneficial outcomes of multicultural practice and learning opportunities supported by migration," and it fully endorsed the International Council of Nurses' position statement and guidelines on the ethical recruitment of overseas nurses (Canadian Nurses Association 2005).

To respect these ethical codes of conduct, Canada must avoid targeted and active recruitment of IENs from source countries with human capital and health human resources at critically depleted levels. Yet Canada has not created legislation directly aimed at regulating the recruitment process of IENs from abroad (nor within other sectors), and instead relies heavily on professional regulatory bodies within Canada to monitor entry into the profession, and on visa officers abroad to assess student visa and work permit compliance. Nevertheless, as the pathways into nursing practice evolve in response to changing conditions in sending countries and shifting immigration policies in receiving nations, it will become imperative to assess and monitor the ethical implications of this transfer of nursing skills between sending, transit, and receiving nations.

Nursing Shortages and Professional Regulation in Canada

The CNA estimates that by 2022, without policy intervention, the nursing shortfall will reach 60,000 full-time RNs (Canadian Nurses Association 2009). In nursing, labour market planning is challenging due to training lags, retirements, enhanced technological change, and skilled labour migration into and out of the sector (Kingma 2006). Documenting how new migrant pathways interact with labour markets is vital for any analysis of skills development and future labour market needs in Canada. Appropriate policies leading to the timely inclusion of migrants with relevant skills offers a buffer for the purposes of planning for workforce renewal under conditions of an aging population and rapid technological change. Incorporating highly skilled international migrants may also offer opportunities for constant upgrading and enhanced training of domestic labour in areas where training is subject to time lags in entry into practice, and under conditions where labour market exit is ongoing and unpredictable. These characteristics are evident in nursing.

The Nursing Profession in Canada

There are three categories of nursing professions across Canada: registered nurse, licensed practical nurse (LPN) (or registered practical nurse in Ontario), and registered psychiatric nurse (RPN). Each of these professions is regulated at the provincial and territorial level by a self-regulated nursing body. Registration with one of the corresponding nursing bodies is required in order to become a practising nurse in Canada. Regulated nurses represent the single largest category of health-care professionals in Canada, and of all professions in Ontario alone, it has the third-largest number of internationally trained members (Office of Fairness Commissioner 2013, 64). It is also a sector of the labour market that suffers structural and cyclical shortages. Despite an assessment at the beginning of the twenty-first century that Canada needed to produce 18,118 RNs annually between 2001 and 2016 (Canadian Nurses Association, 2002, 70–1), in 2012 entry-to-practice programs documented the highest number of graduates at 11,777 RNs, which was a record high for Canada since 1963 – this in contrast to a record low in early 2000 of only 4,816 (Canadian Nurses Association 2013, 8).

Underlying this shortage is a multitude of correlated factors, including retirement of the older nurse workforce, high stress and burnout resulting in early retirement, high rates of absenteeism, high levels of staff turnover due to working conditions and dissatisfaction (O'Brien-Pallas et al. 2010), and high rates of in- and out-migration that add "churning" costs to the system (Gordon 2005). Canada's nursing workforce will also be pressured to meet the demands of evolving demographic shifts, with greater numbers of individuals facing increased risk of illness, injury, or other health problems (CFNU 2008, 13). There will also be significant demands for community-based palliative and long-term care, which will require different health-care skill sets and models of inter-professional, team-based care (Stall, Nowaczynski, and Sinha 2013). Commonly cited solutions to address the nursing shortage include increasing nurse recruitment, retention, and productivity by modernizing health-care service-delivery models through technology, creating flexible and quality workplaces in order to (re)position the nursing profession as an attractive career path, and, most critically, to optimally harness the skills of the existing nursing workforce (ACHDHR 2009).

Developing and retaining existing human resources in nursing will be central (Vaughn 2006; CFNU 2008, 233), although Canada's investment in training new nurses alone will not overcome the anticipated nursing shortage. In addition to new domestically trained nursing graduates, Canada's nursing supply includes the in-migration of IENs. In 2009, IENs made up 8.3 per cent of the overall Canadian nursing workforce and nearly half were working in Ontario (Home 2011, 40). In 2007, one-third of IENs working in Ontario were documented as residing and working in Toronto, comprising 25 per cent of Toronto's local nursing workforce (Home 2011, 40). Integrating IENs will be an important part of labour force planning in this sector, as will understanding and assessing the migration routes those IENs use to enter the profession. Over the last few years there have been a number of changes in the regulatory landscape for IENs in Ontario. There has been a convergence in both regulatory and immigration policy changes related to IENs that has had the effect of restricting certain immigration pathways to practice.

The Two-Step Migration Model: The International Student Program

In recent years, Canada's approach to international students has undergone dramatic changes. Previously, international students were barred from working off campus and were required to leave Canada following the end of their program of study if they wished to apply for permanent residence. Today, international students are viewed as "ideal immigrants" or "future citizens of Canada" who tend to have higher levels of English or French proficiency, academic credentials that are easily recognized by employers, and higher rates of successful integration compared with their counterparts in the foreign worker category (Tamburri 2013).

As such, new strategic policy shifts are aiming to capitalize on the ability of international students to integrate well into the Canadian workforce while also being net contributors to the economy. For instance, in 2010 international students contributed an estimated $8 billion through tuition, living expenses, discretionary spending, and in additional tourism-related benefits (Government of Canada 2012).

International student enrolment reached 265,000 in 2012, constituting a 94 per cent increase from 2001 (Canadian Bureau for

International Education 2013). In keeping with Canada's desire to remain an attractive destination for international students,[1] and also bolstering the quality of the international student program to manage the exponential growth of international students in recent years, Immigration, Refugees and Citizenship Canada (IRCC) has extended the range of institutions permitted to accept international students (CIC 2013b).[2] The opportunity for IENs to enter Canada as international students who can then enter the profession through status conversion is emerging as an important channel for IEN entry into Canada. Monitoring progression into the labour market will be an important element in assessing these policy changes.

The temporary worker and foreign student categories are two-step immigration transition pathways that have significantly changed the immigration system in Canada to one where immigrants are viewed first and foremost as workers (or potential workers) who must earn their permanent status by successfully integrating into the labour market. Due to the complex web of stakeholders involved in the regulated professions, these two-step migration processes demand that governments, academic institutions, professional and career colleges, regulatory and stakeholder bodies all be involved in streamlining the immigration, foreign credential assessment, licensing, and bridge-to-work processes to create coherence at each step (Egenes 2012).

Nursing bridging and postgraduate programs are effective tools not only for preparing IENs for the licensure process, but also for positioning IENs for workplace success as practising nurses. IENs can enter Canada as foreign students enrolled in a postgraduate or nursing bridging program, where they gain the required training that prepares them for the licensure process in Canada without duplicating their entire nursing education. Recent licensure changes have reduced the safe practice window to three years, however, and the implementation of new high-value competency assessments, such as the Objective Structured Clinical

---

1 As of 2018, Canada ranks as the fourth most popular destination in the world for international students (CBIE, 2018).
2 CIC has implemented a regulatory amendment that will provide provinces/territories jurisdiction over designating which schools, programs, and organizations will be recognized as eligible to host international students. As such, CIC will only issue study permits to international students accepted for admission at provincially and territorially approved institutions (in 2016 CIC was renamed IRCC).

Examination (OSCE), suggest some pathways to practice are being constrained for IENs. As entry to practice for RNs becomes more difficult, applicants might be counselled to pursue lower-skilled positions such as RPN positions or unregulated personal support worker (PSW) positions (also known as personal aides, home support workers, or personal care attendants). While PSWs play an important role in the health-care system by meeting other care demands, the ethical concerns of using those RNs trained in the Global South as PSWs in the Global North must be carefully assessed.

Changing Pathways and Pipelines of IEN Migration

Analysis of IRCC data suggests that nursing is one of the professions that is more heavily affected by those transitioning from temporary visa programs, such as the Live-in Caregiver Program (LCP) and international student programs (ISPs), to permanent visa status (Walton-Roberts and Hennebry 2012). Based on immigration and labour force data, we estimate that about 17,500 IENs entered Canada in 2011. According to their final visas, the three main classes by which IENs immigrated were temporary foreign worker (including international students) (49 per cent), economic immigrant (43 per cent), and family class (3 per cent). We estimate that at least 11 per cent of IENs were initially international students. This includes international students who have a work permit explicitly in a nursing occupation (based on the National Occupation Code [NOC] designation 315; 321), and those with student visas who transition to permanent resident visas, stating their intention to work in a nursing NOC category.

The assessment of foreign credentials (the evaluation of the education equivalency and skills qualifications) is often cited as one of the most common barriers that significantly delays or prevents IENs from completing their licensure process (Kolawole 2009, 185). At the start of 2013, the College of Nurses of Ontario (CNO) reduced the safe practice window (the maximum amount of time a candidate can be absent from practising as a nurse) from five to three years, a time frame that makes it difficult for some temporary visa holders to complete registration. Under CNO regulations, IENs who wish to practise nursing in Ontario must have citizenship or permanent resident status according to the Immigration and Refugee Protection Act (IRPA); this limits some temporary visa holders' access to the registration process. CNO regulations will also pose a challenge to the Express Entry program, which launched in January 2015. Express Entry allows employers to search a pool of interested skilled potential migrants for a suitable match, but if IEN candidates must have a valid visa *before* CNO will grant them the right to practise, *how can they be offered a job before they have completed the Canadian licensure process?* This presents a classic catch-22 problem.

In Ontario, the CNO assesses the educational background of IENs and determines if they meet the program equivalency requirements. If they do not, they are required to take the Internationally Educated Nurses Competency Assessment Program (IENCAP), which includes a written multiple choice examination and an Objective Structured Clinical Examination (OSCE), a series of simulations in a clinical setting. Practitioners from educational institutions that offer bridging programs for IENs have attested to the high difficulty level of the OSCE and IENs' subsequent low pass rate. Similar to equivalency examinations in other jurisdictions, the IENCAP can only be taken one time, and unsuccessful applicants are required to complete additional training to address identified competency gaps, which means further time and unanticipated financial commitments. In addition, to fill competency gaps, IENs are required to complete specific university programs, many of which may not have been adequately developed to meet the competencies demanded in the IENCAP. The OSCE is a "high stakes" exam that is assessed in combination with the total application package; that is, rather than having a set "pass rate," the OSCE comprises one part of the larger file that regulators review to assess a candidate's application to practise.

In June 2012, all provincial RN regulators (with the exception of Quebec) entered into an agreement with the US-based National Council of State Boards of Nursing (NCSBN) to replace the Canadian Registered Nurse Exam (CRNE) with the computerized adaptive test, the National Council Licensure Examination (NCLEX-RN). As of January 2015, this has become the entry-to-practice exam required for RN licensure in Canada (CCRNR 2013, 8). Currently, the NCLEX-RN is part of the RN licensure process for the United States and its four territories (American Samoa, Guam, Northern Mariana Islands, and the US Virgin Islands). The new agreement will allow applicants to write the NCLEX-RN at any permanent test site (Pearson Professional Centers) located in Canada as well as any permanent and temporary testing sites in the United States (CCRNR 2013, 8). The NCLEX-RN is also administered in several countries outside the United States, including Germany, India, Hong Kong, Mexico, Puerto Rico, the Philippines, Taiwan, and the United Kingdom.

Given that global mobility is one of the attractions of the nursing profession, and that many OECD countries have relied on IENs to fix structural nurse shortages in the past, it is vital to consider the pipelines and pathways by which IENs enter health systems in order to understand the nature of the global nurse care chain and related ethical factors. Canada has developed a more active policy commitment to promoting international education and using international students as a pool of potential immigrants. Canada's promotion of international education and student-to-worker migrant transition routes will pose new opportunities and challenges to educators and institutions (Brown and Holloway 2008; Egenes 2012). These policy changes for temporary visas and the impact of visa transitions on labour market and migration processes must be assessed in light of the challenges IENs face in nursing.

The immigration process for IENs who intend to work in Canada is complicated, multistaged, and does not end upon arrival in the country. IENs can and do enter under a variety of visas, often transitioning from one status to another. Due to the complexity of navigating the immigration system, the lack of information, the large number of nursing designations, and the way nursing exams are structured in Canada, IENs often enter with unrealistic expectations and revise their plans in the face of difficult circumstances. In order to assess some of these barriers we conducted a survey of IENs who had entered Canada as international students. It is to this case study that we now turn.

Case Study of International Student Pathways into the Canadian Workforce

Our research used both quantitative and qualitative sources of data and focused on a case study of trained nurses from India who entered Conestoga College, a public college located in Waterloo, in southwestern Ontario, that has been actively involved with IENs entering postgraduate professional courses. The study was part of a larger focus on temporary immigrant pathways into the nursing profession (Walton-Roberts and Hennebry 2012). We report on one part of this study, which included Indian trained nurses who had been recruited as international students to a twelve-month postgraduate critical care program through a specialized educational consultant based in northern India. Surveys and semi-structured qualitative interviews were conducted in order to better understand respondent backgrounds and their postgraduate intentions. Through interviews, surveys, and postgraduate data collected in partnership with Conestoga College, we aimed to understand the labour market trajectory of IENs who enter Canada as international students. Below we indicate some of the issues that frame our understanding of their experiences and motivations for studying in Canada and their intentions/experiences with regard to seeking status in the regulated profession of nursing.

Our sample includes 92 students drawn from three cohorts (a total of 162 students) who entered the program between 2010 and 2013. All 92 international students were from India, since the exclusive recruiter for the program at this time was based there. The average number of months the respondent had been in Canada at the time of the survey was 4.6 months. Most had completed a bachelor's of science in nursing, which is the basic qualification needed to be assessed as an RN in Ontario. One held an MBA in hospital management, and one held an MSc. in nursing. Collectively, this group represented a fairly high level of educational attainment. Their previous work experience (gained mostly in India) was an average of 1.8 years, which is a relatively short amount of work experience compared to most IENs, and suggests that these nurses were actively engaged in devising an early career strategy based around international migration. The majority of the sample came to Canada directly from India, which differs from many Filipino IENs who engage in two-step migration and enter Canada from other destinations such as Saudi Arabia or the United Arab Emirates before making their way to more desirable locations that usually offer opportunities for permanent residence (Walton-Roberts and Hennebry 2012; Percot 2006).

The respondents from India were mostly single (74.7 per cent), but 16.8 per cent were married, with just under half of the spouses living in India. Nine of the respondents were engaged to be married. Very few had children, which likely reflected their relatively young age (mostly concentrated in the twenty-to-thirty-year age range). We also asked whether respondents had family members in nursing, as we were interested in exploring ideas of occupational reproduction within families and the cultivation of a culture of migration (Connell 2014; Bhutani, Gupta, and Walton-Roberts 2013). Just under 40 per cent of the sample had a family member (sibling, mother, aunt, or cousin) working in nursing, and of those family members, three-quarters were working overseas.

On the subject of whether respondents intended to remain temporarily or permanently in Canada, 45 per cent intended to remain, while 46.0 per cent were undecided (see Table 12.3). This in itself is an interesting

Table 12.3 Respondents' Intention to Remain Temporarily or Permanently in Canada

	India	%
Yes	42	45.55%
No	8	8.70%
Undecided	42	46.55%
Total	92	100%

Source: Authors' survey

fact, since much of the current debate about international students, especially those from India, assumes that the possibility of permanent residence is the main reason for the growth in numbers. It suggests that the experience of being a student in Canada will play a central role in students' conversion to permanent residents.

We asked respondents about their reasons for entering the nursing profession, in part to explore the intersection of nursing with the growth of overseas opportunities and international migration. The literature is clear that nursing in Western nations is attractive because of the increased salary, higher occupational status, and more opportunities for advancement (Connell 2009). These factors ranked highly with respondents as reasons for entering nursing (23 per cent noted increased salary, 22 per cent improved occupational status), but the desire to emigrate overseas (19 per cent) was also an influencing factor. The issue of providing service was still cited as important (10 per cent) despite the routes these nurses had taken to leave India and go overseas. The importance of family influence with regard to entering the nursing profession was also one of the main factors (20 per cent), which indicates the role of the family in these women's occupational decision-making (Walton-Roberts 2015a; see also Kim and Sondhi in this volume).

We wanted to assess how international education was being funded, and so we asked how students managed the costs of the program in which they were registered (not all respondents chose to answer). The majority of the students indicated that they borrowed in excess of 60 per cent the funds needed to live and study in Canada (see Table 12.4). This level of debt suggests that we should be concerned that students' failure to complete nursing registration examinations might generate a de-skilled pool of indebted migrants (Walton-Roberts and Hennebry 2012; Birrell and Perry 2009).

Table 12.4 Percentage of Funds Borrowed

Percentage of costs borrowed	n	%
0%–15%	17	19.32%
16%–30%	13	14.77%
31%–45%	8	9.09%
46%–60%	14	15.91%
61%+	36	40.91%
Total	88	100%

Source: Authors' survey

In our research the first cohort of the Indian sample of IENs coming through Conestoga College's program had a fairly successful pass rate in the CNO exam (71 per cent for the first cohort of fourteen students who wrote the registration exam in 2011). For those who passed the registration exam, the next challenge was getting their one-year work visa in order to then find a job. Preliminary reports suggest that this group had to contend with inconsistencies between the CNO's reading of a one-year postgraduate visa as not being considered "proof of Canadian Citizenship, permanent resident status, or authorization under the Immigration and Refugee Protection Act (IRPA Canada)" as demanded by the CNO requirements. This suggested a discrepancy between CNO and CIC with regard to international student programs that are intended to create a coherent pathway from education to relevant labour market entry.[3] These visa inconsistencies were eventually resolved, but this cohort's experiences give some indication of the complexities they faced in the process of visa conversion as they attempted to enter a highly regulated sector of the labour force. Subsequent cohorts in 2012, 2013, and 2014 faced an increasingly complex CNO registration process, including the new OSCE assessment and the NCLEX-RN. Anecdotal evidence suggests that the success rate of students in passing these tests has been very low.

---

3 Based on personal communication with faculty at Conestoga College in March 2012.

Conclusion

The process for IENs to obtain licensure is neither an isolated nor insignificant challenge. Moreover, these challenges manifest into a "double ethical" dilemma wherein Canada must seek to avoid causing both a brain drain in source countries (active or even inadvertent recruitment of nurses from countries with severe nursing shortfalls) and brain waste (de-skilling due to inability to enter the workforce at pre-migration equivalent levels) of nursing professionals who migrate to Canada.

Yet in Canada, instances of brain waste manifest most problematically during the licensing process for IENs. For instance, one of the requirements for licensure across all three nursing designations mandates that applicants provide proof of Canadian citizenship, permanent residency, or hold authorization under the IRPA to practise nursing in Canada. This means that the IENs who apply for licensure need to be resident in Canada. Yet, to enter the country, an IEN would have to secure a work visa that, in turn, requires a nursing licence. IENs who are already residing in Canada are being effectively de-skilled if they desire, but fail to complete, their nursing licensure.

Using international student routes to access this process of registration may initially seem to offer an efficient entry system; it is certainly more efficient from the perspective of governments (as this process appears to increase bureaucratic efficiency). But when it comes to migrants and their families, the costs and difficulties faced in entering practice or accessing residency make the system far less streamlined. The long-term costs to migrants and to Canadian society of these disruptions are clearly considered as part of the equation. As the Conestoga case study suggests, the process is more complicated because not only do students have to complete their studies and some nursing practice prior to moving to Canada for further education, they also have to manage the cost of their studies and the process of obtaining the correct visa while also navigating a complex and changing landscape of professional accreditation – all this before they can try to find appropriate employment. This complexity opens the door to a greater propensity for exploitation and abuse from employers, recruiters, and others who might profit from these migrants while they attempt to navigate the system or complete eligibility requirements. For IENs entering as international students, the risks of not getting professional registration are great, and the emotional and financial costs may also be high since many borrow a large portion of the funds needed to pay visa, tuition, and immigration fees. Indirect pathways into Canada for international students involve significant risk, which may delay a migrant's permanent residency application while work and/or study requirements are fulfilled. In some cases this can permanently truncate or deter entry into the nursing profession in Canada. Yet, greater numbers of IENs may well choose this two-step approach in their efforts to enter Canada if other methods fail to meet their needs.

Moving more and more elements of the immigration and licensing processes to a pre-arrival assessment may reduce the churning associated with integrating IENs into the Canadian nursing labour market, but it may also encourage greater recruitment campaigns directed at IEN candidates overseas (the new Express Entry system has already indicated that nurses are on the list of desired occupations despite the complexities of credential assessment).

Regulatory agencies and examination bodies need to continue to acknowledge the international nature of health professions such as nursing. Forging greater cooperation and mutual recognition of international credentials between national jurisdictions creates greater mobility for individuals and facilitates flexibility in human resources planning for health-care professionals. But internationalizing nursing credentials does pose a challenge for national health-care systems when it comes to maintain the integrity of training levels and public safety. For instance, national regulatory agencies have to monitor the in- and out-migration of nurses, as well as the training and regulatory systems in all sending countries, in order to ensure the quality and competency of IENs meet their national standards. Sending states will need to balance nurse emigration against their domestic health human resource needs. They will also need to be more vigilant in overseeing increases in recruitment activities and private training programs geared to overseas migration, which may threaten the quality of training in those locations (Walton-Roberts 2015b).

Governments, educators, and other stakeholders share the overall goal of providing sustainable solutions to nursing shortages in Canada, but it is important to recognize that they each have varying mandates and interests. For instance, while the government may create more diverse two-step migration pathways to convert international students into immigrant labour pools, the nursing regulators appear to be concerned that IENs may jeopardize nursing practice standards in Canada (Canadian Nurses Association 2009). This may represent the thin end of the wedge of internationalization for professional nursing, and indicate the need for greater and more accelerated harmonization both in terms

262 Margaret Walton-Roberts and Jenna Hennebry

of training and entry into the profession. The proliferation of entry systems to include international student pathways makes this process more complex both to monitor and, much more importantly, to negotiate as a migrant.

References

Advisory Committee on Health Delivery and Human Resources. 2009. "How Many Are Enough? Redefining Self-Sufficiency for the Health Workforce: A Discussion Paper." 1–28.

Aiken, Linda H., James Buchan, Julie Sochalski, Barbara Nichols, and Mary Powell. 2004. "Trends in international nurse migration." *Health Affairs (Project Hope)* 23 (3): 69–77. https://doi.org/10.1377/hlthaff.23.3.69. Medline:15160804

Bhutani, Smita, Pradita Gupta, and Margaret Walton-Roberts. 2013. "Nursing Education in Punjab and Its Role in Overseas Migration." In *Readings in Population, Environment and Spatial Planning*, edited by K. Sharma, H. Mangat, and K. Surjit Singh, 203–14. Panchkula, IN: Institute for Spatial Planning and Environment Research.

Birrell, Bob, and Bronwen Perry. 2009. "Immigration Policy Change and the International Student Industry." *People and Place* 17 (2): 64–80.

Brown, Lorraine, and Immy Holloway. 2008. "The Initial Stage of the International Sojourn: Excitement or Culture Shock?" *British Journal of Guidance & Counselling* 36 (1): 33–49. https://doi.org/10.1080/03069880701715689.

Brush, Barbara L, and Julie Sochalski. Feb 2007. "International nurse migration: lessons from the Philippines." *Policy, Politics & Nursing Practice* 8 (1): 37–46. https://doi.org/10.1177/1527154407301393. Medline:17470770

Canada Bureau for International Education (CBIE). 2018. "Canada's Facts and Figures 2018." https://cbie.ca/media/facts-and-figures/.

Canadian Council of Registered Nurse Regulators (CCRNR). 2013. *NCLEX Frequently Asked Questions for Canadian Educators and Students*. NCSBN Examinations.

Canadian Federation of Nurses Unions. 2008. *A Renewed Call for Action: A Synthesis Report on Nursing Shortage in Canada*. 1–96.

Canadian Institute for Health Information. 2011. "Regulated Nurses." *Canadian Trends 2006–2010*:1–153.

Canadian Nurses Association. 2002. *Planning for the Future: Nursing Human Resources Projections*.

– 2005. "Regulation and Integration of International Nurse Applicants into the Canadian Health Care System." Position Statement.

– 2009. "Tested Solutions for Eliminating Canada's Registered Nurse Shortage." https://www.cna-aiic.ca/en/news-room/news-releases/2009/eliminating-canadas-rn-shortage#sthash.4jB0Z6m5.dpuf.

– 2013. "Registered Nurses Education in Canada Statistics 2011–2012. Registered Nurse Workforce, Canadian Production: Potential New Supply." https://www.cna-aiic.ca/~/media/cna/files/en/nsfs_report_2011-2012_e.pdf?la=en.

Citizenship and Immigration Canada (CIC). 2013a. *Temporary and Permanent Resident Entry Data Cubes, 2012.*

– 2013b. "Overview of Proposed Changes to Canada's International Student Program." http://canadaindiaeducation.com/wp-content/uploads/2014/06/CIC_ISP-OVERVIEW-March-2014.pdf.

College of Nurses of Ontario. 2013. *Nursing Registration Exams Report 2012*: 1–15.

Connell, John. 2009. *The Global Health Care Chain: From the Pacific to the World.* New York: Routledge.

– 2010. *Migration and the Globalisation of Health Care.* Cheltenham, UK: Edward Elgar Publishing.

– 2014. "The two cultures of health worker migration: A Pacific perspective." *Social Science & Medicine* 116: 73–81. https://doi.org/10.1016/j.socscimed.2014.06.043. Medline:24983700

Egenes, Karen J. 2012. "Health care delivery through a different lens: The lived experience of culture shock while participating in an international educational program." *Nurse Education Today* 32 (7): 760–4. https://doi.org/10.1016/j.nedt.2012.05.011. Medline:22658373

George, Sheba Mariam. 2005. *When Women Come First: Gender and Class in Transnational Migration.* Berkeley and Los Angeles: University of California Press.

Gordon, Suzanne. 2005. *Nursing Against the Odds.* Ithaca, NY: Cornell University Press.

Government of Canada. 2012. *International Education: A Key Driver of Canada's Future Prosperity.* Ottawa: Advisory Panel on Canada's International Education Strategy.

Home, Glenn. 2011. "Canada's Policy Framework for the Utilization of Internationally Educated Nurses." *Queen's Policy Review* 2 (2): 37–53. https://www.queensu.ca/sps/qpr/sites/webpublish.queensu.ca.qprwww/files/files/15%20canadian%20foreign%20policy%20framework%20foreign%20nurses.pdf.

International Council of Nurses. 2004. "The Global Shortage of Registered Nurses: An Overview of Issues and Actions." *The Global Nursing Review Initiative.* 1–52.

Kingma, Mireille. 2006. *Nurses on the Move: Migration and the Global Health Care Economy.* Ithaca, NY, and London: Cornell University Press.

Kolawole, Bukola. 2009. "Ontario's internationally educated nurses and waste in human capital." *International Nursing Review* 56 (2): 184–90. https://doi .org/10.1111/j.1466-7657.2008.00666.x. Medline:19646167

O'Brien-Pallas, Linda, Gail Tomblin Murphy, Judith Shamian, Xiaoqiang Li, and Laureen J Hayes. 2010. "Impact and determinants of nurse turnover: A pan-Canadian study." *Journal of Nursing Management* 18 (8): 1073–86. https://doi.org/10.1111/j.1365-2834.2010.01167.x. Medline:21073578

Office of the Fairness Commissioner. 2013. "Annual Report." http://www .fairnesscommissioner.ca/files_docs/content/pdf/en/OFC%20Annual%20 Report%202013-14%20English.pdf.

Organisation for Economic Co-operation and Development (OECD). 2007. *Immigrant Health Workers in OECD Countries in the Broader Context of Highly Skilled Migration*. Part III.* 161–228. https://www.oecd.org/migration/ mig/41515701.pdf.

Ortiz, Alejandro, and Rahul Choudaha. 2014. "Attracting and Retaining International Students in Canada. World Education News & Reviews." http://wenr.wes.org/2014/05/attracting-and-retaining-international- students-in-canada/.

Percot, Marie. 2006. "Indian Nurses in the Gulf: Two Generations of Female Migration." *South Asia Research* 26 (1): 41–62. https://doi. org/10.1177/0262728006063198.

Reynolds, Jaratdao, Thunthita Wisaijohn, Nareerut Pudpong, Nantiya Watthayu, Alex Dalliston, Rapeepong Suphanchaimat, Weerasak Putthasri, and Krisada Sawaengdee. 2013. "A literature review: The role of the private sector in the production of nurses in India, Kenya, South Africa and Thailand." *Human Resources for Health* 11 (1): 14. https://doi.org/10.1186/ 1478-4491-11-14. Medline:23587128

Shaffer, Franklin A., and Julia To Dutka. 2013. "Global Mobility for Internationally Educated Nurses: Challenges and Regulatory Implications." *Journal of Nursing Regulation* 4 (3): 11–6. https://doi.org/10.1016/ S2155-8256(15)30124-1.

Stall, Nathan, Mark Nowaczynski, and Samir K Sinha. 2013. "Back to the future: Home-based primary care for older homebound Canadians: Part 1: Where we are now." *Canadian Family Physician / Medecin de Famille Canadien* 59 (3): 237–40. Medline:23486788

Tamburri, Rosanna. 2013. "Changes to Immigration Rules Are a Boon to International Student Recruitment." *University Affairs.* https://www.universityaffairs.ca/news/news-article/

changes-to-immigration-rules-are-a-boon-to-international-student_
recruitment/.

Valiani, Salimah. 2012. *Rethinking Unequal Exchange: The Global Integration of Nursing Labour Markets.* Toronto: University of Toronto Press.

Vaughn, P.W. 2006. *Competency-Based Health Human Resources Planning: Forging a Citizen-Centric Approach.* Health and Human Resources Paper prepared for the Ontario Ministry of Health and Long-Term Care.

Walton-Roberts, Margaret. 2015a. "Femininity, mobility and family fears: Indian international student migration and transnational parental control." *Journal of Cultural Geography* 32 (1): 68–82. https://doi.org/10.1080/0887363 1.2014.1000561.

– 2015b. "International migration of health professionals and the marketization and privatization of health education in India: From push-pull to global political economy." *Social Science & Medicine* 124: 374–82. https://doi. org/10.1016/j.socscimed.2014.10.004. Medline:25445935

Walton-Roberts, Margaret, and Jenna Hennebry. 2012. *Indirect Pathways into Practice: A Comparative Examination of Indian and Philippine Internationally Educated Nurses and Their Entry into Ontario's Nursing Profession.* CERIS Working Paper No. 92.

Yeates, Nicola. 2010. "The Globalization of Nurse Migration: Policy Issues and Responses." *International Labour Review* 149 (4): 423–40. https://doi.org/ 10.1111/j.1564-913X.2010.00096.x.

A Multi-level Perspective on Education Migration

MIN-JUNG KWAK AND ANN H. KIM

As stated at the outset, "outward and upward" remains an apt description of international student mobility (ISM) but it neglects a higher order of thinking that accounts for meso- and macro-level factors that complicate the attainability of geographic and social mobility for students and families. Shifting institutional arrangements and policy frameworks, local businesses, labour markets, and ethnic communities, along with the array of educational actors and institutions, constitute the context within which students migrate and interact. In the introduction of this collection we asked, What is the connection between students and structuring institutions? Which institutions are significant in students' lives and how do they interact with students? It is in the quagmire of government policies and practices that international students face myriad institutions, from their families to communities to businesses, schools, colleges, and universities, all while striving to achieve personal goals.

In this afterword, we highlight three major findings based on the collective work of this volume's contributors: the importance of political membership, the multi-leveled nature of institutions, and the need for a holistic perspective. We then situate our findings in the global context by briefly examining and anticipating trends in ISM among major host countries. Finally, by acknowledging the important and yet limited geographical focus on Canada, we suggest some research directions for the future that emphasizes more comparative and collaborative work on ISM at a global scale.

Students and Structuring Institutions in Canada

We point to three general findings in this collection as a whole. First, international student status as a type of membership in the polity can be important for how students interact with institutions and institutional actors, and thus influences integration outcomes. Legal status, which confers rights to individuals, is an important form of governmental incorporation, and depending on the route of entry for migrants, there is a hierarchy of political membership (Söhn 2013). There are negative implications for those lower on the strata, particularly asylum seekers and undocumented migrants, in terms of various social and economic outcomes (Lomba 2010, Goldring and Landolt 2011; Söhn 2013). Although the 1948 *Universal Declaration of Human Rights* affirms rights with respect to food, health, social services, housing, education, work, and mobility "without distinction of any kind, such as … nation or social origin … birth or other status," Lomba (2010) points out that legal status has primacy over international human rights law (419).

While international students may sit higher, though not high, on Canada's ladder of political membership, they, too, face barriers due to their temporary status, which has historically made them ineligible for many social programs, as well as restricted mobility and work opportunities. Along with higher tuition fees, the authors featured in this volume show that international students struggle with work restrictions (Walton-Roberts and Hennebry), with stigma in co-ethnic communities (Kwak et al.), and with academic and language difficulties in schools (Kim et al.). Moreover, parents' employment, social lives, and interaction with school authorities are also affected (Man and Chou, Kwak et al., and Kim et al.). These studies show that the growing literature on legal status often omits an important group, one that is too often cast as resourced and privileged but which clearly has its own set of issues and challenges. Canada's shift in institutional arrangements that now link the policy spheres of education, immigration, and the labour market, certainly urges us to interrogate these ostensibly firm legal identities and boundaries that are in reality nebulous and more blurred. What happens to retention and transition (from temporary to permanent) rates when students are limited or restricted in the labour market? What about when they cannot access health and social services?

Second, institutions at multiple levels are relevant to students' lives. Here again, this collection demonstrates that international students' social realities shape and are shaped by myriad institutions. Not only do they contend with multiple levels of government gatekeepers and associated policies, they also navigate rules, regulations, and different pedagogical and learning approaches and cultures in academic institutions. At the same time, the presence of students often compels institutions to provide better student support and develop new programs, altering institutional structures and shifting resources in the process. Wintre et al.'s chapter in this volume supports such efforts, revealing the importance of a university environment that is "supportive, structured, and demanding" for positive student adjustment. Their results are consistent with numerous studies that address international students' experiences in classrooms and in broader academic communities (See especially Kim and Sondhi 2015).

Surprisingly, the other types of institutional experiences faced by international students are less well known. Kim et al.'s chapter provides a glimpse in the direction of younger students in schools and compares them to co-ethnic permanent residents and Canadian citizens. Their study raises specific concerns related to younger temporary students, who are likely to confront greater academic challenges, to some extent a relative lack of extra-curricular activities, as well as their parents' more limited involvement in schools. Walton-Roberts and Hennebry, and Lu and Hou, remind us in their chapters that professional and regulatory bodies and labour markets, respectively, also interact with international students beyond their secondary role as unofficial gatekeepers to permanent residence. As gatekeepers to long-term settlement, they have a direct influence on international students' ability to achieve upward social mobility, and students engage in an ongoing and dynamic process of assessment, evaluating and re-evaluating their personal and economic goals in relation to their encounters with such institutions and institutional actors. Added to this are local diasporic communities, whether experienced formally through non-governmental and civil society organizations (Montsion), or informally through work settings, school groups, and other kinds of social relationships (Sondhi). Lastly, there is the institution of the family, perhaps the most influential of all institutions for ISM, as decisions are made and experiences understood, and often constructed, in the family context (Kwak et al., and Man and Chou in this volume). Students consider their options and make decisions in direct interaction with such meso- and macro-level institutions, and we would be remiss to minimize their role in shaping students' experiences and future plans. For these reasons, institutional actors and policies can do more to recognize not only diversity in ethno-national origins but in legal statuses as well, and to consider how policies and practices may discriminate against temporary (and undocumented) residents. Finally, as much as policymakers believe they are "testing" students on their ability to successfully manoeuvre the ins and outs of

Canadian society, students also test Canada. As such, institutions, too, must adapt.

The third key contribution of this volume is its presentation of a more holistic perspective of international students and their families, looking past the dominant image of students as driven solely by educational and economic goals linked to upward class mobility and capital accumulation (Waters 2005). Without diminishing the importance of these motivations for "edugration" – they are of course significant and the inspiration behind this collection – we saw throughout the volume that the process of achieving social mobility is not a straightforward path, but is rather one that is unavoidably entangled with institutions; as a result there are varied trajectories, and students emerge as less unidimensional, as they have begun to appear in other work (Tran 2016).

It is important to view students and their families, and ISM itself, as multidimensional and as leading to multiple outcomes. There is variation in educational and economic achievements, and as both Walton-Roberts and Hennebry's and Lu and Hou's analyses revealed, some international students fare better than others in passing licensing requirements and in the labour market (e.g., those with higher educational attainment in Canada and those from the United States and Europe). Some young respondents continue their journey elsewhere for better educational and employment opportunities (e.g., the United States) and some, particularly those facing blocked and limited mobility, return to their home countries (Kwak et al.). It is also worth highlighting the potentially long-term nature of student migration and the space this leaves for personal changes. Students find their place in different social spaces (Sondhi), give back to local communities (Montsion), and live through family and lifestyle changes (Kwak et al., Man and Chou, and Sondhi). In short, ISM is about more than social mobility.

The studies in this volume used a variety of methodological tools, from linked national administrative data to surveys to ethnography to individual interviews to policy analysis. Despite the historical lack of thought about and subsequent lack of data on temporary residents, including for international students (as demonstrated by Kim, Attieh, and Owen), the authors in this volume found creative ways to address important questions. In order to continue our search for answers on this small but growing group, future work on "edugration" – the intermeshing of education and immigration from state level official discourse and policies to individuals and families – will require states and research bodies to rethink how data infrastructure and content correspond with new social realities. In Canada and elsewhere, data linkages among administrative records and nationally representative survey data may be a move in the right direction.

Education Migration and the Future of the Global Skills Race

Maintaining such an institutional perspective will continue to be important as long as governments, from all over, view internationalization and international student recruitment as a way to achieve economic goals. The internationalization of education (especially in higher education) has gained popularity around the world, and an increasing number of countries have developed and implemented internationalization strategies. Moving beyond the traditional emphasis on international student recruitment, internationalization strategies include student and academic exchange programs, international research collaborations, satellite campuses, and collaborations between schools and international corporations. The role of national governments in these internationalization strategies is particularly noteworthy. According to a report by the British Council (2016), 23 of 26 countries studied have national policies that encourage student mobility and various internationalization efforts. The report identifies the most active governments engaged in such endeavours as Australia, Germany, the United Kingdom, Malaysia, Germany, and China. In this section, we briefly examine and anticipate trends in the United Kingdom, Australia, and the United States, three major ISM countries.

The United Kingdom performs well in implementing internationalization strategies and recruiting international students (She and Wotherspoon 2013). The UK government has, for example, recently developed two major research funding sources, the Global Challenges Research Fund and the Newton Fund (University of Oxford International Strategy Office 2017). Both funds promote research on international topics and international collaborations. The national branding of UK higher education by the government, such as Education UK between 1999 and 2004, and Britain is GREAT since 2010, have attempted to attract prospective international students (Lomer, Papatsiba, and Naidoo 2018). However, even though the United Kingdom has the highest proportion (21.1 per cent) of the international student population among OECD countries, there is a growing concern about the slower growth rate of incoming international students in recent years (Lomer, Papatsiba, and

Naidoo 2018). This reflects the accelerating global competition over international students as more non-traditional host countries pay attention to the growing potential of an export education industry. Some Asian countries like China, Japan, and Malaysia are hosting a growing number of international students from nearby East Asian countries, and Latin American countries are also gaining visibility in the market.

Considering the growing governmental engagement on a global scale, the British Council's 2016 report called for a greater level of coordination between national policies in Europe as well as other international education markets. However, the UK government has been reluctant to advance permanent migration of international students from non-EEA (European Economic Area) countries (She and Wotherspoon 2013). While the United Kingdom is actively recruiting students from non-EEA countries, the government has strictly controlled their postgraduate status change, and they give EEA nationals priority in order to protect European labour markets (She and Wotherspoon 2013). It will be interesting to see how the UK government changes or maintains the existing policy regimes towards international student recruitment and retention after Brexit.

A decade earlier, the Australian House of Representatives Standing Committee on Economics, Finance and Public Administration (2007) made several policy recommendations on its international education industry. These included more aggressive international student recruitment through the lowering of visa fees, the removal of an English-language competency test requirement for ESL students, a quality assurance audit, and the coordination, by the government, of promotional efforts between Tourism Australia and Australian Education International. Australia's international education industry has grown significantly in the last decade, and it is now Australia's third largest export industry overall. In 2015–16, Universities Australia announced that the industry generated a record $20.3 billion (USD$15.5 billion) and supported 130,700 jobs in the country (Universities Australia 2016). The Australian government strives for further growth of the industry. A recent report by Deloitte Access Economics (2015) in partnership with EduWorld and the Australian Trade Commission (Austrade) projected that with a growing portion of the younger population in urban areas, a rising middle class, and the demand for a skilled workforce, the rate of participation in higher education will increase globally. Australia has shown strong performance in the recruitment and provision of onshore international education. Acknowledging the growing competition of the international education industry, however, the report recommends more attention to offshore and borderless opportunities for the future growth of Australia's international education industry. With the industry's existing comparative advantages, Australia will continue to identify potential offshore and borderless markets, provide positive learning experiences, ensure adequate education and training provision for employment opportunities, and establish stable and transparent migration policies to provide international students with a higher degree of certainty when it comes to post-study outcomes.

The United States may be the biggest beneficiary of a rapidly growing international education industry. More than a million international students in the United States contributed to an industry worth over USD$35.7 billion and supported over 400,000 jobs in 2015 (US. Commercial Service 2017). US colleges and universities have a competitive advantage over other similar institutions in the United Kingdom, Australia, New Zealand, and Canada, where English-language instruction is the norm. US institutions, with their reputation for high-quality education, strong curriculum in attractive academic fields (e.g., STEM and business), globally mobile credentials, and top-notch research facilities, attract a significant number of international students from all over the world. According to the 2016 Top Markets Report (International Trade Administration 2016), the top three source countries for the last ten years were China, India, and South Korea, and this trend is expected to remain stable. On the other hand, these advantages are often offset by major fluctuations in the international education market, some sending countries' government funding changes (e.g., Saudi Arabia and Brazil), the strict visa process in the United States and the country's reduced tolerance to outsiders, and concerns about high tuition.

The United States clearly recognizes growing market competition for the "best and brightest" among developed countries and the increasing visibility and market share of other places in the global education industry. However, the US government's market research report projects that the existing advantages enjoyed by US schools will continue to prevail. While other competitor countries are developing and implementing a wide range of marketing and branding strategies by linking governments' migration policies, the United States still identifies the most effective strategy as active recruitment of international students to the country. For one, the US Commercial Service Global Education team publishes an annual report, "Education and Training Services Resource Guide," and assists US educational institutions with comparable and individual market assessments of best prospects as source countries (US Commercial Service 2017). The US government also organizes both live and virtual education fairs and trade missions for education professionals (International Trade Administration 2016). The provision of scholarship programs (e.g., the Fullbright Program) is another of the government's efforts at student recruitment. While the US Department of Commerce has been working closely with the State Department's Education USA program to promote US colleges and universities and diversify markets through research, there seems to be no clear link between recruitment and retention policies. Instead, international students in the United States utilize employment-based programs (e.g., the H-1B visa and the OPT program) to apply for permanent resident status. Historically, the United States has easily fulfilled its immigration goals, and its national government is unlikely to feel any sense of urgency to reform the current retention policy for international students.

Canada is one of the few countries that offer international students a direct pathway to permanent residency. This is a recently adopted government initiative to retain highly skilled international students. Traditionally, Canada relied on skills-based immigration programs that brought in the highly skilled from source countries. Compared to other major destination countries for international students, such as the United Kingdom, the United States, and Australia, Canada still lags behind in terms of a coordinated, nationwide, top-down strategy for the marketing and recruiting of international students (see Trilokekar and El Masri's chapter in this volume). However, this open migration policy for students may increase the role that Canada and Australia play in the global international education market. At least over the past two decades, the absolute numbers of international students have grown for all four countries, including Canada, simply because of the increasing number of international students worldwide (University of Oxford International Strategy Office 2017). If the United Kingdom and the United States continue or intensify their restrictive migration policies towards international students, Canada and Australia will likely experience the benefit of increased numbers.

At the same time, despite Canada's more open edugration policies (relative to the United States and the United Kingdom), the pathways from temporary migrant status to permanent residence have not always been straightforward. International students have to navigate the complex web of government migration policies and locally specific labour market regulations, which often lead to disparities between international and domestic students as well as among international students. Questions related to inequality for international students are shared not only in Canada but also in Australia. For example, Robertson (2011) reported that the issues faced by international students are expressed in the interconnected discourses between human rights and consumer rights. Protecting international students' rights, investing in their welfare, and promoting upward mobility through quality education were all viewed as securing Australia's lucrative market share of the international education industry. Beyond protecting the consumer rights of international students from a neo-liberal viewpoint, Canada needs to approach issues of inequality from an inclusive human rights perspective; appropriate institutional support services, the elimination of barriers to the labour market and to public services, and international students' equitable treatment would make Canada a more realistic option for permanent settlement for a greater number of international students.

Limitations of the Book and Future Directions

The strength of this collection lies in the kinds of questions its contributors ask, ones that go beyond traditional push-pull perspectives – although understanding push-pull dynamics continues to be pertinent for elucidating trends and for making cross-national and cross-group comparisons. And while we believe it stretches the field of ISM to encompass wider ground than is currently covered, we have prioritized depth over breadth.

This is most obvious in the book's singular focus on Canada, where it benefits from the advantages of an in-depth study but perhaps suffers from being somewhat nation-centric. At the same time, it offers a good reference point for comparisons with Canada. More comparative work in the future, particularly among mid-level players in the global drive to attract international students (for the implicit and explicit reasons of economic growth and development), is highly desirable. How institutional frameworks and structures differ across places and differently shape student experiences can provide stakeholders with options for reconceptualizing and restructuring.

In focusing on Canada, the book also displays shortcomings with respect to the limited areas of research based on nationally representative and/or longitudinal data. Although Lu and Hou fill some of this gap, this is an area for further growth. As researchers, we can argue for more data to examine student interactions with multiple institutions across Canada, comparing those in high- and low-density areas, in different types and sizes of educational institutions (e.g., university versus college, fields of study, etc.), and so forth. Conscious of regional representation in the book, we learned about Vancouver and smaller centres in Ontario, but we know international students are an important presence in many other areas within British Columbia, the Prairies, and the Atlantic Provinces. We also know that regionalization is an important part of ISM. In other words, what occurs within Canada mirrors, to some degree, the global skills race. For this reason, a regional perspective is beneficial; we would gain an understanding of how student experiences differ by region and how these experiences are influenced by differences in institutional contexts.

Another shortcoming of the book, and one we expect to be addressed in future work, is the limited range of groups who are represented, both in terms of national origins and professions (and academic disciplines). While the studies discussed in the book reflect student samples from countries that have been the top source countries for years (i.e., China, India, South Korea), we have much to learn from students from different places. Other main source countries include France, Nigeria (one of the fastest growing in recent times), Saudi Arabia, the United States, and Brazil, and these students can broaden our knowledge of the effects of racial, religious, and linguistic dynamics on international student integration. At the same time, the institutional perspective is also relevant for examining differences in experiences according to academic fields and professions such as health care and medicine, science and technology, and business.

Finally, by focusing mostly on the current experiences of international students and their families in Canada, this volume provides limited information on the outcomes of international education with respect to return migration. Some past work and anecdotes suggest that students' experiences upon return to their country of origin are also varied, but more work in the area is needed, particularly in overcoming the challenges of locating returnees (Kim and Sondhi 2015). More specifically, the field of ISM would be more complete with further studies on how international education, credentials, and degrees, along with lived experiences, shape life in home – or third – countries.

We anticipate future work will develop the areas outlined above, particularly those directly related to our findings and limitations: the effect of political membership on both short- and long-term incorporation; a more explicit conceptualization of the student-institution nexus beyond the push-pull model; a holistic and dynamic perspective on international students; data on immigration (i.e., entry) status; and a more comparative perspective on international student experiences among differently positioned countries. As in the past, it will be important to understand how ongoing changes and shifts in policy intersections affect international student experiences with institutions and institutional actors.

This institutional approach brings to the forefront the meso level, as arguably, we cannot dissociate the identity and experiences of international students from structuring institutions. In this book, we attempted to fill the meso-level gap left by the ISM literature, which generally adopts a push-pull framework and emphasizes a binary of individual (and family) and academic or state institutions. Conceptualized in broader terms, international students interact daily with what are often culturally different institutions that yield immense power on the processes of social mobility and which structure students' overseas experiences. We find the connections among the micro, meso, and macro distinctively integrative, conflictual, and transformational.

References

Australian House of Representatives Standing Committee on Economics, Finance and Public Administration. 2007. "The International Education Industry." In *Serving Our Future: Inquiry into the Current and Future Directions of Australia's Services Export Sector.* A report submitted to the Parliament of the Commonwealth of Australia.

British Council. 2016. *The Shape of Global Higher Education: National Policies Framework for International Engagement.* www.britishcouncil.org/sites/default/files/f310_tne_international_higher_education_report_final_v2_web.pdf.

Lomba, Sylvie da. 2010. "Legal Status and Refugee Integration: A UK Perspective." *Journal of Refugee Studies* 23 (4): 415–36. https://doi.org/10.1093/jrs/feq039.

Economics, Deloitte Access. 2015. *Growth and Opportunity in Australian International Education.* A report prepared for Austrade in partnership with EduWorld. https://www.austrade.gov.au/Australian/Education/Services/Australian-International-Education-2025/growth-and-opportunity.

Goldring, Luin, and Patricia Landolt. 2011. "Caught in the Work-Citizenship Matrix: The Lasting Effects of Precarious Legal Status on Work for Toronto Immigrants." *Globalizations* 8 (3): 325–41. https://doi.org/10.1080/14747731.2011.576850.

International Trade Administration. 2016. *2016 Education Top Markets Report.* US Department of Commerce. https://www.trade.gov/topmarkets/pdf/Education_Executive_Summary.pdf.

Kim, Ann H., and Gunjan Sondhi. 2015. "Bridging the Literature on Education Migration." *Population Change and Lifecourse Strategic Knowledge Cluster Discussion Paper Series/ Un Réseau stratégique de connaissances Changements de population et parcours de vie Document de travail* 3 (1), Article 7. http://ir.lib.uwo.ca/pclc/vol3/iss1/7.

Lomer, Sylvie, Vassiliki Papatsiba, and Rajani Naidoo. 2018. "Constructing a national higher education brand for the UK: Positional competition and promised capitals." *Studies in Higher Education* 43 (1): 134–53. https://doi.org/10.1080/03075079.2016.1157859.

Robertson, Shanthi. 2011. "Cash Cows, Backdoor Migrants, or Activist Citizens? International Students, Citizenship, and Rights in Australia." *Ethnic and Racial Studies* 34 (12): 2192–211. https://doi.org/10.1080/01419870.2011.558590.

She, Qianru, and Terry Wotherspoon. 2013. "International student mobility and highly skilled migration: A comparative study of Canada, the United States, and the United Kingdom." *SpringerPlus* 2 (1): 132–45. https://doi.org/10.1186/2193-1801-2-132. Medline:23667802

Söhn, Janina. 2013. "Unequal Welcome and Unequal Life Chances: How the State Shapes Integration Opportunities of Immigrants." *Archives Européennes de Sociologie* 54 (2): 295–326. https://doi.org/10.1017/S0003975613000155.

Tran, Ly Thi. 2016. "Mobility as 'Becoming': A Bourdieuian Analysis of the Factor Shaping International Student Mobility." *British Journal of Sociology of Education* 37 (8): 1268–89. https://doi.org/10.1080/01425692.2015.1044070.

Universities Australia. 2016. "International Education Generates a Record $20.3 Billion for Australia." Press release, 12 November. https://www.universitiesaustralia.edu.au/Media-and-Events/media-releases/International-education-generates-a-record--20-3-billion-for-Australia#.WjM500qnGUk.

University of Oxford International Strategy Office. 2017. *International Trends in Higher Education 2016–17.* http://www.ox.ac.uk/sites/files/oxford/trends%20in%20globalisation_WEB.pdf.

US Commercial Service. 2017. *Education and Training Services Resource Guide: A Reference for US Educational Institutions.* https://2016.export.gov/industry/education/eg_main_108888.asp.

Waters, Johanna L. 2005. "Transnational Family Strategies and Education in the Contemporary Chinese Diaspora." *Global Networks* 5 (4): 359–77. https://doi.org/10.1111/j.1471-0374.2005.00124.x.

Contributors

Reem Attieh is a graduate student in the Department of Sociology at York University.

Saeid Chavoshi is a graduate student in the Department of Psychology at York University.

Elena Chou is a PhD candidate in the Department of Sociology at York University.

Stella Dentakos is a graduate student in the Department of Psychology at York University.

Amira El Masri is a PhD candidate in the Faculty of Education at York University.

Jenna Hennebry is an associate professor at the Balsillie School of International Affairs and the director of the International Migration Research Centre (IMRC) at Wilfrid Laurier University.

Feng Hou is Principal Researcher with the Social Analysis and Modelling Division, Statistics Canada, and adjunct professor of sociology at the University of Victoria.

Abirami R. Kandasamy is a PhD student in clinical child psychology at the University of Windsor.

Ann H. Kim is an associate professor in the Department of Sociology at York University.

Min-Jung Kwak is an assistant professor in the Department of Geography and Environmental Studies at Saint Mary's University.

Eunjung Lee is an associate professor in the Factor-Inwentash Faculty of Social Work at the University of Toronto.

Jeong-Eui Lee currently works as a mental health clinician in a community-based mental health organization.

Sangyoo Lee is a PhD student in the School of Social Work at York University.

Yuqian Lu is Senior Researcher with the Social Analysis and Modelling Division, Statistics Canada.

Guida C. Man is an associate professor in the Department of Sociology at York University.

Jean Michel Montsion is an associate professor in the Department of Multidisciplinary Studies at Glendon College at York University.

Timothy Owen is Deputy Executive Director of World Education Services.

Wansoo Park is an associate professor in the School of Social Work at the University of Windsor.

Gunjan Sondhi is a lecturer in Geography, Faculty of Arts and Social Science, at the Open University, UK.

Roopa Desai Trilokekar is an associate professor in the Faculty of Education at York University.

Margaret Walton-Roberts is a professor in Geography and Environmental Studies and affiliated with the Balsillie School of International Affairs at Wilfrid Laurier University.

Maxine Gallander Wintre is a professor in the Clinical Developmental Area in the Department of Psychology at York University.

Lorna Wright is Executive Director of the Centre for Global Enterprise and EDC Professor of International Business at the Schulich School of Business at York University.

Sung Hyun Yun is an associate professor in the School of Social Work at the University of Windsor.